'This book unravels the multiple meanings of resilience and challenges us to be clear about what we mean. Today's 'striving for resilience' may be akin to yesterday's 'striving for conservation' – a futility in the complex adaptive system within which we live. To prevail, society needs to purposefully use its transformative capacity to embrace a more sustainable pathway. For all in the conservation and sustainable development movements – this is a timely must read.'
Greg Bourne, former CEO of WWF Australia, BP Regional President (Australasia) and currently Chair at the Australian Renewable Energy Agency.

'Resilience, or its importance, are not immediately obvious, even to the resilient. Yet sustainability depends on it. Nothing can be sustained that is not resilient, whether it be natural systems, the efforts to conserve them or those who try to understand the processes and principals involved. Confused? Then read this book!'
John Cortes, Minister for Health and the Environment, HM Government of Gibraltar, Gibraltar

'*Searching for Resilience in Sustainable Development* provides a critical analysis of how the resilience concept is applied in contemporary debates ranging from global climate change to community development. Using a variety of framing devices, the book demonstrates how resilience has come to be understood, applied and re-interpreted across differing contexts and scales. The book is essential reading for scholars and practitioners seeking to understand what the concept of resilience has to offer individuals, communities, businesses and governments as we enter an age of environmental and social transformation.'
Stewart Barr, University of Exeter, UK

'Sustainability must be at the heart of how we do business. We cannot use more resources than our planet can support. This challenging new book seeks to reflect on the value and effectiveness of the conservation and sustainability movement at a time when its own resilience is being tested. Read it!'
Jane Davidson, former Minister for Environment and Sustainability in Wales and Director of the Institute of Sustainable Practice, Innovation and Resource Effectiveness (INSPIRE) at University of Wales, Trinity St Davids

'In its application to sustainable development, the concept of resilience assumes new complexity. In their book *Searching for Resilience in Sustainable Development* Blewitt and Tilbury exhibit healthy scepticism and deepen critical inquiry into resilience beyond the state of the art. A must read for all those interested in critical yet fundamental concepts of resilience and sustainable development.'
Helen Kopnina, The Hague University of Applied Science, the Netherlands

D0024408

'This book is unique in providing a truly interdisciplinary account of the uses and abuses of 'resilience' set within an inspiring sense of commitment to radical change. Resilience emerges as a profoundly humanist – as well as ecological – concept.'

Jenneth Parker, Director of Research, Schumacher Institute, UK

'This book is timely and exemplifies the very strong commitment that we in UNEP have to the world of Universities, both as research centres and intellectual drivers of our sustainable development paradigm, and as centres of training for professionals who will enable us in the future to help societies in making this transition.'

Achim Steiner, Executive Director, United Nations Environment Programme (UNEP)

Searching for Resilience in Sustainable Development

Resilience is a term that is gaining currency in conservation and sustainable development, though its meaning and value in this context is yet to be defined. *Searching for Resilience in Sustainable Development* examines ways in which resilience may be created within the web of ecological, socio-economic and cultural systems that make up the world. The authors embark on a learning journey, exploring both robust and fragile systems, and asking questions of groups and individuals actively involved in building or maintaining resilience.

Through a series of wide-ranging interviews, the authors give voice to the many different approaches to thinking of and building resilience that may otherwise stay rooted in and confined by specific disciplinary, professional or spatial contexts. The book documents emerging trends, shifting tactics and future pathways for the conservation and sustainable development movement post-Rio+20, arriving at a set of diverse but connected conclusions and questions in relation to the resilience of people and planet.

This book is ideal for students and researchers working in the fields of conservation, sustainable development, education, systems thinking and development studies. It will also be of great interest to NGOs and government officers whose interests and responsibilities focus on conserving or reconstructing biodiversity and system resilience.

John Blewitt is Co-Director of MSc Social Responsibility and Sustainability, a member of the IUCN Commission on Communication and Education. He is also a Fellow of the Royal Society of Arts and a Distinguished Fellow of the Schumacher Institute.

Daniella Tilbury is Professor and Director of Sustainability at the University of Gloucestershire. She is Co-Chair of the Sustainable Futures Leadership Academy, a Marie Curie Fellow and President of Copernicus Alliance of Universities.

Searching for Resilience in Sustainable Development

Learning journeys in conservation

John Blewitt and Daniella Tilbury

Routledge
Taylor & Francis Group

LONDON AND NEW YORK

earthscan
from Routledge

First published 2014
by Routledge
2 Park Square, Milton Park, Abingdon, Oxon OX14 4RN

Simultaneously published in the USA and Canada
by Routledge
711 Third Avenue, New York, NY 10017

Routledge is an imprint of the Taylor & Francis Group, an informa business

British Library Cataloguing in Publication Data
A catalogue record for this book is available from the British Library

Library of Congress Cataloging-in-Publication Data
Blewitt, John, 1957–
Searching for resilience in sustainable development : learning journeys in
conservation / John Blewitt and Daniella Tilbury.
pages cm. – (Routledge studies in sustainable development)
Includes bibliograhical references and index.
1. Sustainable development. 2. Sustainability. 3. Human ecology. I. Tilbury,
Daniella. II. Title.
HC79.E5B583 2014
338.9'27–dc23
2013007890

ISBN: 978-0-415-52488-9 (hbk)
ISBN: 978-0-415-52489-6 (pbk)
ISBN: 978-0-203-10951-9 (ebk)

Typeset in Goudy by
FiSH Books Ltd, Enfield

MIX
Paper from
responsible sources
FSC
www.fsc.org   FSC® C013604

Printed and bound by CPI Group (UK) Ltd, Croydon, CR0 4YY

Contents

Figures, tables and boxes

Figures

Tables

Boxes

Acknowledgements

The book has been a long time in the making. 2012 was a busy year, although not exactly a momentous one from the perspective of sustainable development. There were disappointments, but some achievements, at Rio, and there is much more work still to do. We would like to thank the many people who gave us their time to consider our questions and discuss our views. We have provided detailed biographies of our interviewees as recognition of their important contribution to this work. However, we should make it plain that our interpretation of resilience, sustainable development and the related issues discussed in this text are ours, and any failings in understanding or appreciation of what the world is and how it is progressing into the future are likewise ours alone. Other people have also contributed to this book, particularly colleagues and students whose views have helped shape our interests and concerns over the years. These people are too numerous to mention, but we thank them too. Our thanks also go to Earthscan for commissioning this book and for being so patient as deadlines were exceeded and extended. But probably our greatest thanks must go as always to our respective families, for without their support and encouragement we would not have been able to find the necessary resilience to write this work.

John Blewitt
Daniella Tilbury

Author and interviewee biographies

Authors

Dr John Blewitt studied politics, history and sociology at UCW Aberystwyth; film and television at the Polytechnic of Central London; and education at the Universities of Greenwich and Huddersfield. He has 30 years of experience working in adult, further, international and higher education, and has worked at the universities of Huddersfield, Bradford and Exeter. He is presently co-director of the MSc Social Responsibility and Sustainability at Aston University, UK. He is a member of the IUCN Commission on Communication and Education, a founding member of the International Environmental Communication Association, a distinguished Schumacher fellow, and a fellow of the Royal Society for the Arts and of the Higher Education Academy. His research interests include urban sustainable design, new media and public space, and the future of the public library. As a 'Face' he is an ambassador for the new Library of Birmingham – the biggest public library in Europe.

Professor Daniella Tilbury is a University Director at the University of Gloucestershire and holds a Chair in Sustainability. She is responsible for the University's sustainability performance. She also leads the International Research Institute for Sustainability and the United Nations University Regional Centres of Expertise based at the University. Her expertise lies in areas of education and learning and leadership and organisational change for sustainable development. Daniella has an extensive portfolio of consultancy work in sustainable development having attracted over 4.5 million pounds from funding sources such as European Union, United Nations, World Conservation Union (IUCN), World Wide Fund for Nature (WWF), British Council and several government agencies. Daniella has been the recipient of several awards, including the Macquarie Innovation Award, the 2008 and 2010 Green Gown Award for institutional change for sustainability and was named a Marie Curie International Professor by the European Commission in 2010 for her work in the University sector.

Interviewees

Phil Beardmore is a highly experienced and respected sustainability consultant. He was one of the founders of Birmingham Social Enterprise Energy Network in 2005. He was a co-founder the renewable energy co-operative CoRE50. He is a director of the think-tank Localise West Midlands. He specialises in thought innovation, developing new environmental business models, bid-writing, strategic planning and evaluation. He has considerable experience of advising consumers on energy billing, and integrating billing and tariff advice into programmes such as Stay Warm Stay Well, on which he was a project manager.

Greg Bourne graduated as a chemist and trained as a drilling engineer. After 32 years as a senior executive at BP, he took up the position of CEO of one of Australia's most influential environmental organisations, WWF. He was CEO of BP Marine, London, and later president and general manager (exploration and gas) for BP Developments Australia Ltd; and he was director of BP Scotland and then regional director for Latin America, based in Caracas. He returned to Australia in 1999 to become regional president of BP Australasia the position from which he retired from BP in September 2003. Greg was CEO of WWF-Australia from 2004 to 2010. Greg was seconded to the prime minister's Policy Unit at 10 Downing Street in 1988 for two years. He is chair of the Australian Renewable Energy Agency; a member of the CSIRO Climate Adaptation Flagship advisory council; and a member the BHP Billiton Forum on Corporate Responsibility. He was awarded the Centenary Medal for services to the environment and an honorary doctorate from the University of Western Australia for services to industry.

Keith Budden, strategic partnership manager, joined E.ON in 2011 to develop and manage city partnerships in the south of the UK. He has helped to deliver Birmingham's largest commercial photovoltaic scheme, large-scale domestic energy efficiency projects in Coventry as well as district energy schemes in Exeter. In 2001 Keith moved to Birmingham to become director of an environmental charity and in 2005 joined Be Birmingham, the city's Local Strategic Partnership as head of sustainability working across the public, private, voluntary and community sector. Keith helped Birmingham win a Green Flag from the Audit Commission for tackling climate change. Keith established Birmingham Energy Savers as the UK's largest local authority-run renewable energy and housing retrofit programme. He was invited to become a fellow of the Royal Society of Arts in 2006 in recognition of his work in tackling climate change.

Dr Paul Clarke is professor of education at St Mary's University College, London, and director of sustainable leadership at Mott MacDonald/ Cambridge Education. Paul is a co-director and founder of the Pop-Up-Foundation. This initiative encompasses a portfolio of projects (Pop-Up-Farm, Pop-Up-Coffee, Pop-Up-Orchard, Pop-Up-Power), which distil ideas and action around core sustainability challenges of energy, water, waste, food, well-being and buildings, and disperse them worldwide. Schools, communities and organisations adopt the core challenges and develop activities, enterprise and new insights around these themes, and in so doing take practical understanding and solutions to sustainability into the heart of their daily lives. The findings of this work are now being used to formulate a pedagogy for sustainable living.

Uchita de Zoysa is researcher, activist, communicator, author and social entrepreneur in the area of sustainability. He is the executive director of the Centre for Environment and Development (CED) and chairman of Global Sustainability Solutions based in Sri Lanka. In 1991 he led the then largest environment and development NGO coalition in Sri Lanka, called the Public Campaign on Environment and Development, and conducted a large public hearing process, which led to a Citizens' Report on Environment and Development. The report was presented to UNCED in 1992 in Rio de Janeiro. He led the 'People's Sustainability Treaties' at Rio+20, as an alternative process setting sustainable development pathways and goals.

Ann Finlayson is the CEO of SEEd (Sustainability and Environmental Education) and successfully restarted it in 2008 from the umbrella organisation CEE. She was also the only commissioner for education and capability building for the UK Sustainable Development Commission (2005–2011). Prior to this Ann was the head of education at WWF-UK for 5 years. Ann has worked in the environmental field for over 30 years both in academic research, education, facilitation and management. After a stint as a countryside ranger in Scotland, she began travelling the world teaching, facilitating and consulting in places such as Papua New Guinea, Australia and Canada. With a working knowledge of formal, informal and non-formal education, Ann's particular interests are in the role of learning, communication and evaluation in sustainability and social change, and the methodologies needed for adoption of effective sustainable living strategies. She has won awards with colleagues in North America for development of training and evaluation tools.

Professor Herbert Girardet is co-founder and former director of programmes of the World Future Council (WFC). He is leading consultant on sustainable development and a recipient of a UN Global 500 Award 'for outstanding environmental achievements'. For many years he has focused mainly on the challenges of sustainable urban development and he is often called the world's leading urban ecologist. He has been a consultant to UNEP and UN-Habitat, and has developed sustainability policies for major cities such as London, Vienna and Bristol. In 2003 he was inaugural 'thinker in residence' in Adelaide, developing sustainable development strategies for South Australia. At present he is a senior consultant to the Saudi Sustainability Initiative, based in Riyadh. From 1996 to 2008 Herbert was chairman of the Schumacher

Society, UK. He is an honorary fellow of Royal Institute of British Architects, a patron of the Soil Association, UK, and a visiting professor at University of the West of England.

Anne Hannaford is director of public and university learning services and engagement at the University of Worcester, and responsible for the joint civic university library The Hive. After a degree in English and history at the University of Kent at Canterbury, Anne began working in the public library sector. After two years, she moved into higher education, where she has extensive management experience in library and resource centres. She has published in the field of information literacy and converged services, and is currently working on an exciting development with Worcestershire County Council and other partners on a collaborative new library project for the city and region of Worcester.

Peter Head is a civil and structural engineer, and champion for sustainable development principles, promoting the idea that the way public and private money is invested in the built environment could be very much more effective if the public and private sectors adopted such principles. Peter is a world leader in the construction of major bridges, the application of advanced composite technology and sustainable development in cities. He has won many awards for his work as an engineer, and has been a judge for the Prince Philip Designers' Prize, the Holcim Awards and the Earth Awards. In 2009 Peter was awarded the Sir Frank Whittle medal of the Royal Academy of Engineering for a lifetime contribution to the well-being of the nation through environmental innovation. Formerly head of global planning at ARUP, he is now founder of the Ecological Sequestration Trust and chairman of the Institute for Sustainability.

Rob Hopkins is the co-founder of Transition Town Totnes and of Transition Network. He was named by the *Independent* as one of the UK's top 100 environmentalists. He is the winner of the 2009 *Observer* Ethical Award for the Grassroots Campaigner category, and in December 2009 was voted the Energy Saving Trust/*Guardian*'s 'green community hero'. In February 2012, Rob and the Transition Network were among NESTA and the *Observer*'s list of 'Britain's 50 new radicals', and in 2012 won the European Economic and Social Committee Civil Society Prize. He lectures and writes widely on transition, and recently completed a PhD at the University of Plymouth.

Francine Houben is architect/creative director at Mecanoo Architecten, Netherlands. She began formulating the three fundamentals of her lifelong architectural vision while studying at the Delft University of Technology. Always looking for inspiration and the secret of a specific location, Francine bases her work on both analyses and intuition. She is known as one of the most prolific architects in Europe today. Her wide-ranging portfolio comprises an intimate chapel built on the foundations of a former nineteenth-century chapel in Rotterdam (2001) to Europe's largest library in Birmingham (2013).

She was granted lifelong membership to the Akademie der Künste, Berlin in 2010. In 2008, she received the Veuve Clicquot Business Woman of the Year award. Her commitment to research and education is evidenced in her instatement as professor in architecture, chair of aesthetics of mobility at the Delft University of Technology (2000), her professorship at the Universitá della Svizzera Italiania, Accademia di architettura, Switzerland (2000), and her appointment as visiting professor at Harvard University (2007).

Dr Anne Kerr is director of the Environment Division of the engineering company Mott MacDonald, and is based in Hong Kong, but works in Asia Pacific, Australasia and the Middle East. She is the group's champion for Future-Cities initiatives, sustainability practice leader for Asia Pacific and Australasia, and long-time proponent of an integrated approach to improving the way we plan, design, build, and live and work together. The holistic approach to planning through the consideration of sites and resources before buildings is a key component in creating world-class cities.

Stephen McKenna is Head of Town Planning at Mott MacDonald. He is a chartered town planner and chartered surveyor with over 30 years of experience in planning and implementing major urban regeneration and development planning projects, as well as infrastructure schemes. He has worked in both the public and private sectors, as client as well as consultant, and is also a specialist in EU funding. Stephen sits on the RICS Environment and Resources Board, commenting on policy directions, consultations and educational development of the institution. He is passionate about making places that are socially just, economically vibrant and increasingly that are in harmony with their natural hinterland. Climate change, urbanisation and cultural change are all issues of great concern and, working on projects abroad, including in India, Stephen has an acute sense and understanding of the challenges facing new mega-conurbations and the capacity of places to become more resilient.

Philip Monaghan is founder and CEO of Infrangilis, which is part think-tank, part consultancy, and whose work focuses on resiliency strategies. Philip is a recognised leader with over 18 years of international experience as a strategist and change manager in the fields of economic development, corporate social responsibility, and environmental sustainability. This includes half a decade with AccountAbility, where he helped establish the think-tank's global leadership on corporate governance standards. Philip has worked as a lead advisor on a variety of consultancy and research assignments across the public, private, civil society and academic sectors over the past two decades.

Jonathon Porritt was born in 1950. The next couple of decades flowed by effortlessly at Eton, Magdalen College, Oxford, and dossing around planting trees and farming in New Zealand and Australia. He first got involved with environmental issues in 1974, at the same time as he became a teacher in a west London comprehensive. Ten years later, he left teaching to become director of Friends of the Earth where he stayed until 1991, just prior to the Earth

Summit in Rio de Janeiro in 1992. In 1996, he helped set up the sustainability organisation Forum for the Future, which remains his 'home base' in terms of all the different things he does today. He is also co-director of the Prince of Wales's Business and Sustainability Programme, and was chair of the UK Sustainable Development Commission between 2000 and 2009.

Mahesh Pradhan was appointed head of UNEP's Environmental Education and Training Unit (EETU) in January 2011 and is based within the Division of Environmental Policy Implementation in Nairobi. In close coordination with UNEP's Regional Office for Asia and the Pacific, Mahesh oversees the partnership with Tongji University through the joint UNEP–Tongji Institute of Environment for Sustainable Development (IESD) in Shanghai. The core focus of his work at UNEP is enhanced engagement with universities through GUPES. Prior to this, Mahesh has more than 16 years of experience as UNEP's regional environmental affairs officer for Asia and the Pacific, based in Bangkok, Thailand. In 2009, he was assigned as interim director of the AIT-UNEP Regional Resource Centre for Asia and the Pacific (RRC.AP), which is located on campus of the Asian Institute of Technology (AIT) in Pathumthani, Thailand.

Pamela J. Puntenney is founder and CEO of Environmental and Human Systems Management, a private sector consulting firm that seeks to facilitate and support the further implementation of sustainability strategies through learning processes, research and influencing policy, provision and distribution of key information, and training and capacity building. She currently serves as co-chair of the UN Commission on Sustainable Development Education Caucus and head of delegation on climate change and environmental security. As a member of the IUCN Commission on Education and Communication she has contributed her expertise on policy and advocacy, as well as management and evaluation of environment and education for sustainable development strategies. Pam's work focuses on cross-cultural solutions, the impact of world systems on local communities, public choice and public responsibility, learning systems and sustainable solutions. She has served as a lecturer and research scientist with the University of Michigan.

Roel van Raaij is a senior policy officer and adviser in the national government in the Netherlands, responsible for policies and strategic development of environmental education (EE) and education for sustainable development (ESD). Starting as a teacher, educator and lecturer, Roel worked in several organisations, and was appointed in the Nature Department of the Ministry of Agriculture, Nature Management and Food Quality, which recently merged with the Ministry of Economics. As EE and ESD in the Netherlands are interdepartmental and intergovernmental responsibilities, Roel is responsible (as national secretary of the steering committee Learning for Sustainable Development) for the EE and ESD policies, public participation, interaction between government and NGOs, and knowledge management portfolios. As chair of the United Nations Economic Commission for Europe (UNECE) Expert Group on ESD Indicators, he has led a team of experts who advise on the process of monitoring and evaluation of the UNECE Strategy. He is an active member of the IUCN Commission on Education and Sustainable Development.

Sue Riddlestone is chief executive and co-founder of BioRegional and managing director of BioRegional MiniMills. Sue is also a Skoll, Schwab and Ernst & Young award-winning social entrepreneur. As a founder of BioRegional's One Planet programme, she has worked to create sustainable communities in the UK and in countries from China to the USA and with leading businesses, such as B&Q, on their sustainability strategies. As a member of the Mayor's London Sustainable Development Commission, Sue has set targets for reducing London's CO_2 emissions and the London 2012 Olympic bid – and subsequently helped to write the sustainability strategy 'One Planet Olympics'. Sue is included in *Building Design*'s top 50 green leaders for 2012.

Stephen Robertson has been CEO at the Big Issue Foundation since July 2007. His previous role was director of commercial operations at Shelter, where he had responsibility for a chain of 100 charity stores, a mail-order business and a training business primarily focusing on housing professionals. Stephen was a member of the senior management team with cross organisational responsibility for the strategic management of the charity. Stephen was at Shelter for 13 years. Stephen helped found and ultimately chaired the professional body that represents the majority of charity retailers in the UK, the Association of Charity Shops. Stephen is also a trustee of the homeless health care charity London Pathway, and a trustee of TRAID, a charity committed to protecting the environment and reducing world poverty by recycling and campaigning at home.

Kartikeya V. Sarabhai is the founder director of the Centre for Environment Education (CEE), established in 1984 as a centre of excellence of the Ministry of Environment and Forest, Government of India. Mr Sarabhai is a member of the UNESCO Reference Group for UNDESD and a member of the International Steering Group for the End of the Decade Conference 2014. CEE is the nodal agency for implementation of UNDESD in India. He was a member of the Indian delegation to UN Conference on Environment and Development at Rio in 1992 as well as the World Summit at Johannesburg in 2002. Mr Sarabhai is a member of the Earth Charter International Council. He is a trustee of the Sabarmati Ashram set up by Mahatma Gandhi. He is the vice-chair of the Indian National Commission of IUCN. Mr Sarabhai received the Tree of Learning Award from IUCN in 1998 for his work in environmental education. In 2012, the Government of India awarded him the Padma Shri, one of the country's highest civilian awards, in recognition of his distinguished service in education for sustainability.

Molly Scott Cato is professor of strategy and sustainability in the Business School at the University of Roehampton. She is a green economist who is also well-known in the field of co-operative studies. Molly's primary area of work is into the green economy, addressing the question of how we might design and organise an economy that fits comfortably within planetary limits and achieves social justice. Molly is a member of the UK Society of Co-operative Studies and a former member of the editorial board of the *Journal of Co-operative Studies*. She is a board member of Meadow Prospect, the regeneration subsidiary of a housing mutual based in the Welsh Valleys, and was recently appointed to Wales' Co-operative Commission. She is interested in developing work in the areas of the bioregional economy and participatory planning within the context of climate change. She is also engaged with practical sustainability via her involvement with Transition Stroud and her role as a Green councillor on Stroud District Council.

Simon Slater is executive director of Sustainability West Midlands. Previously head of sustainable development at Advantage West Midlands, he helped produce the UK's first regional low-carbon economic strategy, secured carbon reduction targets for all Regional Development Agencies (RDAs), and the first sustainable development action plan for a Regional Development Agency. Prior to this he was at the UK's leading sustainable development charity, Forum for the Future, where he advised Jonathon Porritt (then chair of the Sustainable Development Commission), Ken Livingstone (then London Mayor) and Rhodri Morgan (then Welsh first minister) on aspects of regional sustainable development. His other experience includes over 15 years working in the private, public and voluntary sectors on issues such as regional development, natural resource management, regeneration, planning, participation and change management.

Dr Rachel Suissa is an assistant professor at the National Security Program in the School of Political Sciences at the University of Haifa, and a research fellow in three different academic affiliations due to her multidisciplinary professional background: Center for Public Management and Policy (University of Haifa), the Department of Geography (University of Haifa) and Samuel Neaman Institute – Technion, Haifa. Her research interests encompass multi-disciplinary security and strategy studies, emergency studies, peace studies, conflict cognition, psychology and behaviour, technology and society, and philosophy of social sciences.

Dr Mitchell S. Thomashow devotes his life and work to promoting ecological awareness, sustainable living, creative learning, improvisational thinking, social networking and organisational excellence. He was the president of Unity College in Maine (USA) from 2006 to 2011. Thomashow is currently director of the Second Nature Presidential Fellows Program, which is the lead supporting organisation for the American College and University Presidents' Climate Commitment. He is a fellow of the Salzburg Global Seminar and a member of the Sustainable Futures Leadership Academy.

Farooq Ullah joined Stakeholder Forum in September 2011, and took over formally as executive director on 1 September 2012. Before this, Farooq was at the UK Sustainable Development Commission (SDC) for nearly five years. Farooq worked on strategic assessment at the SDC; key elements of this work included policy advice, stakeholder engagement and capability building. In all, Farooq has nine years of public sector experience at international, national and local government levels, with a further three years of private sector consultancy experience. Currently, Farooq is a specialist adviser to the UK Parliament's Environmental Audit Committee and a member of the Alliance for Future Generations. Additionally, he is a founding member of Brighter Future, a climate-change action group in London. Farooq holds a BComm in management science from the University of Alberta and an MSc in public policy from the London School of Economics.

Graham Wallington is the co-founder and CEO of WildEarth.tv. Graham has worked in Australia and the United States, and a few years ago directed a three-part series in the Serengeti, Tanzania for *National Geographic*. Late one night, while following lions using infra-red imaging, Graham and Emily, the producer of the series (and also Graham's future wife), began discussing the content, channel and business that would become WildEarth. These discussions and dreams continued during post-production in London, and then in Johannesburg after Emily decided to move out to South Africa.

Keith A. Wheeler has over 35 years of professional experience in the fields of sustainability, conservation, technology and the environment. Currently, he is chairman and CEO of ZedX, a knowledge management and IT company that focuses on sustainable resource management designing interactive, web-based decision support systems for the agricultural, water and energy sectors. He served as chair of IUCN's Commission on Education and Communication from 2006 to 2012. Wheeler was appointed to President Clinton's Council for Sustainable Development and served as co-chairman of the White House.

Dr J. Morgan Williams is a New Zealand ecologist, agricultural scientist and environmentalist who served as the New Zealand Parliamentary Commissioner for the Environment (PCE). Dr Williams completed 10 years as PCE in March 2007, following an earlier career in the Ministry of Agriculture and Forestry, the South Pacific and research in Antarctica. He is currently an adjunct professor at the universities of Canterbury and Queensland, positions he has held for 10 years. Williams obtained an MSc from Canterbury University, studying ecology, and a PhD at the University of Bath in population ecology. He worked in Antarctica and Fiji before returning to New Zealand, where he worked for the Ministry of Agriculture and Fisheries in research, management and policy for 21 years. He is currently chair of WWF New Zealand.

Dr Juliane Zeidler is co-founder of Integrated Environmental Consultants Namibia (IECN) and Namibia-based Natuye Institute for the Environment.

She is well known for her expertise in biodiversity, land management and climate change research, natural resources management, community development and sustainable development. Among others she helped develop Namibia's third National Development Plan and she was instrumental in the drafting of Namibia's National Biodiversity Strategy and Action. She was strongly involved in Namibia's National Programme to Combat Desertification, and at the global level she supported the strategic plan preparations of the UN Convention to Combat Desertification. She was elected chair of the IUCN Commission on Education and Communication in 2012.

1 Introduction

Learning journeys and resilience in times of change

> **Search:** to try to find something by looking or otherwise seeking carefully and thoroughly.
> **Resilience**: ability to withstand or recover from difficult conditions.
> **Learning:** the acquisition of knowledge or skills through study, experience, or being taught.
> **Journey:** an act of travelling from one place to another.
> (adapted from *Shorter Oxford English Dictionary*)

Times are changing. We are living through a moment in history where the risks associated with upsetting natural climate processes, the erosion of the quality and diversity of life on Earth and the injustices that plague our world are beginning to have an influence on social practices and economic decisions.

At a superficial level, various examples can be cited to suggest that the influence has been a positive one. Governments in developed countries across the globe are taking ambitious steps to reduce their carbon footprint as they begin to experience the extremes in natural patterns associated with human inducted climate change (for example, as encountered through Hurricane Katrina and Hurricane Sandy in the USA) and experts assess the financial costs of climate change impact at £190 billion (Parry *et al.* 2009; Stern 2007). Consumer demand for organic, fair-trade and ethical products is on the rise (Co-operative Bank 2011; Hainmueller *et al.* 2011), as is the use of car sharing, waste recycling and energy conservation (Department of Energy and Climate Change 2012; SGS 2012). Businesses such as Alliance Boots, Symantec, BP and UPS join national and international banks, supermarkets, energy and utilities companies to embrace and report annually on corporate social responsibility.[1] A global study shows a growing number of universities and colleges are committing to ethical investment, sustainable energy and the greening of campuses (Global University Network for Innovation 2011). There has also been a rapid growth in the number of action groups (such as Transition Towns and Cool Communities) that are carrying out the necessary groundwork and mobilising communities to adopt sustainable practices.

A macroscopic look at these trends, however, indicates that they do not yet reflect a deep cultural shift in core practices (Worldwatch Institute 2012a) and that increasing awareness and assessment of sustainability risks has had a negative impact on quality of life (Knowles 2012). For example, recent events and reassessment of probabilities have been accompanied by an increase in insurance premiums as well as taxes and other impacts that are also influencing family life (Australian Government 2011).

Figure 1.1 Rio+20 Sustainable Development Summit: Welcome Wall
Source: Daniella Tilbury

The Worldwatch Institute identifies twenty-four positive trends from organic farming to high-speed rail to wind power in its 'Vital Signs' for 2012 (see Box 1.1), but concludes that despite these developments the evidence is that we have never been closer to ecological collapse. It reminds us that a third of humanity lives in poverty, and another two billion people are projected to join the global population over the next 40 years.

The United Nations Global Pulse is an initiative of the United Nations (UN) secretary-general. This initiative utilises digital data and real-time analytics to: gain a better understanding of changes that affect human wellbeing; and, 'strengthen resilience to global shocks' (United Nations Global Pulse 2012: 1). Its Sustainable Development Indicators Project recently confirmed what many suspected: that there is a gap between the positive trends towards more sustainable practices and the lack of impact on the overall health of the planet. In

Box 1.1 Vital signs

- Global energy intensity rose 1.35 per cent in 2010 – a rare exception to a long-term positive trend that saw energy intensity drop by just over 20 per cent from 1981 to 2010.
- In 2010, global oil consumption reached an all-time high of 87.4 million barrels. At 37 per cent of primary energy use, it remains the largest single source of energy, though its share has declined for 11 consecutive years.
- Fossil fuel consumption subsidies fell 44 per cent in 2009, to US$312 billion – reflecting changes in international energy prices rather than a change in policies.
- Continuing its rapid ascent, installed global wind power capacity increased 24 per cent to 197,000 megawatts in 2010 – nine times as much as a decade ago.
- Solar photovoltaic generating capacity grew even faster. The 16,700 megawatts that were newly installed in 2010 surpasses the total photovoltaic capacity that was in place in 2008.
- The production of passenger cars and light trucks reached a new peak in 2010, surging from 60 million to 74.7 million.
- High-speed rail lines expanded from 10,700 kilometres in 2009 to almost 17,000 kilometers in 2011. High-speed trips accounted for 7 per cent of all rail passenger travel in 2010.
- Global biofuel production increased by 17 per cent in 2010 to reach an all-time high of 105 billion litres. Rising portions of the US corn harvest and Brazil's sugarcane production are turned into ethanol – giving rise to fears of increasing food and fuel trade-offs.
- Organic farming methods were used on 37.2 million hectares worldwide in 2009. This represents a 150 per cent increase since 2000, yet the organic area amounts to just 0.85 per cent of global agricultural land.
- Per capita meat consumption in the developing world doubled to 32 kilograms over the past quarter-century, but this is still far below consumption levels in the industrial world.'
- Fish farming has increased some fifty-fold since the 1950s and now accounts for 40 per cent of total fish catch.
- The number of overweight people age 15 or older worldwide jumped 25 per cent since 2002, to 1.93 billion.

Source: Worldwatch Institute (2012: 4–6)

response, the UN secretary-general's High-Level Panel on Global Sustainability have assembled a unique dataset to signpost progress in ways which can drive policy and thinking towards sustainable development and scale up the changes. The data uses traditional signposts such as gross domestic product (GDP), but also includes social, economic and environmental indicators informed by people's use of mobile phones or accessing of online services which leave real-time data trails:

> These digital trails are more immediate and can give a fuller picture of the changes, stressors, and shifts in the daily living of a community, especially when compared with traditional indicators such as annual averages of wages, or food and gas prices. This is especially crucial during times of global shocks, when the resilience of families and their hard-won development gains are tested.
>
> (United Nations Global Pulse 2012: 1)

Achim Steiner (2012), United Nations Environment Programme (UNEP) executive director, defines the problem in a different way. He argues that the international community is able to understand the issues on paper and has sufficient data to respond but it does so with a series of discrete measures. He argues that the ambition (and the associated actions needed) to transform, rather than merely respond, proves elusive. The ongoing financial and economic crisis, Steiner believes, is further undermining international determination and changing the goalposts (2012). These views were shared by many of the stakeholders in attendance at Rio+20 in July 2012, who were frustrated by the pace and scale of global change towards sustainable development.[2]

The UN Rio+20 Summit

The world leaders gathered once again in Rio, twenty years after committing to changing the future of the world and reverse unsustainable patterns of human activity on the planet. Those present understood the legacy of the first Summit and the expectation that the 2012 gathering would be equally ground-breaking. In 1992, the world leaders signed the Convention on Biological Diversity and the Framework Convention on Climate Change, and made broad pledges to solve some of the most complex problems facing humanity (Tollefson and Gilbert 2012). Countries also agreed to build sustainable communities as defined in a document known as Agenda 21 which lacked formal commitments but which eventually spawned the Convention to Combat Desertification and international processes such as the UN Decade in Education for Sustainable Development. Ten years on, the 2002 Johannesburg Summit recognised that actions had not been far reaching and that poverty continued to deepen and environmental degradation worsening. What the world wanted, the UN General Assembly (2002) said, was not a new philosophical or political debate but rather, a summit of actions and results: what it generated was a series of partnerships with business and non-governmental organisation (NGO) entities that reshaped action plans for sustainable developments. This resulted from a realisation that legal frameworks were only part of the solution and that engagement and empowerment of civil society was key to sustainable futures as reflected in the

Johannesburg Plan of Implementation. The 2012 Summit built on this engagement theme and had its focus on the green economy and institutional frameworks. It also privileged discussions about water, energy and employment given the rise in energy prices, the unprecedented concern about water resources and economic downturn which had left many struggling to earn a living.

Uchita De Sousa, an NGO leader who was present at all three summits, reminds us that the arduous negotiations which took place in Rio 2012 did not broker any new agreements or targets, leaving many deflated by the polarised viewpoints often fuelled by the 'green economy' discourses (De Sousa 2012). UNEP led the green economy proposals seeking to drive sustainable development, and pushed to make the environment and wellbeing the determining factors of economic production, value and long-term prosperity. Given that the green economy was often narrowly interpreted by those at the summit as the clean energy economy, many doubted that it would lead to equitable growth and address sustainable development needs. As a participant, it was clear that the focus on 'green' concerns (associated mostly with nature, natural resources and climate change) troubled stakeholders concerned with social justice agendas, who often called for an alternative (rather than an adaptation) of the existing economic and human development paradigms.

The notion of the green economy was popularised by the Pearce Report (Pearce, Markandya and Barbier 1989) developed for the UK government over 23 years ago. It proposed ways in which the environment could feature as a variable in economic analysis and proposed taxation systems to protect life. It was evident at Rio+20 that today there are a diversity of meanings assigned to the notion of a green economy, many equating it to a low carbon economy and investment in green technology while others associate its environmental strands more strongly with development and meeting the needs of the most vulnerable in our society.

Farooq Ullah, executive director of Stakeholder Forum, who was an official delegate at Rio+20, argues that the green economy as an idea is very valuable and could lead to the redesign of capitalist schemas so that wealth generation can be more equitable and address the social issues of our day. He acknowledges that discussions around the green economy at Rio+20 were highly contentious and explains that ideas were rushed through without the necessary opportunities to digest and engage with the concept in meaningful ways.

For another Rio+20 delegate and former chair of the IUCN's Commission on Education and Communication, Keith Wheeler, the debates around the green economy are not about fundamental and systemic change: 'The Green Economy is understood by many to be about investment in green technologies rather than a rethink or our current systems of production and consumption' (Wheeler 2012).

UNEP clearly sees the green economy as an expression of an ecological modernisation project that will leave the essential economic dynamic unchanged but would nonetheless ensure a greater degree of efficiency and social equity. Its Green Economy initiative offers the following understanding:

Figure 1.2 Rio+20: in front of the Theatro Municipal do Rio de Janeiro, close to Parque
do Flamengo (location of the People's Summit)

Source: Philipp Schoffmann

> Practically speaking, a green economy is one whose growth in income and
> employment is driven by public and private investments that reduce carbon
> emissions and pollution, enhance energy and resource efficiency, and
> prevent the loss of biodiversity and ecosystem services. These investments
> need to be catalysed and supported by targeted public expenditure, policy
> reforms and regulation changes. This development path should maintain,
> enhance and, where necessary, rebuild natural capital as a critical economic
> asset and source of public benefits, especially for poor people whose liveli-
> hoods and security depend strongly on nature.
>
> (United Nations Environment Programme 2012: 1)

For Karen Chapple (2008: 1), faculty director of the Center for Community
Innovation at the University of California, Berkeley, and author of *Defining the
Green Economy*, it is about generating economic activity and eco-efficiency in
such a way that both preserves but more importantly enhances environmental
quality. We already have the knowledge to allow us to reduce our own impact on
the planet but we are not so clear how we might develop our economies in such
a way that is truly equitable for everyone on the planet, she argues.

Perhaps the most popular interpretation of the Green economy is that encap-
sulated by the Green Economy Group (Box 1.2).

Box 1.2 Definition of a green economy

What is the green economy? The green economy is defined as a sustainable economy and society with zero carbon emissions and a one-planet footprint where all energy is derived from renewable resources which are naturally replenished. A green economy rigorously applies the triple bottom line of people, planet and profits across all corporations at the microeconomic level and throughout the entire economy at the macroeconomic level. In contrast to a green economy, a traditional 'black' energy economy is based on carbon-intensive fossil fuels such as coal and petroleum. By definition, a low carbon economy is distinct from a green economy because it still generates carbon emissions. A green economy exhibits the following characteristics:

- An energy infrastructure with zero carbon emissions that is powered by 100 per cent renewable energy – made possible through a combination of proven, renewable energy technologies; breakthrough cleantech solutions; as well as enabling regulation and carbon markets.
- The water, waste and wastewater infrastructure is based on long-term sustainability.
- The preservation and protection of the world's ecosystems, biological diversity and forests in partnership with indigenous peoples and all relevant stakeholders through the creation of sustainable governance models, markets and business models for delivering, maintaining and paying for ecosystem services.
- Sustained and successful adaptation to climate change at a local, regional and global level.

Source: The Green Economy Group (2012)

While the world leaders wrestled with forging positive outcomes for economy and environment at Rio+20, those involved in the conservation movement continued to push for clear biodiversity outcomes after decades of negotiations. The International Union for Conservation of Nature (IUCN), for example, expected better-defined aspirations and a link with the Aichi Targets (see Box 1.3), as well as pathways for marine biodiversity conservation that went beyond national jurisdictions (International Union for the Conservation of Nature 2012). These did not materialise.

WWF International launched its 2012 *Living Planet Report* on 'the road to Rio', in an attempt to scale up the momentum and depth of commitment. The report provides scientific evidence of the cumulative effect of human activity on the planet, and the consequent decline in the health of the forests, rivers and oceans that are having an irreversible impact on ecosystems and biodiversity as

Box 1.3 Aichi biodiversity targets

The 10th Convention of Parties (CoP) held at Nagoya, Japan in 2010 adopted a Strategic Plan for Biodiversity with a defined time frame to achieve twenty specific targets before 2020. These targets are referred to as the Aichi targets:

- Strategic Goal A: Address the underlying causes of biodiversity loss by mainstreaming biodiversity across government and society.
- Strategic Goal B: Reduce the direct pressures on biodiversity and promote sustainable use.
- Strategic Goal C: To improve the status of biodiversity by safeguarding ecosystems, species and genetic diversity.
- Strategic Goal D: Enhance the benefits to all from biodiversity and ecosystem services.
- Strategic Goal E: Enhance implementation through participatory planning, knowledge management and capacity building.

Source: Convention of Biological Diversity (2012)

well as our own quality of life. WWF was also seeking a new global course for sustainability after Rio+20 given evidence in the report that humanity's use of renewable natural resources exceeded the Earth's capacity to renew them by 50 per cent. As James Leape, director general of WWF's international secretariat writes:

> It is also a unique opportunity for coalitions of the committed to step up – governments in regions like the Congo Basin and the Arctic, joining together to manage the resources they share; companies which are competitors in the marketplace nonetheless joining forces to drive sustainability into their supply chains and offering products that help customers use less resources; and pension funds and sovereign wealth funds investing in green jobs.
>
> (WWF 2012: 2)

Despite its shortcomings, Rio+20 did meet some of these expectations; stimulating engagement through fresh analysis and policy pathways, reframing governance and reporting relationships and establishing regional partnerships with the potential to broker green initiatives for economic development (Steiner 2012). It also gave us the promise of global Sustainable Development Goals (see Box 1.4).

The Rio+20 outcomes document, *The Future We Want* (United Nations 2012), did not catalyse the global transformation many were expecting, but it did lay significant tracks for change. Resilience surfaced as an important concept on the road to Rio+20, as confirmed by its presence in the summit's outcomes

---

Box 1.4 Sustainable Development Goals

Currently there is no single, universally accepted definition or assessment matrix for sustainable development. One of the main outcomes of the Rio+20 Conference was the agreement by member States to engage in a process to develop a set of Sustainable Development Goals (SDGs), which will build upon the Millennium Development Goals (that sought to end poverty by 2015) and converge with the post-2015 development agenda. The goals were to serve as a tool for countries to measure their progress in implementing the principles of what was agreed in Rio in 1992. It was thought that SDGs could focus international collaboration and co-operation at a practical level.

The governments of Colombia and Guatemala initially proposed the development of SDGs suggesting that priority should be given to themes that are seen as critical to the attainment of sustainable development such as: combating poverty, changing consumption patterns, promoting sustainable human settlement, biodiversity and forests, oceans and water resources, advancing food and energy security.

The world civil society organisations (CSOs) followed this with a document that included 17 key thematic goals, such as climate sustainability, sustainable livelihoods, youth and education, subsidies and investment, and health, as well as many identified by the initial document. Each goal included sub-goals, reasoning and clarifications which articulate the detail of these international framework. Over 1400 official CSOs support this more extensive document.

Those present at Rio+20 further agreed that SDGs must be:

- *Action-oriented*
- *Concise*
- *Easy to communicate*
- *Limited in number*
- *Aspirational*
- *Global in nature.*

Universally applicable to all countries while taking into account different national realities, capacities and levels of development and respecting national policies and priorities.

---

document, where it is referred to on thirteen separate occasions and conveyed as critical to the attainment of sustainable development. This is notable given its absence from the Johannesburg Key Outcomes document or Plan of Implementation (both 2012), but not unexpected given its positioning as a key theme in the stakeholder documentation circulated at Rio, the presentations at the official side events and the discussions of the high-level panels.

Understanding resilience

The term 'resilience' takes on multiple meanings but is most often associated with disaster management and the ability to bounce back from events or incidents that threaten the globe, a country, an economy, a community, an ecosystem or a business. Rio Tinto (2012), the mining engineering company, for example, uses the term to refer to business resilience and recovery from incidents that threaten its own existence. The Red Cross locates resilience in the context of victims of natural disasters and see it as necessary to protect the poor from scenarios that threaten their lives and livelihoods. The UN uses resilience to refer to climate adaptation and links it to 'smart choices' which help communities recover from disasters and make them less vulnerable to the impacts of climate change. Informing this notion of resilience is an intention to shape decisions on how food is grown, where and how homes are built, how financial and economic systems operate, as well as how we educate (United Nations 2012). Following this theme, the Stockholm Resilience Centre, a research body based at the University of Stockholm, is engaged in the quest for knowledge of how resilience can be strengthened in society, and in nature, so as to cope with the stresses caused by climate change and other environmental impacts.

The concept has also entered a number of popular cultural discourses, leading to a diversity of self-help books, manuals and toolkits designed to help individuals, groups, businesses, governments and organisations to cope with risk, adversity and hardship. The 'bouncing back' metaphor is a particular favourite of those writers who offer advice on personal development, growth and survival. Jane Clark and John Nicholson (2010) offer readers a guide to self-knowledge and a means of discerning their own 'personal resilience quotient'.

For American guru and pundit Andrew Zolli (2012), the importance of resilience is that in requires people to recognise that the world is constantly changing and that it is imperative to be able to learn from modest disruptions and failures. Human communities can learn for the widespread resilience of the natural world, which he also poignantly suggests many sustainability practitioners have not done. Not wishing to point the finger at 'traditional bad guys', Zolli looks towards pragmatic and provisional solutions telling 'Wired magazine' (Wohlsen 2012), 'let's create a grand vision for humanity' and is more focused on how we make sure that the future is survivable.' For Zolli resilience is both a conservative and optimistic notion.

For sustainability opinion leaders such as Keith Wheeler, Mitch Thomashow and Greg Bourne, who were interviewed for this book, resilience offers possibilities of progressive, radical and genuinely transformative change.

The speed with which resilience has become embedded in the conservation and sustainable development discourse is not surprising, given that resilience has become meaningful to various communities, in the context of recent natural disasters in Japan, China, Haiti in particular but also to populations across Africa, Europe and the US that have felt the impact of changing weather patterns. The term has become part of the vocabulary of sustainable development, specifically at the international and national policy levels, with an unchecked assumption that resilience as a concept is understood and embraced by stakeholders on the ground. Often associated with the notion of resilience are terms such as 'risk', 'mitigation', 'adaptation',' vulnerability', 'critical thresholds' and 'transformation' (see Figure 1.3). However, the concept is complex and its various meanings range from the metaphorical and figurative to the strictly scientific. An analysis of key terms associated with 'resilience' used in over fifty documents distributed at the Rio+20 conference and official side events in June 2012 show that 'coping' and 'risk' are by far the most prominent.

Figure 1.3 Rio+20 wordcloud: key terms associated with resilience in the documentation circulated at Rio+20

Source: Analysis by Daniella Tilbury of leaflets, papers and PowerPoint presentations distributed at Rio+20

This book searches for the meaning of resilience in the context of sustainable development, asking how the concept is understood and used by influential actors within the movement. It searches for the ways in which resilience can be created within the web of ecological, socio-economic and cultural systems that make up the world in which we live and upon which all living creatures depend.

It offers an exploration of both robust and fragile systems at several levels, asking questions of individuals and groups who have been actively involved in building or maintaining resilience. The primary material was generated through a series of wide-ranging interviews.

Our interviewees come from all walks of life, but what they have in common is an experience and commitment to promoting environmental sustainability and conservation. Some, during their careers, have worked in a variety of roles in the private, public and voluntary sector, many have had direct experience of working with local communities in both the Global South and Global North, and many interviewees have had considerable responsibilities at high levels within international organisations, national government, NGOs and corporate businesses. All are well-respected experts in their fields who have helped frame policy and discourses or establish communities of practice. In some ways our research has offered some additional space for these people to deliberate further on what is occurring in our world and an opportunity to reflect openly on their own engagement with it, their own learning and development, their own futures and possibilities for all. A full list of interviewees and a brief biography of each can be found on pages ix–xviii.

The book works as an investigative documentary in written form using the voices of some key players in a variety of fields, to take the reader on a journey through real life experiences, into deeper analysis and critical questioning. This is framed by our own interpretations, analyses and reflections on current and emerging trends in conservation and sustainable development, arriving at set of diverse but connected conclusions, ideas and questions in relation to resilience

The book also aims to provide a platform upon which key stakeholders express their views and concerns about resilience in relation to sustainable development, and demonstrate the practical and successful ways in which resilience may be established, reworked or rearticulated.

The book therefore aims to empower readers with knowledge, understanding and a sense of the possible. We explore what can be done to recognise:

- how rigidity and brittleness can undermine resilience;
- how systems can bounce back against adversity;
- how communities can reconnect to address challenges head on; and
- how a movement must reinvent itself as goals and priorities shift.

In doing this, the book attempts to capture the dynamic nature of conservation and sustainability.

By embarking on a series of learning journeys, the book intends to show that answers and solutions are not ready-made; they are based on learning from experience in practical, pragmatic but nonetheless theoretically informed ways. Through interviews, observations and reflections, the authors give voice to the many different approaches to understanding and building resilience, that might otherwise stay rooted in, and confined by, specific disciplinary, professional or spatial contexts. The book emphasises the paramount importance of social learning and creative co-operation in the success of conservation and sustainable development practices throughout the world. The intention is to contribute to all fields of education and learning, systems thinking and development studies, where the relationships between human society and the environment are of crucial significance.

Above all this book is seeking to spark a 'grown-up' conversation about conservation and sustainable development, twenty years on from the pivotal moment at Rio in 1992, when agreement was reached about the necessity of international vision and global collaboration on sustainable development, for the sake of humanity and the planet. It maps some stages of that journey, reflects on progress and asks whether conservation is a resilient concept in the context of sustainable development. It recognises that conservation is changing in the face of contestation and adversity. The discourses have changed from pollution and limits to growth to poverty reduction, food security and the green economy. The book asks whether has this been as a result of experience and learning to adapt to a changing landscape or whether this is a sign that conservation is struggling to resist co-option and the dilution of it central mission to preserve life on earth. We explore the connections between the personal, the professional and the political. It investigates whether the agents for sustainability are themselves resilient. The interviews ask whether there has been too much compromise or too little, whether is adaptation necessary for the survival of the conservation movement or whether a stronger, more radical and ideologically courageous approach is required from all of those people who believe that a more sustainable, just and equal world is the only one that has long-term prospects.

In the course of this investigation we explore a number of key themes, such as the dominating interest, in the global North, in climate change, peak oil and green economic activity. We ask about the resurgence of interest and activity in the areas of participation, democracy, human rights in the global South over recent years. The present chapter introduces the context and key themes of resilience, green economy, international collaboration, conservation and sustainable development. In Chapter 2 we explore how the concept of resilience has been developed in a number of disciplinary and professional fields and how systems theory has formed the template for its various applications and practical expressions. Some themes and issues developed in later chapters are introduced here. Chapter 3 maps both the resilience and journey of the conservation movement by examining the tactics and politics involved, the influence of faith and other value-based belief systems and showing how attentions has seemingly shifted from a concern with biodiversity to climate change. The ways in which these shifts connect to the particular stories of key actors in the movement will also be analysed as will the changing emphasis from knowledge exchange to problem solving and to resilience building within both conservation theory and practice. Chapter 4 develops the discussion started in earlier chapters by focusing on the way resilience has been addressed by, and forms a background to, the development of responses to the economic recession, green business practices including ecotourism and the often self-defining significance of meaningful work, or it absence, for individuals and communities in the twenty-first century. The belief that another world is possible emerges from this examination and this belief is taken up in Chapter 5 where the contrast of resilience and regeneration, sustainability and practical utopias, implicitly informs many debates and practices around eco-cities, design, technology and other environmentally sustainable urban ventures in China, the Middle East and other parts of the developed and developing world. Chapter 6 looks at resilience both as a quality and a variable in a context of largely urban community development, behaviour change and the idea of transition as articulated by the growing Transition Movement. The importance of local food production as a means of fashioning a more socially sustainable, democratic and perhaps resilient city-region is also discussed, and through this the sometimes contrasting and sometimes complementary understandings of resilience are give critical scrutiny. Chapter 7 draws on, and develops, a number of references to education and learning that have appeared in preceding chapters but here the focus is sharper on the value of conservation education initiatives. As well as identifying leading programmes, the chapter seeks to deconstruct the purpose and models of educational systems more generally. It uncovers educational assumptions that have influenced investment in conservation education and those that could shape educational responses to resilience. Chapter 8 returns to a discussion of resilience in context and starting with an examination single homelessness and the role of *The Big Issue* begins a deliberation on the metaphorical uses and implications of resilience for both the vulnerable homeless person and the vulnerabilities and transformative potentials of other individuals, groups and collectives. Indeed, by revisiting some moments of critical concern identified earlier, the discussion moves towards a fundamental questioning of the value and efficacy of the concept itself. It asks: what forms of critical thinking and practical action are needed to achieve a more sustainable and just future for all creatures on this planet?

The ninth and final chapter attempts some resolution to our exploration of the series of challenges that we all will have to address this century. We recognise that positive change does occur, that hope and faith are important, but ultimately what is of greatest significance is perhaps not so much what we all say, or even perhaps what we believe, but what we all do.

Through the chapters, the book addresses questions such as: What is resilience? Is it a process, frame of mind, a set of skills or all of the above? What defines resilient systems, communities or individuals? Do we come to learn about resilience through studying communities that have demonstrated resilience against all odds? Or do we need to turn to the natural world to fully understand this concept? Is resilience something that needs rebuilding – in other words, something we have lost and need to regain or construct (International Institute for Educational Planning 2009)? Is adaptability a strength or have the compromises made along the journey explain the lack of tangible progress in areas? Is constant adaptation and accommodation a force for genuine change or the end of conservation?

The debate we document seeks to reflect on the value and effectiveness of the conservation and sustainability movement at a time when its own resilience is being tested.

2 Resilience in theory and practice

Introduction

In her posthumously published primer *Thinking in Systems*, Donella H. Meadows (2009: 76) defined resilience as 'the measure of a system's ability to survive and persist within a variable environment'. For Meadows, resilience is a product of a system being able to draw upon a rich series of feedback loops that works to bring a system back to a desirable balance following a disturbance of some description. Those feedback loops that are able to restore or rebuild operate at a high level and may be said to learn, create, design and evolve. They can fashion structures that are increasingly restorative and complex in their constitution. Resilient systems are said to be self-organising. Meadows, and other systems thinkers, often use the example of a human body or a natural ecosystem as a way of making concrete a notion that can be quite difficult to grasp in the abstract. The human body can repair itself after injury or a cut, can withstand a variety of different temperatures and can accommodate itself to any loss of specific functioning. The human person is also intelligent in that it can learn, create, socialise and design new things. It can enhance natural physical resilience with its capacity to invent and develop aids through technological and other innovations. Ecosystems are also, on the whole, remarkably resilient holding in balance a variety of species organisms that may otherwise multiply to a greater or lesser extent according to fluctuations in nutrient supply, weather patterns and so on. Ecosystems too have the capacity to 'learn' through genetic variability and temporal variation but this learning is of a different order to that of the affective and cognitive variety experienced by humans and other higher primates. Resilient systems are never static. They are constantly in the process of change and transformation; they evolve, oscillate, peak and collapse according to the various factors that impact upon its functioning. However, only when a violent or catastrophic change to context and the wider environment occurs does resilience become obvious either in its presence or absence. For Meadows, resilience is therefore a quality that may exist in all manner of social, biological, economic, ecological, political and technological fields. Consequently, a business can be resilient, so can a city, so can an individual person's or community's health and wellbeing. Thus, it is argued that awareness of resilience in both theory and practice enables an individual, a community group, a government or a business to see ways in which in they may preserve or add value to a system's inherent restorative capabilities. They will not only survive perturbation but recover.

In recent years resilience has increased its salience in many sustainability discourses. In *Resilience Thinking*, Brian Walker and David Salt emphatically believe that resilience is a key to sustainability, if not *the* key:

> The bottom line for sustainability is that any proposal for sustainable development that does not explicitly acknowledge a system's resilience is simply not going to keep delivering the goods (or services). The key to sustainability lies in enhancing the resilience of socio-ecological systems, not in optimising isolated components of the system.
>
> (Walker and Salt 2006: 9)

Holistic thinking is consequently an essential element to both thinking sustainably and becoming resilient. But this thinking cannot, or rather should not, occur as if human beings, together with their cultures and civilisations, are somehow outside the system itself. Holistic thinking means that we are 'all in it together', being able to recognise and act upon the fact that everything is in some way interlinked and connected. Jared Diamond's history lesson *Collapse* (2005) purports to show what happens to socio-ecological systems when human beings think and act otherwise, when resilience is undermined or destroyed by excessive resource exploitation, the failure or refusal to learn and the inability to think and act differently. The massive statues lining the coast of Easter Island may have been erected by the island's inhabitants to show respect to their gods, but they have become iconic and powerful testimonies to the consequences of unsustainable development. They have become a visual metaphor for our times, but the stories of Easter Island and the other societies Diamond writes about, such as the Norse in Greenland or the city of Uruk in Mesopotamia, or the Indian culture of the American southwest, also perhaps offer other lessons. Environmental mismanagement, climate change, drought and natural environmental factors certainly did play a part in their 'collapse' but more important were the deleterious impacts of these society's own social and economic arrangements. Indeed, many of the societies that Diamond studies only collapsed after a significantly long period of time – far longer in fact than our present social and economic arrangements of free market capitalism has dominated the globe. In fact, the people of Easter Island survived, if not flourished, for more than five hundred years in one of the remotest areas on the planet and their demise was probably triggered by the economic exploitative and politically oppressive actions of the European colonisers and proto-capitalists rather than by their own behaviour. Perhaps the real story is one of resilience rather than collapse (McAnany and Yoffee 2009)?

The history of resilience

In the growing body of literature on the concept of resilience a great deal has been written about the capacity of systems to absorb shocks but from the perspective of many sustainability practitioners what is of equal, if not more importance, is the capacity for change, renewal, development and reorganisation. Disturbance is not always a negative for it provides opportunities to do new and different things. Old ways of thinking that may have been seen as natural or traditional may find themselves under a sharp critical scrutiny. This is what started happening in the 1960s when a number of scientists, most notably C.S. Holling (1973), introduced the concept of resilience to the study of ecological systems and processes at a variety of temporal and spatial scales. He outlined measures by which system resilience (stability domains) could be assessed and communicated. His work was quickly taken up by those working in boreal forest dynamics in North America, rangelands, freshwater systems and fisheries. The implications for developing effective tools for natural resource management were obviously but other academic disciplines also saw the value of developing and applying a resilience perspective – anthropology, education, defence studies, childhood development, ecological economics, environmental psychology, community development, cultural theory, organisation studies, leadership, business and property management. However, it was with ecosystem analysis and management, complexity theory, engineering, systems science and later sustainable development that resilience had the most purchase. The idea of non-linear dynamics, alternate domains of attractions and regime shifts began to change the hegemony of steady state equilibrium theory in mainstream ecology. However, for some years, ecology tended to interpret resilience as something like return time following a system disturbance. It was also combined with a growing concern for engineering resilience through changing human behaviour in order to maintain constancy, predictability and system efficiency. Increasingly, however, systems were being perceived as complex rather than predictable or deterministic with multiple feedbacks allowing for self-organisation. As Folke (2006) explains, a number of scientists developed theories of far-from-equilibrium system dynamics, with up to six properties of complex adaptive economic systems being identified. These were: dispersed interaction, the absence of any global controller, cross-cutting hierarchical organisation, continual adaptation, perpetual novelty and far-from-equilibrium dynamics. Links between complex systems, thermodynamics and ecology were also made. Biodiversity and ecosystem services became an essential ingredient to fully appreciating system dynamics, complexity and the ability to self-organise (Holling *et al.* 1995). For instance, as Folke *et al.* (1996) discovered, species that may seem unnecessary for ecosystem functioning at one stage of ecosystem development may become really critical at other times such as when a system is in the process of regeneration and reorganisation following perturbation or disturbance. Cross scale interplay, discontinuous patterns, processes and structures became not only central to the study of ecology but also to the study of the diversity and redundancy of human institutions.

The growing sophistication in the study of the dynamic development of complex adaptive systems saw two further important concepts emerge: the concept of the adaptive renewal cycle and that of panarchy (Gunderson and Holling 2002). Panarchy was conceived as the antithesis of hierarchy. The term derives its name from the Greek god of nature Pan, who was unpredictable and changeable. It is an attempt to rationalise the relationships between change and persistence, what is or what can be predicted and what is and what cannot. Holling and his co-authors believed there are hierarchies of influence between embedded scales (panarchies) that constitute a cycle of adaptive change generating new and different activities or experiments at different connected levels. Thus, there are potentially multiple connections between temporal phases at one level and phases occurring at another. Some levels operate quickly and others more slowly. The quick ones are generative and essentially experimental in nature and the slow ones stabilising and conserving. This means that panarchy is simultaneously creative and conserving, adaptive and changing. The structure in which natural systems such forests, grasslands, rivers, and seas and those of human beings such as nation states, social groups and cultures, together with environmental management and related systems controlling natural resource use, are interlinked in continuous and continuing adaptive cycles of growth, accumulation, restructuring, and renewal. These transformational cycles take place in nested sets at scales ranging from the micro to the macro, from the leaf to the biosphere and over periods of duration lasting from minutes and days to eons. For Holling and others, by understanding these cycles and their scales, it becomes possible to identify points at which a system is capable of accommodating positive change and which can help foster resilience and sustainability. Sustainable development is, therefore, the combination of these elements and processes. Gunderson and Holling (2002) write:

> Change and extreme transformations have been part of humanity's evolutionary history. People's adaptive capabilities, have made it possible not only to persist passively, but to create and innovate when limits are reached.
>
> The reason for the astonishing resilience of natural ecosystems can be found in examining the scales at which processes (including humans) operate to control the system. For example, in most terrestrial systems, geophysical controls dominate at scales larger than tens of kilometers. At scales smaller than this, biotic processes, interacting with abiotic ones, can control structure and variability. They produce volumes and patterns of vegetation and soil, for example, that moderate external extremes of temperature, conserve moisture and nutrients, and even affect regional climate and the timing of seasons. These are also the scale ranges where human land use transformations occur so that the arena where plant and animal controlling interactions unfold is the same arena where human activities interact with the landscape. That is why human population growth and development is so inexorably interconnected with terrestrial ecosystem resilience.

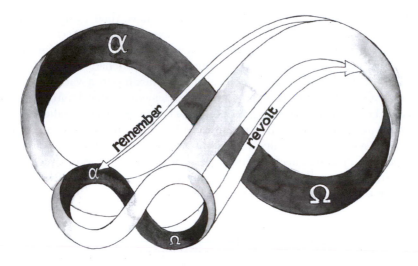

Figure 2.1 Panarchy: the *Revolt* and *Remember* connections are important at times of change. When a level enters its omega phase and experiences collapse, that collapse can cascade to the next larger and slower level by precipitating a crisis, particularly if that level exhibits low resilience

Source: Lorna Blewitt

Resilience thinking provides an integrated perspective for analysis, emphasising the potential of nonlinear changes and the interdependency of social and ecological systems. When resilience thinking combined with optimisation outcome orientated tools in conservation and sustainability practice that recognises resource scarcity and the need to make rational and transparent decisions then cost effective and enduring sustainability/conservation results are arguably quite possible. Such practice will enhance system adaptability and resilience (Fischer *et al.* 2007). Holling (2001: 393–4) writes in detail about the adaptive cycle arguing that three properties shape its functioning and by extension the future state of the system. These properties include:

- The inherent potential or 'wealth' of a system that is available for change, since that potential determines the range of future options possible.
- The internal 'controllability' of a system or the degree of connectedness between internal controlling variables and processes, a measure that reflects the degree of flexibility or rigidity of such controls, such as their sensitivity or not to perturbation.
- The adaptive capacity or 'resilience' of the system, a measure of its vulnerability to unexpected or unpredictable shocks. This property can be thought of as the opposite of the vulnerability of the system.

Human, as opposed to natural ecological, systems have their own peculiarities and systemic characteristics. These include the existence and impacts of human foresight and intentionality, the human capacity to communicate ideas and experience, and the application of sophisticated and system-changing technologies (Holling 2001). Developing the ability to learn flexibly in a variety of ways, contexts and circumstances is an important element of developing adaptive capacity. However, some learning is not always for the good, and resilience itself is not always a good thing as it is quite possible that an undesirable social or ecological system may be highly resistant to change. Learning and adaptive management processes may depend on political will and political action, as power structures and dominant economic interests, ways of producing and consuming, are both robust and aggressively persistent.

Table 2.1 Sequence of resilience concepts

Resilience concepts	Characteristics	Focus on	Context
Engineering resilience	Return time, efficiency	Recovery, constancy	Vicinity of a stable equilibrium
Ecological/ecosystem resilience, social resilience	Buffer capacity, withstand shock, maintain function	Persistence, robustness	Multiple equilibria, stability landscapes
Socio-ecological resilience	Interplay disturbance and reorganisation, sustaining and developing	Adaptive capacity, transformability, learning, innovation	Integrated system feedback, cross-scale dynamic interactions

Source: Adapted from Folke (2006)

There have been a number of attempts to examine the processes of socio-ecological resiliences. Studies have been made of coastal communities, cities, patterns of migration, changes in social capital and social trust networks, economic management, famine and the vulnerability of food systems and land use and degradation over time. In these explorations the importance of undertaking risk assessments seems of paramount importance but these are too often not done adequately or done at all. Socio-ecological systems have powerful multi scalar reciprocal feedbacks. Human institutions and organisations consequently need to construct sophisticated models for analysis in order to build knowledge, learning and capabilities, so that integrated adaptive management can occur at local, regional and global ecosystem levels. However, as Folke writes, a distinction needs to be made between adaptability and transformability:

> In resilience work adaptability is referred to as the capacity of people in a socio-ecological system to build resilience through collective action whereas transformability is the capacity of people to create a fundamentally new

socio-ecological system when ecological, political, social, or economic conditions make the existing system untenable.

(Folke 2006: 262)

Holling's concept of panarchy complements what is known as 'world systems analysis', developed by Immanuel Wallerstein and others a number of years ago (Wallerstein 1974; Chase-Dunn and Hall 1997; Gotts 2007). Although not necessarily planetary in scope, world systems analysis takes into account multiple societies, and long-term and highly structured interrelationships even though the most important unit of world systems analysis remains the entire world-system itself. Within this world-system there are core, semi-peripheral and peripheral regions with the latter tending to service the former. Individual nation states may move within the system but upward mobility is constrained by trade relations and the exercise of geopolitical power. Large corporations are major economic actors and with the military–industrial complex they work to ensure that the existing world order, as far as possible, maintains its resilience and their economic interests. Long and short economic cycles are central to understanding global hegemony, and the distribution of political, military and economic power, and the world system as it is recognizable today, more or less came into being with the growth of European capitalism in the sixteenth century. However, having emerged from the study of ecological systems, the panarchical perspective does not directly address the ways in which dominant social and political elites maintain themselves even though these elites, and sometimes violent conflict, are extremely important to social and economic dynamics and clearly relevant to understanding the nature of and prospects for improved environmental sustainability. It should also be noted that the panarchical perspective has said little about the long-term growth of the world's population. However, having said that, connectedness and interrelationships are pivotal to understanding present problems and challenges and applying a historical world systems perspective may enable analysts to model potential future directions and transformations including highly significant demographic ones. For Holling (2004), the world is presently moving towards a period of major transformation only seen three or four times before in the whole of human history. Consequently, Holling sees it as imperative that businesses, governments, NGOs, scientific institutes, universities, political parties and citizen groups need to be engaged at all levels not so much to predict the future but to experiment, innovate and create the future that we need and desire:

> The present responses of the world community at large to the possibility of transformation have been at best adequate or bad. The question is how to tip the scales more toward adequately good and achieve a better balance in the world by improving the lot of poverty-stricken populations, reducing extremes of population growth and collapse, and nurturing inventive solutions. What I observe is that the good approaches are less in ascendance at the present, and narrow, powerful, military and protectionist economic

approaches are taking precedence. In the late economic bubble of the 1990s, business and government combined and dangerously usurped the balance normally provided by government. That does threaten the breadth of influence needed in a democracy. There is a tendency toward greater extremism, which ignores the broad inequities within society, or toward narrow approaches that preclude attempts to address diversity. The scale of the issues is such that they are beyond the reach of any one company, sector of the economy, or government. There is a need for a co-operative international effort that involves a major contribution to transformation by people of vision or groups of people thinking deeply about the nature of risk and finding novel ways to approach it.

(Holling 2004: 19)

For Holling, the Internet is a new means for international co-operation and sharing, invention and creativity. It is where a considerable amount of hope may lie. Unfortunately, corporate colonisation and government censorship of the Net has increased markedly in recent years which may make this optimism a little misplaced (Blewitt forthcoming 2014).

Differing and partially overlapping mental models such as panarchy and world systems thinking can indeed be extremely valuable heuristic devices which may themselves change and adapt over time as new knowledge and understanding accrues and as new crises emerge (Walker *et al.* 2006). A problem comes when key concepts such as resilience, or for that matter sustainable development, become subject to a wide range of sometimes competing, sometimes contradictory and sometimes complementary definitions. When this happens, meaning can become quite vague, diffuse and malleable. Brand and Jax (2007) identify ten definitions of resilience each respecting a certain degree of normativity some of which having multiple characteristics.

For resilience to remain useful, the concept must retain a clear descriptive capability even though it has been elevated in many disciplines to be a way of thinking, or even an analytic paradigm in itself. In some ways it has become a 'boundary object' which, like the concept of sustainable development, may provide a common ground for academics, politicians and professionals to come together to discuss and perhaps reconcile different or contrasting interests. However, if the meaning of resilience, again like sustainable development, remains unclear or confusing, or if differing groups fail or refuse to recognise the value of this common ground, scientific and political progress may be hard to realise. In this case, fudges and confusions are the most likely outcome if agreement is still to be sought. Learning and discussion may lead not to consensus but to compromise, and the degree to which this compromise is satisfactory will be determined by what is done with the future.

Generally speaking, it may be said that narrow definitions are preferable to scientists and broader ones, which invariably include normative dimensions, to social scientists. For Brand and Jax (2007: 33), however, 'increased vagueness and malleability of resilience is highly valuable because it is for this reason that

Table 2.2 Ten definitions of resilience with respect to the degree of normativity

Categories and classes	Definitions
ECOLOGICAL SCIENCE	
1. Original ecological	Measure of the persistence of systems and of their ability to absorb change and disturbance and still maintain the same relationships between populations or state variables
2. Extended ecological	The magnitude of disturbance that can be absorbed before the system changes its structure by changing the variables and processes that control behaviour; the capacity of a system to experience shocks while retaining essentially the same function, structure and feedbacks, and therefore identity
3. Systemic–heuristic	Quantitative property that changes throughout ecosystem dynamics and occurs on each level of an ecosystem's hierarchy
4. Operational	Resilience *of* what *to* what? The ability of the system to maintain its identity in the face of internal change and external shocks and disturbances
SOCIAL SCIENCES	
5. Sociological	The ability of groups or communities to cope with external stresses and disturbances as a result of social, political and environmental change
6. Ecological–economic	Transition probability between states as a function of the consumption and production activities of decision makers; the ability of the system to withstand either market or environmental shocks without losing the capacity to allocate resources efficiently
HYBRID CONCEPT	
7. Ecosystem-services-related	The underlying capacity of an ecosystem to maintain desired ecosystem services in the face of a fluctuating environment and human use
8. Socio-ecological system	The capacity of a socio-ecological systems to absorb recurrent disturbances so as to retain essential structures, processes and feedbacks; and/or a perspective or approach to analyse socio-ecological systems
NORMATIVE CONCEPT	
9. Metaphoric	Flexibility over the long term
10. Sustainability-related	Maintenance of natural capital in the long run

Source: adapted from Brand and Jax (2007)

the concept is able to foster communication across disciplines and between science and practice'. For this to work an intellectual division of labour is probably required: on the one hand, resilience conceived and articulated as a clear, well-defined and specific descriptive concept (i.e. as in 'ecological resilience/ecosystem resilience') will satisfactorily form the basis for application and operationalisation within ecological science; on the other, resilience conceived and articulated as a boundary object (i.e. as in 'socio-ecological resilience') will enable transdisciplinary learning, research and development.

Resilience in cross-cultural perspective

In order to understand and act effectively to combat the acute social and environmental problems that confront us, we must be able to recognise the importance of, and develop, a range of higher-order thinking skills and capabilities. Such thinking will include an appreciation of personal epistemological beliefs (i.e. the beliefs we hold about the nature of knowledge and how we come to know what we know, or at least think we do). These beliefs in large part shape how we relate to each other and how we relate to the wider world of complex socio-ecological systems.

For Fazey (2010), resilience thinking is potentially a principle component of developing increasingly sophisticated personal epistemological beliefs. This requires equally sophisticated approaches to formal learning, cross-cultural and transdisciplinary understanding and spaces for discursive public communication and discussion. However, it should also be recognised that a systems view is only one of a number of qualitative and quantitative ways of understanding complex processes. Systems thinking tends towards positivist world views, and resilience thinking may not necessarily be able to accommodate the various ways different groups and individuals may experience the same set of circumstances or series of events. Neither is systems thinking adept at applying concepts of political power, philosophical intentionality and human subjectivity.

There is also a danger, perhaps, despite Brand and Jax's (2007) useful discussion of the variable nature of the resilience concept itself, that resilience thinking may overemphasise biophysical structures of a system and underplay the dynamic influence of human subjects. If resilience is to be a key component in scientific and non-scientific higher-order thinking then it will also have to create a profound understanding of human social processes that other concepts are unable to do. Resilience should not be seen as a universal answer, a concept that will unlock the door to all knowledge and wisdom, although it may well be an element of the knowledge and wisdom that must inform future processes of sustainable development and in our growing understanding of the processes and stages of human psycho-social development (Cook-Greuter 2000).

However, as Arve Gunnestad (2011) shows in his comparative study of South Africa and Norway, different cultures generate resilience in different ways. For children growing up in the world today intellect, physical robustness, social and familial networks, belief systems, and emotional stability are frequently cited as the basic ingredients for resilience. These factors interact with each other and with the external cultural environment by building up a positive self-image and by reducing the effect of actual and perceived risk factors. For Gunnestad, culture consists of the norms, values and ways of life that we are born into and which each generation interprets and adapts to in their own times. Cultural processes are inevitably diverse and in a moment when global communications are opening up alternative cultures to view facilitating new forms of do-it-yourself bricolage, cultural change and identity can be fraught with many individual, group and national tensions.

Consequently, the different elements of each specific culture or sub-culture may be combined with others. The complexity of their wider interactions will therefore contribute to how and why resilience is articulated in the way it is in different cultures, contexts and historical moments. Thus, although the family is an important protective family found in most if not all areas, the extended family is of far greater salience in South Africa than it is in contemporary Norway where the nuclear family remains the dominant institution. Individualism is also far more central in Norwegian culture than in many other cultures, such as in southern Africa (or, for that matter, among Latino and Indian First Nation peoples). Complexity also increases with globalisation and migration where biculturalism often sees groups and individuals moving in and out of two, or more, cultures, languages, sets of norms, values and expectations. Thus, culture is inevitably dynamic and changing, often hybrid and always in the process of becoming. Culture is, or at least can be, a source for individual and societal resilience however defined.

In 2011 the International Society for the Study of Behavioural Development published a series of short articles on children and young people's reaction to various stresses, ranging from war to natural disaster. Personal and societal vulnerability often lead to less rather than more resilience, but as Masten and others have shown in a number of articles, the processes that build resilience are in fact quite ordinary relating closely to basic human adaptation systems (Masten *et al.* 1990; Masten 2001).

This is further confirmed in the comparative study of street children in India, the Philippines, Indonesia and South Africa by Verma *et al.*(2011) with the caveat that resilience plays out differently in different cultural settings and in different situations. For example, the street becomes the solution for children whose families are unable to or cannot support them because of domestic violence or abusive parents or parents who may be completely absent as is invariably the case with AIDS orphans. Children who live in shelters tend to cope differently from those who live at home but what is needed by all are supportive networks and representations, and hope that a better world is possible and not just a dream.

This better life may come from formal and informal learning as well as the cultivation of certain personal attributes, a sense of personal worth and the capability of engaging in productive work activity of some description. People may learn from the past and do not necessarily return to the same point after having had stressful experiences. People may tend to combine bits of knowledge and emotional experiences to develop ways and means of coping in the future that work to overcome vulnerabilities, risks and hardships. Social and psychological resilience is often a product of individual and collective learning that, unlike that applied to the biophysical sphere, is not metaphorical but actual. A recognition and experience of a sense of personal and collective efficacy is extremely important and, apart from family, friendship, community and other social networks, there is a role for government at various levels to ensure that this sense of efficacy can be realised.

These points will be revisited in Chapter 8, but for now it is worth noting that in her overview of the field Silvia Koller (2011) notes that whatever scales, measures, and data frameworks researchers employ, the information gained on lifestyle and life satisfaction, wellbeing, hope and optimism, sense of efficacy and so on will always be partial. These can only describe a few elements of a more dynamic and broader process:

> Strictly speaking, we cannot conclude much about resilience because it seems to depend on the circumstances, the local culture, and the individual's subjective perception. Perhaps it is time to abandon resilience as a variable per se and, instead, either qualify it through adjectives or replace the term 'resilience' with more descriptive variables, so that the circumstances, culture, perceptions, and value assessments of the benefits and harm of stressful events can be described more precisely.
>
> (Koller 2011: 18)

The psychologist Michael Unger (2011) believes there is clear evidence that resilience is not so much an individual trait but rather a quality of a child's environment, and perhaps it can be extrapolated further to include adult social and spatial communities, social and physical ecology. Applying an ecological understanding to, and of, resilience could possibly help resolve, to some extent, both definitional and measurement problems for a major issue with resilience is that the term is used by many writers, policy makers, practitioners and researchers to describe both the outcomes and the processes that lead to these outcomes. A clear distinction should be made therefore an individual's internal traits and resilience which is process orientated, invariably complex and quite probably culturally relative. This leads Unger to offer a revised definition of resilience, which places the locus of control for positive development on a shared experience of both individuals and their social and physical ecologies:

> In the context of exposure to significant adversity, resilience is both the capacity of individuals to navigate their way to the psychological, social, cultural, and physical resources that sustain their wellbeing, and their capacity individually and collectively to negotiate for these resources to be provided and experienced in culturally meaningful ways.
>
> (Unger 2011: 10)

It seems that preparing societies for major disasters, natural or otherwise, requires the integration of social learning and human research on resilience in a transdisciplinary manner that is able to derive benefit and insights from all those disciplines and professional fields concerned with resilience in complex and dynamic socio-ecological systems (Masten and Obradovic 2007).

Resilience in conservation and sustainable development

The World Conservation Union (International Union for the Conservation of Nature, IUCN) is one of the leading bodies in developing and applying this type of connected resilience thinking. The long-term sustainability of ecosystems and their attendant eco-system services depend in large part on the maintenance of biodiversity. Thus, a sustainable ecosystem needs, as insurance, a large number of substitutable species the dynamic interactions between each of the species and the environment as a whole. All this together with that combination of structures that enable resilience or reorganisation to occur after a disturbance is known as the system's 'ecological memory' (Bengtsson *et al.* 2003).

Through linking its work on biodiversity conservation to building resilience in human (particularly rural) communities, the IUCN aims to help people deal effectively with the massive changes to life and livelihoods that are occurring as a result of climate change and periodic natural disasters. Some communities have been historically located in hazard prone areas such as the foot of volcanos, or on or near flood plains, eroding coastal areas or at the banks of major river systems but anthropogenic climate change and other risks derived from irresponsible economic development are putting increasing numbers of people in a situation of uncertainty and potential danger. Coastal areas are often rich in food and other natural resources but may also be subject to ferocious whether systems with delta cities subject to an increasing incidence of seriously destructive flooding.

However, living in the path of cyclones or subject to the possibility of a tsunami or gradual sea level rise does not mean that a life of perpetual struggle is the only thing human beings can expect of the future. For the IUCN's Commission on Education and Communication, as Bradley Smith (2011) notes, human communities need to build their own social, environmental and spatial resilience: first, by developing a sufficient buffering capacity; second, by being able to regroup and reorganise after experiencing the impact of a natural or other disaster; and third, by developing the capacity to learn and adapt after each disturbance.

Resilience can be nurtured by taking appropriate precautions, developing and implementing contingency plans, by communicating effectively and again by learning. Indeed, it is the environmental learning that is possibly the most important thing a community can undertake and unfortunately something that frequently gets overlooked or underemphasised. When a resilience perspective is integrated into environmental learning and in more formal educational processes and institutions, attention shifts from identifying an individual's learning outcomes to exploring how this learning interacts with the other components of the social and ecological systems humans inhabit (Krasney *et al.* 2010).

However, although resilience is becoming increasingly common in many fields with, in recent years, a veritable explosion of academic publishing in this area, the main finding of the bibliographic research of Janssen *et al.* (2006) was that the resilience knowledge domain was only weakly connected with the two most closely related knowledge domains, that is of vulnerability and adaptation, at least in terms of co-authorship and specific citations. Academic work on resilience emerged predominantly from the fields of ecology and mathematics together with their familiar penchant for theoretical modelling, whereas those focusing primarily on vulnerability and adaptation seem to have a background in geography and natural hazards research, where case study methodologies and climate change research flourishes. It seems that disciplinary boundaries, professional and scholarly networks remain of determining significance. Resilience is increasingly pervasive but interpretations and salience varies and this can also be seen in the way the term is applied in practice and used in professional discourse, political actions, economics, public policy and media discussion.

The devastating impact of Hurricane Katrina on the city of New Orleans not only showed up the vulnerability of a city located in a risk prone areas but also the inadequacy of the city's artificial and natural defences, its dams and levees, its degraded wetlands and mangroves which had made way for luxury hotel construction and economic growth. Katrina also clearly demonstrated that the city's lack of resilience was the product of discriminatory economic, housing, political and social policies that compounded and amplified the impact of the 'natural disaster'.

However, the city survived, as virtually every modern city has done in modern times, whether the havoc has been wrought by natural forces or the atomic bomb. Buildings can be rebuilt, property lines rediscovered but what is most important in a city, and this was the case in New Orleans, was the resilience of the people – their communal institutions, family and friendship networks, intangible and tangible cultural heritage and so on (Campanella 2006). We must, however, learn about and from the environment on which we depend and this learning cannot be divorced from politics, culture, economics and social arrangements. Smith concludes his IUCN article by stating that:

> Our communities' exposure to natural hazards will be increasingly frequent in the coming decades. With our human population continuing to rise and increasing numbers congregating along coastlines, fault lines, and river boundaries, a greater number of humans are living harm's way. These hazard-prone regions provide bountiful natural environments where we can find food, shelter, and engage in commerce. Yet we need to foster community resilience in order to address our vulnerability to the threats that are also part of these environments.
>
> (Smith 2011)

Thus conservation of the natural environment is intimately connected to the wellbeing of human communities whether they be in the 'developed' global North or the 'under' developed global South. The IUCN's approach to area biodiversity conservation links human social and economic wellbeing to that of endangered flora and fauna at site level. The areas identified by the IUCN as being of primary global significance involve intergovernmental agencies, national governments, civil society organisations, private sector business, and local and indigenous community groups. The IUCN Red List of Threatened Species, the UNESCO Man and Biosphere Programme, the World Heritage Convention, the Ramsar Convention on Wetlands combined with the 2010–2020 Strategic Plan for the Convention on Biological Diversity are part of a global effort to protect and conserve planetary ecosystems.

The 'key biodiversity areas' have been incorporated into various tools such as the Integrated Biodiversity Assessment Tool for Business that aims to ensure business decisions that may affect critical natural habitats are informed by the best available scientific information. The tool can be used to develop action plans that manage the impact on biodiversity from such operations as mining and drilling for oil.

Social arrangements and community participation is key to the IUCN's work, and although the IUCN acknowledges that it is difficult to comprehensively record the emergence and activities of local 'site support groups' to implement conservation measures, it is clear that they are part of a much wider series of positive developments. These include conservation related employment and income, stabilisation of land tenure, maintenance of ecosystem services, educational opportunities and the nurturing of community pride in proximate natural environments. Inevitably, the enhancement of resilience and ecosystem-based adaptation to climate change is central for many groups in many areas (International Union for the Conservation of Nature 2012).

One of the main challenges in both the theoretical and practice work around climate change adaptation is understanding what the implications are for resilience beyond the technological and infrastructure developments that are often constructed in the wake of crises and disasters. Hard flood defences may have negative impacts on biodiversity as modified ecosystems embark on a process of maladaptation although, equally, if appropriate environmental and natural resource management strategies are implemented there may occur highly positive feedback for both biodiversity and people. Climate change is already having discernible impacts on biodiversity at various organisational and spatial levels with species distribution and composition altering to accommodate changes in temperature and rainfall. The increase in invasive formerly non-native species is a major driver of ecosystem change locally and globally.

More generally, those ecosystem services upon which human communities depend, such as water flow regimes, fish stocks and carbon sequestration processes, are now clearly evident, as the Millennium Ecosystem Assessment (2005) exhaustively detailed. Biodiversity and climate change is indubitably linked (Campbell *et al.* 2009). Adaptation strategies recognise the inevitability of change and include a number of processes, tools and procedures, one of the most important of which are vulnerability assessments i.e. an assessment of the degree to which a system is susceptible to and/or unable able to cope with the negative impacts of climate change. As is stated in the IUCN's book of case studies on climate change adaptation, *Building Resilience to Climate Change*, these assessments should:

- Assess the nature and magnitude of the climate change threat;
- Identify the key sources of climate change vulnerability;
- Identify, analyse and evaluate the impact of climate change and variability on natural resources, ecosystems, socio-economic systems and human health;
- Understand the vulnerabilities that relate to institutional capacity and financial resources of affected communities (e.g. farmers, foresters, and fishermen);
- Assess the possible adaptive responses of human and ecological systems;
- Develop technical, institutional and financial strategies to reduce vulnerability levels for ecosystems and human populations.

(Perez *et al.* 2010: 14)

There is perhaps a residual faith in the techno-rationalist model of thought, action and development that has also proved problematic. It is now virtually accepted universally that anthropogenic climate change is currently occurring at an unprecedented and alarming rate and although human societies have adapted to climate variability in the past quite successfully, the issues and problems now confronting human society are of a different order. The risks and uncertainties are not natural as such, but induced by human action – largely industrial developments, which, for the German sociologist Ulrich Beck (1992), are the product of persistent and consistent 'organised irresponsibility'.

An ecosystems approach to climate change adaptation attempts to integrate social and environmental systems in a way that leads to comprehensible, comprehensive and practical action. At the collective level this involves establishing effective governance and management structures which enables capacity building within, and by, organisations, groups and individuals (Nelson *et al.* 2007). Above all, it involves transforming capacity into action and much current research and development in this area is predicated on the assumption that the inevitable rise in global temperature can be contained within a band of 2–3 degrees centigrade. In excess of that, the tipping points for many socio-ecological systems will come on furiously as there are not the institutions, technology or finance available that could prevent the devastating consequences from occurring.

Given the structural social, political and economic inequalities that have characterised the first part of the twenty-first century, despite nearly ten years of action on the Millennium Development Goals, it is certain that the world's poor, particularly those who eke out a living on US$2 a day (or less), will suffer the most. What needs continually emphasising is that economic development as presently practiced often occurs at the expense of the natural ecosystems which is still aided and abetted by a tacit worldview that aggressively posits nature as something that needs to be tamed and whose riches are there to be exploited and extracted.

Consequently, for the IUCN, resilience is an essential condition for sustainable economic development and environmental responsiveness. A resilient global economy needs inclusivity and diversity as well as competitiveness and co-operation. Any meaningful transition to a green economy must promote equity, environmental conservation and participatory democracy as overriding principles. In a position paper on the transition to a green economy prepared for the Rio+20 summit in 2012 the IUCN stated that ecosystem management necessarily endorses the keen dependency of human society on natural resources and ecosystem services,

> A truly resilient economy preserves and enhances its natural capital and invests in the restoration of landscapes to support local as well as global livelihoods. Resilient economies enhance the quality of life, and optimise the delivery of 'regulating' ecosystem services (e.g. water filtration, carbon and nutrient cycling, storm mitigation). A nature-based economy is one which thrives on these ecosystem services by empowering those communities who depend directly on natural resources and processes. Indigenous communities in general – and women in particular, often play a central role in the management of natural resources. A Green Economy needs to recognise and value their role as stewards of our precious natural capital and biophysical systems.
>
> (International Union for the Conservation of Nature 2012: 3)

For the UN too, resilience is at the heart of sustainable development (United Nations 2012). Real choice for people is only possible when human rights, basic needs, security, equity and resilience are assured. The UN argues that governments need to integrate resilience into their planning, budgetary, conservation, agricultural and economic developments. There needs to be a greater degree of crop diversification than has occurred recently. Social protection systems or safety nets will need to be developed in order to minimise hardship and ameliorate the impact of risk and shortage brought on by extreme weather events, financial instability, food and resource scarcity. Global planetary boundaries, such as those delineated by the Stockholm Resilience Centre, must be recognised and adhered to. These boundaries include:

- climate change,
- global freshwater use,
- biogeochemical flows,
- rate of biodiversity loss,
- stratospheric ozone depletion,
- ocean acidification,
- change in land use,
- chemical pollution and
- atmospheric aerosol loading.

These boundaries are clearly interlinked and changes in one may impact on others causing these others to exceed what the centre firmly believes to be safe operating spaces for humanity.

However, as the authors of an important paper conclude, 'the evidence so far suggests that, as long as the thresholds are not crossed, humanity has the freedom to pursue long-term social and economic development' (Rockström *et al.* 2009: 475). In terms of global governance these boundaries are not necessarily or effectively static and multilateral negotiations, adaptation policies and actions at multiple scales recognising that there is a degree of fluidity in what may be safe operating spaces (Galaz *et al.* 2012). Resilient systems are able to absorb large shocks without changing in fundamental ways; resilience is generally associated with diversity and with things that can be restored albeit slowly.

Fortunately, changes do tend to occur slowly but this is not always the case and the great fear today around tipping points is that shocks may push a system dramatically over into an undesirable state quite different to the previous more comfortable one. Maybe the fish will not return, the ice will not reform or soil recuperate, the city will not bounce back...What is clear to some systems analysts, and those that explore governance and management implications, is that control and adaptation mechanisms must be flexible lest naturally occurring ecological variables and disturbance regimes, social capital and social memory are irreparably harmed or even destroyed.

Thus it is argued that conservation and sustainability knowledge can be constructed from learning from past mistakes, crises and problems brought on by resource depletion, habitat destruction and species loss and new means of dealing with future problems and perhaps rectifying earlier human impacts can be enacted. In this way, more resilient and integrated socio-ecological systems may emerge (Berkes and Turner 2006). People must be enabled so they can envisage future possibilities, develop scenarios for change that incorporate alternate perspectives and build resilience into decision making processes and, most importantly, be able to act appropriately and wisely (Peterson *et al.* 2003). Innovation and collaboration is essential, meaningful indicators will need to be developed and applied and policy needs and tools to be socially owned as well as politically implemented (Folke *et al.* 2002). There is a lot to do.

The future of people on Earth

In a background scientific paper for the 2002 Johannesburg Earth summit, Folke and his co-authors identified four critical factors essential to sustaining the capacity for socio-ecological resilience:

- learning to live with change and uncertainty;
- nurturing diversity for resilience;
- combining different types of knowledge for learning; and
- creating opportunity for self-organisation towards socio-ecological sustainability (Folke *et al.* 2002).

These factors interact and cross different spatial and temporal scales, and are necessary for successfully dealing with natural resource dynamics in periods of change, uncertainty and reorganisation. For these authors learning and appropriate indicators are key to flexible adaptive management processes.

However, where resilience is concerned the indicators need to relate to underlying variables rather than the current state of the system. Understanding and, wherever possible, directing these variables are important to building both resilience and adaptive capacity. Certain events, such as droughts and hurricanes, are not easily predicted, so building resilience is probably the most pragmatic and effective way of managing socio-ecological ecosystems. Thus Folke *et al.* (2002: 44–45) suggest that the main attributes a complex adaptive system ought to include actions and strategies that are cognisant of:

- Ecological resilience which can be assessed by the amount of variability that can be accepted without patterns changing and controls shifting to another set of keystone processes.
- Keystone ecosystem processes interacting in an overlapping, apparently redundant manner. They should not be evaluated by the efficiency with which any one process functions.
- Resilience within a system that is generated through major changes and renewal of systems at smaller, faster scales.
- Essential sources of resilience lying in the variety of functional groups and the accumulated experience and memory that provides for reorganisation following disturbances.
- Resilience residing in slowly-changing variables such as soils, biological legacies, and landscape processes, which provide ecological memory and context for critical life processes.

So the capacity of adaptive management is central to all our futures. The environment, natural ecosystems cannot be separated from human action, society, political institutions or economic arrangements. Culture, society, government, social and physical ecologies of individuals everywhere are unsurprisingly central to the highly ambitious aims of the IHOPE project, which identifies as its main objective:

> to use new and existing data sources to produce an integrated historical account of changes in climate, atmospheric chemistry and composition, ecosystem distribution, material and water cycles, species extinctions, land-use systems, human settlement patterns, technologies, patterns of disease, patterns of language and institutions, conflicts and alliances, and other variables. To achieve this ambitious goal, it will be necessary to create a framework that can be used to integrate perspectives, theories, tools and knowledge from a variety of disciplines spanning the full spectrum of social and natural sciences and the humanities.
>
> (Hibbard *et al.* 2010: 1)

Current knowledge suggests that societies tend to lose resilience as they get larger geographically, that is, expand spatially or become ever more structurally complex. This means that the same environmental stresses that could be dealt with relatively easily in earlier times, when society was less developed and complex, can in later times become sufficient to cause collapse. To gain a clear and comprehensive understanding of this will involve a careful consideration of the concept of systems complexity, a concept which Gleick (1998) has likened to walking through a maze whose walls rearrange themselves as one proceeds. As the walker adjusts his direction, so do the walls of the maze, and often this is compounded by the development of new technologies, the persistence of a spuriously confident faith in technical fixes, the reformative potential of the capitalist economic system and an incapacity or reluctance to learn reflexively. As John Urry (2005: 238) states, in complexity theory, 'order and chaos are often in a kind of balance where the components are neither fully locked into place but yet do not dissolve into anarchy'. The IHOPE project intends to explore this Zone through seeking answers to a number of specific questions:

1   What are the resilience characteristics of socio-ecological systems that lead to either sustainability or collapse? What makes socio-ecological systems resilient or brittle at various points in their evolution?
2   How do societies respond to resource limitations? Can technology create new frontiers indefinitely? What is the role and path of technology in the evolution of socio-ecological systems?
3   What causes socio-ecological systems to be more or less successful in adapting to ten year period and longer changes (e.g., land use, climate, disease)?
4   Are some types of environmental stress inherently more likely to cause collapse than others?
5   What might have been the long-term human contributions to changes in the rates and composition of Earth processes?
6   Historically, what are the effects of humans on the dispersal of other species (i.e. diseases, invasive species), and vice versa?
7   How can we use our understanding of past socio-ecological interactions to help map modern spatial variations in resilience, system trajectory and sustainability worldwide, thus allowing classification and ranking of the state of world systems at different scales?

In attempting to answer these questions, IHOPE will have to accommodate, and perhaps reconcile, a number of different academic and disciplinary cultures if shared conventions between biophysical and social science research communities are to emerge. Issues relating to spatial and temporal scales, the conciliation of impacts and drivers among the different components of a coupled socio-ecological system and differing views of the resulting analytical framework will have to be resolved.

To some extent this has already been achieved within the Millennium Ecosystems Assessment and within the developing discipline of sustainability science, but a great deal has still to be done in terms of gathering, interpreting and converting tools and data into knowledge and wisdom across disciplines. The groundwork for some of this has already been undertaken (Costanza *et al*. 2007), forming the backdrop to the ongoing project to make sense of and practically realise the idea of sustainable development for which resilience has increasingly become a central component.

In the United Nations' *The Future We Want* (United Nations 2012), published at the conclusion of the Rio+20 Earth Summit, 'resilience' appears throughout as both a means and an end. It appears thirteen times. We need to be resilient in order manage natural disasters and climate change and we need to ensure our social and ecological systems are themselves resilient. Cities, oceans, ecosystems, natural habitats, the global economy and society need resilience but perhaps our present way of organising and financing economic development is itself too resilient at least in terms of being able to accommodate change, resist or deflect criticism. Resilience then is not an easy concept but then the world in all its cultural and physical complexity is not a particularly easy place either. In *The Future We Want,* the United Nations reaffirmed its holistic, ambitious and common vision:

> We recognise that poverty eradication, changing unsustainable and promoting sustainable patterns of consumption and production, and protecting and managing the natural resource base of economic and social development are the overarching objectives of and essential requirements for sustainable development. We also reaffirm the need to achieve sustainable development by: promoting sustained, inclusive and equitable economic growth, creating greater opportunities for all, reducing inequalities, raising basic standards of living; fostering equitable social development and inclusion; and promoting integrated and sustainable management of natural resources and ecosystems that supports *inter alia* economic, social and human development while facilitating ecosystem conservation, regeneration and restoration and resilience in the face of new and emerging challenges.
>
> (United Nations 2012: 2)

3   Shifting tactics?

Testing the resilience of a movement

Introduction

Resilience, although difficult to comprehend as a concept, concerns every human being, community and ecosystem, explains Uchita De Zoysa (2012), a Sri Lankan and international activist. Many, such as Juliane Zeidler (2012), IUCN Commission on Education and Communication chair and Namibian conservationist, interpret resilience as a competence or way of thinking that only becomes visible when a major challenge or crisis is faced. Farooq Ullah (2013), executive director of Stakeholder Forum, explains that testing resilience is about ascertaining how well people and communities bounce back from a shock to social, economic as well as environmental systems. The interviews that inform this text suggest that resilience is embodied in the story of the conservation movement itself, and reflected in the personal and professional journeys of its key advocates and champions.

The lack of progress towards the conservation ambitions first agreed at the UN Summit in 1992, and the absence of systemic social change necessary to achieve internationally agreed conservation targets, led Greg Bourne (2012), Keith Wheeler (2012) and Morgan Williams (2012) to conclude that in the aftermath of Rio+20, conservation is facing an uncertain future.[1] The resilience of the conservation movement itself is being tested, as many point to the failure of conservation strategies (Kareiva et al. 2012) and a reluctance, in some quarters, to question traditional paradigms in conservation (Bourne 2012; Wheeler 2012). In parallel, leading conservation organisations, such as IUCN and WWF, face a future without the financial backing from development agencies and government initiatives that they have come to rely on in the last two decades. New conservation alliances with the corporate sector and governments with questionable human rights records plague the conservation community with controversy, as was highly evident at the September 2012 IUCN Jeju Conference (Box 3.1).

Box 3.1 Jeju: dividing IUCN interests and support

'World's largest environmental organisation in ethical quandary: should it answer to conference sponsors Samsung and Korean government, or to its historical mission to protect environment and social justice?'

Pressenza International Press Agency, 14 September 2012

'IUCN officially blocks participation by Jeju villagers who oppose naval base construction near convention.'

Global Forest Coalition, 5 September 2012

'Jeju-island navy-base controversy divides IUCN.'

Sukhyun Park, 14 September 2012

'Jeju Island Base Divides Korean, International Green Groups.'

Jon Letman, 20 August 2012

The 2012 World Conservation Congress (WCC) brought together conservationists, governments, businesses, indigenous groups, journalists and scientists from across the globe with an interest in ecology, biodiversity and sustainable development. Over 8,000 participants arrived in Jeju Island in early September 2012 to attend the event, which was held at Jungmon resort, seven kilometres from Gangjeong. The 'Nature+' theme of the congress focused minds on 'boosting the resilience of nature'. The congress, which is the world's largest and most important conservation event (Toulmin 2012), proved to be the most controversial IUCN gathering in its history.

Jeju lies 80 km southwest of the Korean peninsula and is an area of special biodiversity, cultural as well as scientific interest. It is home to multiple UNESCO World Heritage sites and was named one of the 'New Seven Wonders of Nature' in 2011. The site is also the location of various daily protests and frequent arrests, as the Korean Government took the decision to construct a naval base which threatens Jeju's fragile ecosystem, its rare wildlife, as well as local culture and livelihoods.

The proposed naval base, which has the support of the US government, will accommodate multiple submarines and up to 20 warships, including US Aegis-equipped destroyers. Experts advise that the development would inflict irrevocable damage to this lava coastline and bio-diverse habitats; that it would contaminate one of the cleanest and most abundant freshwater sources in the world; and that it would threaten bottle-nosed dolphins, narrow-mouthed toads, red-footed crabs, Jeju freshwater shrimp and dozens of species of soft coral that live in this landscape.

Protesters include scientists, community groups, grassroots NGOs,

Catholic nuns and Gangjeong's mayor, who have been arrested and brought to trial as they seek to challenge Korean government's decision (Letman 2012). Human rights organisations have joined the long list of opponents, as the Korean Government is seizing farmland and destroying traditional farming and subsistence diving by Jeju's iconic *haenyo* women divers.

Figure 3.1 Jeju: dividing IUCN interests and support

Source: IUCN

Fifty-five Korean environmental and civic groups wrote to the IUCN asking it to justify its decision to hold the 2012 WCC at Jeju and clarify its position on a number of underpinning issues. Another group, the Jeju Emergency Action Committee, submitted an open letter to the IUCN calling for the postponement or relocation of the congress, unless the base construction is halted. The letter argues that to hold the congress at Jeju undermines IUCN's position as well as historical purpose.

IUCN director general Julia Marton-Lefèvre responded to the controversy, stating that no country has a clean record on the environment. The official IUCN line is set out in the statement that it 'trusts the Korean government has complied with all relevant domestic laws in planning and developing this port' (Toulmin 2012). IUCN's director of communications, John Kidd, reminds critics that 'IUCN is not a campaigning organisation like Greenpeace or Friends of the Earth. We're a membership organisation that exists to promote scientific research and facts and to bring different groups in society together' (Letman 2012: 1).

The controversy reached fever pitch when Dr Imok Cha, an American scientist, was deported on arrival in South Korea and on the first day of the conference. Dr Cha was expected to give presentations on an independent environmental assessment that exposed the flaws in the Korean government's environmental impact assessment for the base construction (Park 2012).

IUCN's human rights as well as conservation reputation was further challenged when it confirmed that Samsung C&T and Hyundai were among the sponsors helping the South Korean government to offset the cost of hosting the congress. It is no coincidence that Samsung is the lead contractor at the base and Hyundai Heavy Industries is contributing to the production of the Aegis Combat System to be deployed on warships at the Jeju naval base (Letman 2012).

Camille Toulmin, director of the International Institute for Environment and Development, and a congress participant, asked 'Is it best to boycott an event because of such controversy?' She concluded that there are no easy answers, but hoped that 'the potential outcomes from going to such a meeting, and of making the dispute visible to observers from around the world, makes it a better option than staying away' (Toulmin 2012: 1).

The Jeju experience has divided IUCN's membership, as the events brought into question the values and partnership decisions of the largest conservation organisation in the world.

Conservation at a crossroads

The American Association for the Advancement of Science (AAAS), which sees itself as the world's largest scientific society, has captured the sentiments of many in the light of Rio+20, as conservation efforts continue to fall short of key targets and fail to halt the global decline in biodiversity. At a recent symposium, the question was raised as to whether the conservation battle is being lost; AAAS called on opinion leaders to contribute to a paradigm shift aligned with more integrative and innovative human-centred approaches to conservation (American Association for the Advancement of Science 2013).

In the US, these debates are being informed by the work of Peter Kareiva, Michelle Marvier and Robert Lalasz (2012). In their *Breakthrough Journal* essay, 'Conservation in the Anthropocene', they poignantly argue that 'By its own measures, conservation is failing'. Their analysis of various authoritative studies confirms the rapid decline in biodiversity:

> We continue to lose forests in Africa, Asia, and Latin America [Food and Agricultural Organisation of the United Nations 2011]. There are so few wild tigers and apes that they will be lost forever if current trends continue [International Union for the Conservation of Nature 2011]. Simply put, we are losing many more special places and species than we're saving. Even as we are losing species and wild places at an accelerating rate, the worldwide number of protected areas has risen dramatically, from under 10,000 in 1950 to over 100,000 by 2009 [United Nations Environment Programme 2011]. Around the world, nations have set aside beautiful, biodiverse areas where human development is restricted. By some estimates, 13 per cent of the world's land mass is protected, an area larger than all of South America [ibid.].
>
> (Kareiva *et al.* 2012: 1)

Peter Kareiva, lead author and chief scientist of the Nature Conservancy,[2] has come under attack by others in the movement for this 'myth-busting' work. However, Butchart's 'Global Biodiversity: Indicators of Recent Declines' (2010) confirms that biodiversity loss over the last twenty years has been significant and continues to escalate. Keith Wheeler (2012), former chair of the IUCN's Commission on Education and Communication, believes that conservation is facing a 'perfect storm' as an increasing number of policy-makers and the public see the all-important IUCN Red List as an actuarial mortuary and conservation dies a slow death in traditional strongholds such as Europe and the United States. The problem, he argues, is that many in the generation of conservationists who are in important decision-making roles cling nostalgically to 1960s and 1970s approaches to conservation and to the idea of purchasing pristine landscapes to protect natural havens and the biodiversity of these key global hotspots. These affiliations continue, despite the fact that history has shown that these strategies are not working:

We may protect places of particular beauty or those places with large numbers of species, but even as we do, the pace of destruction will likely continue to accelerate. Whether or not the developing world sets aside a large percentage of its landscapes as parks or wilderness over the next hundred years, what is clear is that those protected areas will remain islands of 'pristine nature' in a sea of profound human transformations to the landscape through logging, agriculture, mining, damming, and urbanisation. In the face of these realities, 21st century conservation is changing.

(Kareiva *et al.* 2012: 1)

The movement's obsession with cataloguing species has also plagued it:

We can keep counting for 60 years and so what...becoming aware of the problem is not making a difference to the survival of these species. Tools like the IUCN Red List are a part of the solution, because you cannot change what you cannot measure, but the conservation movement must embrace the entire suite of business management tools including marketing and education.

(Wheeler 2012)

Wheeler reminds us that public support for conservation continues to wane, for what is perceived as a concern of those at the top of the socio-economic pyramid. Kareiva *et al.* (2012) call for conservationists to stop clinging to 'old myths'; they predict that, as a movement, conservation is facing a turning point. It must, they argue, continue to shed traditional strategies and face the reality that nature can, and must, exist amidst a diversity of human landscapes.

To understand the current predicament in conservation, there is a need to understand its origins as well as the journey which has led to the existing scenario. Those interviewed for this book have cast our minds back to the roots of conservationism and to early nineteenth-century Europe and North America, where the expansion of cities and widespread air, land and water pollution degraded environments and quality of life, while many longed to escape to nature (see for example Mumford 1962). The nineteenth-century Romantic view of nature as God and its transcendental valuation of natural landscapes underpinned the initial conceptions and can be seen has formative in the movement's obsession with parks and pristine environments. This explains the practice of buying places, erecting fences and protecting natural places from human development. Conservation was, and some argue still is, about fences, limits and far-away places.

Uchita De Zoysa (2012) recognises that conservation is essentially a Western construct and that underpinning traditional conceptions of conservation is an assumption that local people cannot often be trusted to care for their land.[3] Juliane Zeidler agrees, as her experience of living in Southern Africa showed that conservation was traditionally very exclusive of people, and black people in particular. Conservation programmes have actively resettled large numbers of people, mostly indigenous, who lost homes, farmlands and often their identities; it is believed that between 5 and 14 million people have been displaced over the last century by conservation initiatives in Africa alone (Dowie 2009). Indigenous groups have been speaking out against this injustice over decades and gained public as well as intergovernmental support, which in turn have challenged traditional conservation practices. It would be fair to say that conservation has learnt lessons, and that today, most conservation organisations have policies intended to protect the rights of local communities and programmes that actively seek to involve social scientists and anthropologists (see Gardner and Lewis 1996). However, issues relating to human rights still haunt the conservation movement. The complexity and intensity of these challenges, Keith Wheeler (2012) argues, were tangible at Jeju: 'the movement still often behaves like an ostrich sticking its head in the sand.'

Kareiva *et al.* (2012) remind us that the conservation movement's binaries of growth *or* nature, prosperity *or* biodiversity, are:

> pitting people against nature, conservationists actually create an atmosphere in which people see nature as the enemy. If people don't believe conservation is in their own best interests, then it will never be a societal priority. Conservation must demonstrate how the fates of nature and of people are deeply intertwined – and then offer new strategies for promoting the health and prosperity of both ... people are actually part of nature and not the original sinners who caused our banishment from Eden.
>
> (Kareiva *et al.* 2012: 1)

Roel Van Raaij (2012), a senior civil servant in the Dutch government engaged in UN and IUCN work for some years, concludes that the tide is turning on a movement that has enjoyed a special status at the intergovernmental level. Conservation organisations were vital in the brokering of ambitious agreements such as the Convention for Biological Diversity, despite the fact that conservation has never experienced majority support in any nation. The economic downturn challenging Western lifestyles is heightening this lack of stakeholder support; conservation NGOs are struggling to make persuasive arguments to funders at a time when the number of people living in poverty is on the increase. The lack of examples of genuine sustainable development programmes that also benefit communities economically and socially in the donor countries – and not just in far-away and remote places – is having consequences. Leading conservation organisations such as IUCN and WWF, the high-profile voices of the conservation movement, are being forced to re-prioritise and restructure their own operational contexts in the short term. Echoing arguments made by Borrini-Feyerabend in the late 1990s, Keith Wheeler (2012) calls for a rethink of the business models that underpin the movement, as recent social developments have accentuated the ineffectiveness of present models.

Evolving models or shifting tactics?

Rethinking the funding of a movement is one of the significant consequences, although in itself this is not a new challenge. In its early days, conservation was funded by a small number of high profile and wealthy individuals who cared about the environment; their monies built these organisations (Wheeler 2012).

Over time, this funding was made available to the conservation movement through Foundations and Trusts for projects they were prepared to support, or may propose which meant that conservation organisations had to respond to their specific interests sometimes at the expense of more pressing needs (Williams 2012). By the 1990s, conservation organisations were heavily reliant on government funding, as various environment ministers and international development departments channelled funds for environment and sustainable development. The organisations competed for funding with development NGOs until the language of sustainable development forged greater co-operation with economic and health development groups.

Bourne (2012), Wheeler (2012) and Williams (2012) concur that the decade of 2010–2020 is likely to see another shift in business models as conservation organisations are forced to forge partnerships with the private sector to fund their activities. There are potential dangers here, for although corporates may learn a great deal from conservation NGOs and a number (most prominently WWF International) work closely with many big corporations, conservation and the protection of nature may compromise too much with neo-liberal market logics, processes of capital accumulation and the ideology of capitalist economic growth (Heynen *et al.* 2007).

The conservation movement has to reposition itself among communities that are wrestling with poverty brought on by economic challenges as well as natural disasters, Roel Van Raaij (2012) reminds us. There is a need to align scientific assessments (traditionally associated with conservation) with cost–benefit analysis and socio-economic approaches, and work actively to enhance natural systems that could benefit the most vulnerable communities – including the poor in our cities. Protecting biodiversity for its own sake has not worked and measuring success by the number or scale of protected areas is no longer sufficient. The large conservation organisations, such as WWF, publicly acknowledge this and are moving on to new territory (WWF 2013), but Kareiva *et al.* (2012) remind us that conservation must do more to monitor its achievement in large part by its relevance to people and everyday life.[4]

Some of our interviewees question whether there is the commitment and ability within the conservation world to deeply revisit its core principles, while others – such as Mitch Thomashow (2012), a leading author and adviser – remind us that shifting tactics is not a new experience for the movement, and that conservation organisations have already embarked in this journey before. Indeed, the conservation movement has faced significant challenges in the past and responded to these wake-up calls, sometimes incrementally, and at other time rapidly, as it learns to become more impactful and take action to regain relevance in contemporary contexts.

The interviews undertaken to inform this book, reveal that there have been several key shifts over time relating to the place of science in conservation, the scale and operational frames of conservation programmes, the levels of (and approaches to) stakeholder engagement, the role of economic instruments and assessments, and relationships with funding partnerships. Some of these shifts are evident in the story and experience of the WWF (see Box 3.2).

Box 3.2 Shifting tactics? The WWF story

Science has always underpinned the work of leading conservation organisations such as WWF. The 'Morges Manifesto', which called for urgent action to stop wild animals being hunted out of existence, became the platform for the establishment of WWF in 1961 (WWF 2013). This document was underpinned by the perspectives of Julian Huxley (a respected biologist) and Peter Scott (a renowned ornithologist), which framed the future for WWF.

WWF International, on its own webpages, acknowledges the critical role of science in the first Decade of the organisation's life. In the 1960s it focused its efforts on a range of initiatives mostly around science research, trials and education. Key initiatives of the time include the establishment of a research station in Galapagos Island in 1962 and a reintroduction programme of the white rhino in the southern and east African region in 1965.

In the 1970s the investment in science continued, but by then the organisation shifted strategies, moving away from ad hoc support to individual projects and investing in conservation efforts for entire biomes as well as species across their range (WWF 2013).

In the late 1970s WWF stepped up its policy and advocacy work as it became an important presence at intergovernmental meetings and shaped global environmental treaties. The international policy arena became a two-way sphere of influence, shaping WWF's frames of reference as well as positioning conservation concerns centre stage in global conversations.

WWF celebrated its twentieth anniversary in 1981. It was celebrating the launch of 'Caring for Earth' and was able to showcase its global influence; it had secured 1 per cent of the Earth's surface as protected areas. On reflection, WWF admits:

> As impressive as this was, the organisation realised that parks and crisis-led conservation efforts – while important – were not enough. Now with an expanded global presence and starting to run its own projects, WWF began more heavily promoting the ideas of its

founders; that conservation was an the interest of people and needed to be integrated into, rather than viewed as in conflict development, a philosophy that now permeates conservation, development and even corporate strategies.

(WWF 2013: 1)

There is evidence to suggest that the conservation movement did change its course in 1990 to respond to people-centred approaches; although some would refer to it as a change of discourse rather than practice (De Zoysa 2012). Key strategic directions and groundwork remained unchallenged for a little longer. For example, in the 1990s WWF turned its focus to the world's most critical eco-regions and in six key areas – species, forest, marine and freshwater conservation, climate change and toxic chemicals – not exactly human centred concerns. The 1990s also saw a move away from country based projects to what was perceived as a more unified and bigger picture conservation effort.

WWF did venture into new territory in the late 1990s as it became involved in the global effort to curb carbon emissions and embrace community-based natural resource management programmes more extensively thanks to funding from USAID and other donors. Notably, WWF led the way with the certification of forest and marine products to assist consumers to make more environmentally acceptable choices. Prior to this, and with a few exceptions,[5] people's engagement strategies were limited to those who lived and worked in national parks or ecological sensitive areas. Taking strides to make conservation relevant to consumers marked an important milestone.

WWF had over the years invested in awareness raising and nature education. Daniella Tilbury formed part of a team of evaluators that was asked to assess the value and impact of education across the WWF family in the late 1990s (Fien *et al.*1999, 2001). The study showed that WWF had sought to integrate conservation issues into school and teacher education curricula as well as through school nature clubs in countries such as Madagascar, Malaysia, China, Hong Kong, UK and US with a degree of success. A handful of other social learning programmes had located conservation issues within a sustainable development frame and were successful in engaging learners and in changing stakeholder practices. The study provided evidence that WWF had begun to connect environment and development in a meaningful way and engaged people in the resolution of issues.

Science continued to be a cornerstone of its work. Its 1998 *Living Planet* report (now a biannual publication) is one of the leading science-based analyses of biodiversity health. The report brought some home truths; WWF and other conservation organisations faced the reality that its efforts were not having an impact on what they cared for most about biodiversity:

'the first report found that global biodiversity had declined by 30 per cent since 1970 –highlighting for the first time that while the conservation movement had won many battles, it was nevertheless losing the war' (WWF 2013: 1).

The turn of the century saw further changes, with WWF adopting the twin goals of conserving biodiversity and reducing ecological footprints. In some quarters, bright green environmentalism brought the view that through technology, good design and more thoughtful use of resources, people can live responsibly. It also embarked on a £12.7 million five-year partnership with HSBC to protect freshwater habitat.

It was the early 2000s when it recognised the need to put a price on nature. In 2003, WWF estimated that coral reefs provide nearly US$30 billion in net benefits each year through their provision of goods and services to the world economy. WWF was now assessing the economic value of ecosystems and species, and informed the development of payments for ecosystem services, where local people are compensated for the maintaining and managing natural habitats. This was a brave move, as the monetising approach, reflecting the growing influence of business models on conservation practice, is not widely embraced by WWF members or supporters.

By 2010, the sustainable lifestyle discourses had made their way into WWF's vocabulary, and influencing people's choices and ways of living had become centre fundamental for some WWF offices (e.g. WWF UK). Climate change had gained greater currency within the WWF family, following the success of WWF Australia's Earth Hour. This now global WWF annual event started in Sydney, urging politicians to act on climate change. Daniella Tilbury, who at the time was a governor of WWF Australia, recalls how on the 28 March 2007 the Australian government leaders congregated in Sydney to see the skyline plunged into darkness – a show of people power.

In 2013, Earth Hour has extended its reach, and every year landmarks across the world, including the Acropolis, the Pyramids, Big Ben and the Empire State Building, participate in this global initiative, which reaches out to 6 million people and calls for climate action. In WWF's own words: 'WWF's focus has evolved from localised efforts in favour of single species and individual habitats to an ambitious strategy to preserve biodiversity and achieve sustainable development across the globe' (WWF 2013).

Changing paradigms?

Although scientific analysis and monitoring has been a core strand of its work since 1961, WWF's strategic approach has evolved, becoming more global, political and people-centred over time. The tensions that exist between the new and old were palpable at Rio+20[6] as the conservation movement experienced the transition to a new paradigm. These are also subtly visible across WWF webpages today; some national offices have carved new strategic pathways embracing sustainable living and tackling climate change at its roots while others still rely on species centred awareness campaigns. Liz Shanahan, a political science professor from Montana State University argues that the public is no longer responding to the 'Chicken Little sky-falling' narrative or the images of polar bears that are used to incite a response to climate change (Person 2011). The discourse has changed but leading conservation organisations must experience deeper shifts to respond to current scenarios.

So what are these deeper shifts that are needed to help conservation organisations gain greater public support? Juliane Zeidler (2012) believes that there is a need to match the global efforts of the leading conservation organisations with more work on the ground by recruiting an increasing number of practitioners to the central offices that are mostly composed of scientists and administrators. These parallel strategies are embodied in the work of faith organisations that are gaining ground across local communities by offering opportunity and optimism about the future of the planet and becoming global opinion leaders promoting values and ethics based approaches to conservation. Their presence at international dialogues and UN policy platforms has been felt over the last decade as they offer people- and values-centred frameworks that resonate with the goals of sustainable development.

Faith groups and religious organisations have been connected to conservation and environmental agendas since the 1970s, but it was 1986 that saw the first gathering of the five major world religions (Buddhism, Christianity, Hinduism, Islam and Judaism) in Assisi. Father Serrini's welcoming address at the gathering reminds us how the frames of operation that underpin these religions differ from the scientific roots of WWF and IUCN among others:

> Each religion will celebrate the dignity of nature and the duty of every person to live harmoniously within the natural world. We are convinced of the inestimable value of our respective traditions and of what they can offer to re-establish ecological harmony; but, at the same time, we are humble enough to desire to learn from each other. The very richness and diversity lends strength to our shared concern and responsibility for Planet Earth.
>
> (Father Serrini speaking in 1986, cited in ARC 2012)

This initial gathering laid roots for an inter-faith platform – the Alliance of Religions and Conservation (ARC) – a secular body that supports the major religions of the world develop teaching beliefs and practices in the area of conservation and sustainable development. By drawing on holy books, sacred sites, community networks and faith assets they engage people in conservation issues and support forest management, organic and permaculture farming, low-carbon community development, protection of cultural and environmental heritage, advocate for Green Pilgrimage and develop curriculum to support a values based approach to conservation. ARC (2013) reminds us that faith groups hold the attention of communities in many parts of the world where few others are heard. In fact, there are a number of compelling reasons why leading conservation organisations should take the role of faith groups seriously and partner with them to achieve change. Religious and faith groups:

• are the largest organised sector of civil society worldwide (over 85 per cent of the world's people describe themselves as belonging to a faith);
• own 7–8 per cent of the habitable land surface, including 5 per cent of commercially run forests worldwide, and have influence over 15 per cent of forests that are considered to be sacred;
• are involved in more than half the schools worldwide (in sub-Saharan Africa they run or contribute to 70 per cent of the schools);
• are among the largest investment blocks in the global stock market;
• produce more newspapers than the whole of the European Union.;
• are involved in their communities in the long term (they think in terms of generations rather than short-term projects); and
• can bring real, pragmatic changes and sustain action and projects for the long-term.

(ARC 2013)

This may explain why foundations such as Pilkington and Rufford, as well as government donors from Denmark and Norway, finance the work of the ARC. Indeed, WWF has a history of supporting faith initiatives, but mostly at the fringes of its activities[7]: it has much to learn from the people focused approaches and levels of social engagement commanded by these groups. A UNEP regional officer recently acknowledged the importance of these new alliances:

> I really realised, just coming this morning, we that could be more successful, we could be more relevant to the needs and aspirations of the continent, we could have more impact, in all African countries if we can work with you [the faiths] hand in hand.
> (Mounkaila Goumandakoye, September 2012, cited in ARC 2012)

The influence of faith groups is not limited to the developing world. In the US, for example, the Baha'i community has been promoting sustainability education across the core and extracurricular activities through school and neighbourhood partnerships which count with the support of the White House. The US has also seen the inter-faith rallies for action against climate change, where Baha'i, Baptist, Buddhist, Catholic, Evangelical and Hindu worshippers gather at Earth week events to rally against climate change. They use ethical and spiritual ideas (rather than science) to engage people in change and advocate for action with hope and optimism (rather than doomsday scenarios or red lists). Through this approach they are winning hearts and minds – a battleground many would argue has been lost by conservationists. Faith organisations have shown how grounded,

Figure 3.2 The launch of the Indian Green Pilgrimage Network at Rishikesh, on the banks of the Ganges, India, in December 2012

Source: N P Jayan

Figure 3.3 Buddhist monks in Cambodia ordaining a tree in order to protect it as part of their care of a community forest

Source: Monks Community Forest

long term approaches to community and stakeholder engagement can work (Podger 2009). The mainstream conservation organisations have much to learn from these religious movements.

Greg Bourne (2012), previously CEO of WWF Australia, advises that it is not just a programmatic shift or change in engagement approaches that is required but that organisational change will be essential, he argues. Comparing his WWF experience with his time at BP, Bourne explains:

> When you join BP or a company like it, you join as an engineer, accountant, HR person and so on. If you like them and they like you, over time the values align and individuals will identify with the company and eventually share common values. If you look at conservation NGOs what you find is that the values do not necessarily identify with the organisation. Let me give you an example, the WWF turtle specialist will remain in the organisation as long as WWF has a turtle programme that suits their paradigm. If not she or he will leave to follow their passion in a different organisation which satisfies their personal needs. What you have at these conservation, and some environmental, NGOs, is passion and values going in multiple different directions- all trying to save the world. The challenge for these NGOs is to harness that energy.
>
> (Bourne 2012)

Bourne believes that for an organisation to become resilient in times of change, it needs to draw deeply on its values, identify and address blind spots, and use the commitment that drives its existence to move forward 'Introspection and drawing on inner strength are critical', he notes, reflecting upon his own experiences; 'this is especially relevant at times when there have been shocks to the system and key fundamental principles underpinning the organisation are tested'. Mitch Thomashow (2012) reminds us that resilience is about adaptation and embedding flexibility into the system. This, he argues, is exactly what the conservation movement has done over the years and needs to do at this moment in time.

Transposing this to current scenarios could mean that conservation organisations, such as IUCN, need to revisit their values, reassess recent experiences (such as Jeju) to learn from them, and consolidate their own positions going forward. Did IUCN adopt a pragmatic stance at Jeju given that an economic recession makes it difficult to find sponsorship for a world congress? Or did it misjudge the complexity of the scenario and undermine the values of its membership? To build its own resilience, should WWF continue to put a price on nature and its extend its relationships with the corporate sector which may secure its financial future? Alternatively, should it scale up its partnerships with faith organisations and other grassroots NGOs to extend its influence and improve its social relevance? Should it adopt more values-centred frameworks for promoting biodiversity and conservation goals? Should it do all of the above?

The conservation movement has never been at the cutting edge or a leader of innovative practice; it is often slow to adopt and adapt new ways of thinking and doing. However, history has shown how it has subtly diversified and, at times, shifted tactics (Table 3.1). Contemporary issues facing conservation suggest that this journey continues. Time will tell whether these changes will harness greater public support, improve the effectiveness of its strategies, and protect nature, natural resources and biodiversity.

Table 3.1 Building resilience – shifting tactics? It has been suggested that conservation organisations have extended the range of their work and at times changed tactics. In some cases, the diversification or shifts mapped below are still taking place and may be evident in some conservation efforts, but not in others. Many of the critics cited early in the chapter would argue that the shift in tactics has not been as mainstream or deep as required

Expertise	From the development of a science knowledge base → to the monitoring of threatened species → to shaping biodiversity policy and investment → to undertaking ecosystem value assessments and shaping models for a green economy.
Strategy	From purchasing land and creating national parks → to advocating for new national and regional legislation → to brokering international agreements → to promoting mitigation and adaptation to climate change → to brokering socio-economic change.
Programmatic focus	From programmes focused on preserving wilderness and individual iconic species → to protecting habitats and biomes → to lowering ecological footprints and promoting ecosystem services → to promoting sustainable lifestyles and linking conservation to poverty alleviation.
Education	From promoting personal connections with nature → to awareness-raising around conservation issues → to promoting people and government actions → to buildings contexts and for social and economic change.
People engagement	From excluding people from protected areas and its management → to knowledge communication → to community problem-solving → to citizen science and consultation → to influencing consumer choices and engaging the public in policy advocacy → to resilience building and building social contexts for sustainable development.
Funding	From wealthy individuals → to foundation and trusts → to government and aid agencies → to corporate donors, product sales and membership fees.
Human resourcing	From a group of scientific experts and naturalists → to the inclusion of species and habitat specialists → to the incorporation of public and inter-governmental policy experts → to inclusion of anthropologists, communication and education experts.

4 Contesting market logics

Changing the economics of conservation

For over thirty years neoliberal market ideology has dominated the nature of economic growth and development throughout the world. The key values of the free market economy have become, at least until recently, hegemonic, hardly being seen for what they actually are; namely, the masks and veils of a corporate capitalism dominated by its financial sector. Costs and efficiencies, labour and capital mobilities, the spatial division and distribution of wealth and power, and, if not the continuing degradation of labour, then there certainly a relentless drive to make it, and everything else, 'competitive', insecure, precarious and hard.

As the global population increases and the imperative of economic growth remains firmly embedded in the consciousness of global political elites and business leaders, productive and meaningful work is in increasingly short supply. The planet's ecosystems are considerably stressed for in monetising the environment we tend to know the price of everything and the value of less and less. The very building blocks of life are themselves commoditised; it is necessary to go beyond the market logic and the superficial shibboleths of trickle-down economics.

However, for many economists the price mechanism and market economy is the most efficient, and perhaps even the fairest, way of allocating scarce resources. Green economists themselves have argued over how best to value nature, to put a price tag on the global commons, to make the polluter pay, as sure ways of instilling some frugality in to the mentalities of producers and consumers of all descriptions. The idea that the price mechanism rations scarce resources is clearly a powerful one, as anyone in the oil-based and car-obsessed societies of the developed world know full well. Put up the price of diesel or petrol and drivers become more circumspect in terms of how, and how much, they drive.

On the other hand, valuing nature and commoditising certain practices aimed at conserving what remains has double-edged consequences. For example, ecotourism is perhaps, like the concept of sustainable development, yet another oxymoron, another ideological sweetener beloved by sustainability practitioners in the somewhat bittersweet environment of working with business. Conservation and capitalism have, over the years, clearly shaped the institutions and practices aiming at protecting nature and fostering the emergence of a sustainable development economic practice. Neoliberal market logics and the ideology of capital accumulation and economic growth are evident in wildlife and habitat conservation movements as everywhere else (Igoe *et al.* 2010).

However, as Duffy and Moore (2010) show in their study of elephant back tourism in Thailand and Botswana, the tourist industry has provided valuable employment for both elephants and their mahouts. In Thailand, because of the importance of the god Ganesha, which takes the form of the elephant, elephants are perceived as being far more than a means to increase shareholder value. In fact, the operation of neoliberal business and management processes here have, albeit inadvertently, revived and partially reinvented some traditional values and mores. Some conservation entrepreneurs, however, want to go further looking to explicitly and intentionally develop a business model and conservation-tourist project that does no ecological harm and also ensures that local communities are genuine beneficiaries.

The South African media company WildEarth TV, with its internet-based wildlife safaris, is a pioneering and adventurous project (Blewitt 2011). Graham Wallington, CEO and co-founder of WildEarth TV, believes that many different ecotourism businesses are facing similar problems:

> And the real problem is this: the economics of [eco]tourism is that delicate habitats are fundamentally vulnerable and the problem lies in the fact that in order to build a business you need to constantly grow your profits. That is currently the definition, unfortunately, of a good business that it keeps making more and more profit. Some profit is never enough. It has to be growing for the business to have value. In an environment with a limited resource, there are two ways you can increase your money. Either you continue to add more people or you charge them more – those that you have. In many parts of the world and where we operate in Kruger Park South Africa, you have reached a cap in what you can charge. You are talking thousands of dollars per person per night. Extremely expensive. You can't charge more. So more people are the only way you can go on the tradition model and the more people you have the more you damage your resource. Either your business is going to suffer or the environment is going to suffer, and if the environment suffers, your business suffers. So you've got a flaw. Now virtual tourism is different because instead of having eight people on a safari vehicle you can go to eight thousand or eight million. It is a totally scalable model. Others might find ways of making money by making wildlife content, a wildlife film, but not a cent, zero, of that makes its way back to the ground...So what we did was change the media model and the tourism model. We proposed a solution. Wildlife Media is split into two layers of business. One lay is the distribution network WildEarth. The layer below that is the production company, Safari TV, which currently belongs in the main to WildEarth but our intention is to have 50 per cent of that company belong to a combination of the wealthy white landowners (25%) and to the

communities that surround that area (25%). We will distribute shares on an equal basis to every adult, male or female, that lives within a five kilometre radius of the area and can prove they have lived there for at least one generation. What we are doing now is putting the idea out there, including the white landowners and communities, and we are trying to build a consensus that this will work.

(Wallington 2010)

Wallington and his colleagues still have a lot of work to do in identifying exactly who will become share/stakeholders, but the ideas and values informing such a form of entrepreneurial business activity are firmly based in a commitment to social, economic and environmental justice. More often, though, it seems the capitalist exploitation of nature and local communities goes hand in hand with the products of exploited labour often being made available to consumers in the marketplace without any evidence of the sweat equity that went into their production. Thus, as Castree (2003: 284–5) writes, 'the materiality of the commodification process "ignores" the material specifics of environmental inputs and outputs as if they did not exist or did not matter'. External nature becomes an accumulation strategy for capital and it doesn't matter in this context whether the industry is (eco) tourism, bioprospecting or copper mining. Additionally, in other production processes hybridisation is of key importance. Nature is incorporated into the actual production and commodification processes themselves as with the genetic modification of commercially produced crops or the systemic use of growth hormones in beef production. If such ecologically questionable and economically exploitative processes become resilient to contestation and the possibilities of sustainably sound alternatives, it becomes incumbent on sustainability practitioners to take a more critical look at the political application of the concept of resilience and of systems theory itself. There is a clear danger that an unwanted and undesirable political functionalism will, or has already emerged. In other words, sustainability practitioners need to adopt a realist critical political ecology that questions 'scientific' and discursive explanations and assumptions alike. They need to reflect on whether, or how, they may be operating as the ventriloquist's dummy for the dominant economic and political power blocs (Forsyth 2005).

Economics, business and sustainability

The credit crunch of 2007 and the deep global recession following it has dented but not destroyed the resilience of neoliberal ideology. Despite a resurgence of green economic thinking, and a partial rehabilitation of John Maynard Keynes and Marxian economics, and although neoliberal economic policies and practices may be increasingly redundant, they have certainly not yet disappeared. The business economist Colin Crouch (2011) has perceptively written of neoliberalism's strange non-death, but it is the Marxist geographer David Harvey (Harvey 2011) who arguably offers the most coherent explanation of the current economic crisis, and for that matter, every other recent crisis of late capitalism. As Harvey (1998: 23) has written:

> The risk and uncertainty we now experience acquires its scale, complexity, and far reaching implications by virtue of processes that have produced the massive industrial, technological, urban, demographic, lifestyle and intellectual transformations that we have witnessed in the latter half of the twentieth century. In this, a relatively small number of key institutions, such as the modern state and its adjuncts, multinational firms and finance capital, and 'big' science and technology, have played a dominant and guiding role. For all the inner diversity, some sort of hegemonic economistic-engineering discourse has also come to dominate discussion of environmental questions, commodifying everything and subjecting almost all transactions (including those connected to the production of knowledge) to the singular logic of commercial profitability and the cost benefit calculus. The production of our environmental difficulties, both for the working class, the marginalised and the impoverished (many of whom have had their resource base stripped from under them by a rapacious commercialism) as well as for some segments of capital and the rich and the affluent, is broadly the result of this hegemonic class project (and its reigning neoliberal philosophy).
>
> (Harvey 1998: 23)

If Marx was anything, he was certainly a systems thinker, but one who clearly recognised the significance of human agency and political power. John Urry (2005) argues that the structure of Marx's arguments illuminates what may be described as a 'complex rationality', and although he may have been wrong in his 1848 prediction of a worldwide proletarian revolution, it is highly probable that relatively small perturbations in the capitalist system may have produced minor but still significant and emergent properties that have caused capitalism to branch off into directions that he could not have anticipated. The post-Fordist welfare consumerism that dominated the late twentieth century is perhaps one example of this effect. For Marx, and those analysts who have found his thought valuable, the contradictions of capitalism are systemic. The dialectical relations between the system's various spheres of activity – the labour process, intellectual production, the socially constructed environment, revolutionary technologies, organisational forms and social relations – produce a creativeness and destructiveness that maintain a necessary dynamic necessary for the system's survival, and potential prosperity. This dynamic can be quantified and David Harvey (2011) has calculated this to be in the region of a 3 per cent compound rate of economic growth. Without new areas for productive investment this necessary growth rate may not be achieved and the system and its elites, who have benefitted so spectacularly from the disposal of public assets, policy induced national indebtedness and the huge structural inequalities, will be in trouble. However, as history shows, capitalism is immensely resilient, being able through innovation and technological invention to transcend its inherent contradictions and crises to emerge if not stronger, then certainly fit enough to fight another day.

However, there are well-known social and ecological limits to growth, as was clearly articulated long ago by Fred Hirsch (1977), and famously by Donella Meadows and her co-authors in their *Limits to Growth* report for the Club of Rome in 1972 (Meadows *et al.* 1972). Other writers, particularly those exploring the theoretical legacy and insights of classical Marxist philosophy and economics, have demonstrated the existence of an ecological or metabolic rift in the relationship between human production and consumption to nature. Ultimately, for these critics, no amount of entrepreneurial invention, technological innovation, expropriation or exploitation will gainsay the compelling logic that flows from that system dynamic (Foster *et al.* 2010). The Jevons paradox has therefore returned to plague both the natural capitalists and ecological modernisers: increased resource efficiency will be most likely to lead to ever more resource use as production and consumption increases to satisfy the systemic need for continuous growth. Advertising and marketing will keep consumers in a continual state of want; and, what has also been apparent in recent years is the geographic expansion and deepening of capitalist relations of production destroying the more traditional forms of capitalism.

This has led Saskia Sassen (2010) to characterise this process as a contemporary form of primitive accumulation but of a form of capitalism that is also 'advanced' in that it is dominated by the logic of finance. Unlike earlier forms of capitalist development which tended to value human populations as both workers and consumers this phase does not, for large numbers of people are being brutally 'expulsed' from the system as is clearly evidenced by the huge populations of the abjectly poor, the unemployed, economic and political (and environmental) refugees, and those disabled in some way through the pressures and experience of long working hours and loss of labour rights. Accompanying this has been increased environmental degradation as natural resources have been mercilessly and thoughtlessly extracted. Vast areas of land in South America and sub-Saharan Africa have been purchased by the big corporations for agriculture, and the extraction of underground water, metals and minerals. Neoliberal structural adjustment policies have led to crippling levels of debt servicing for many countries in the global South, which has been ironically mirrored in the global North by the millions of households who have struggled, and failed, to service their debts following the 2007 subprime mortgage crisis in the United States and its systemic multiplier effects elsewhere. What this crisis has achieved in the deepening of advanced finance capitalism is its extension to, and throughout, all forms of social, economic and political life and its material and natural expressions – homes, neighbourhoods, forests, oceans, and so on. For Sassen, this latest phase of capitalism 'is akin to wanting the horns of the rhino, and throwing away the rest of the animal, devaluing it, no matter what its multiple utilities. Or using the human body to harvest some organs, and seeing no value in all the other organs, let alone the full human being – it can all be discarded' (Sassen 2010: 46).

For the green economist and UK Green Party spokesperson Molly Scott Cato, if the economy is to evolve beyond its habit of excessively pressurising people and the environment it will need to abandon some of its principle traits, features and characteristics. To some extent this is happening but slowly and modestly. The real question is one of power in a world that is increasingly stressed environmentally and economically.

> There is a real struggle going on now at the heart of international capitalism over how much accommodation has to be made for the system to survive. I am finding myself agreeing with Mervyn King, the current Governor of the Bank of England, and Adair Turner [chairman of the Confederation of British Industry] who are basically calling for adaptations because they know that otherwise the system is not resilient and it will crack and crumble. The smarter ones are seeing that some accommodations need to be made but unfortunately the people who really invested in the existing system and are really gaining a lot of money and power from it are fighting for everything to remain as it is. I am really outside of this argument but look at Davos this year [2012]. Look at who they invited to perform for them. It's all a performance, but it is nonetheless important in terms of the signals they think they need to be sending. I don't think the neoliberal model can adjust in a way that will make it just and sustainable but it obviously recognises the stresses at the moment... What is interesting is how much people have wised up about all this stuff. It's astonishing. I used to teach about money creation and three or four years ago people would think I was a complete nutter but after 2008, suddenly, I was not a nutter anymore because they see the reality of it. By 2010 they have spent hours on the internet working out how banking works because it is their money that is at stake – pensions, savings. We need to know how this system works. It is amazing how the financial crisis has led to this awareness raising at least for the banking side of it, although the environment has been put into the pale a bit.
>
> (Scott Cato 2012)

The National Audit Office (2011) in the United Kingdom reported in July 2011 that the total outstanding support explicitly pledged to the banks as at 31 March 2011 was £456.33 billion, which was down from £612.58 billion at 31 March 2010 and from an earlier peak of some £1.162 trillion. In March 2011 the total outstanding support was 31 per cent of gross domestic product. The value of the state investment in the banking sector was showing a steady decline. In the United States, the total value of federal bail outs to the banks and to the big corporations such as General Motors and Chrysler totalled somewhere in the region of US$30 trillion by October 2010. It was with this in mind, together with the coming of the Rio+20 summit on sustainable development, that the world's business and political leaders congregated at Davos in Switzerland for the World Economic Forum's annual meeting in January 2012. The theme for the gathering was 'The Great Transformation: Shaping New Models', with sustainability,

climate change, resource use joining the perennials of economic growth, employment and security on the agenda. The natural capitalist's notion of 'doing much
more with less' had been earlier legitimised somewhat by the McKinsey and
Company's publication *Resource Revolution: Meeting the World's Energy, Materials,
Food and Water Needs* (Dobbs *et al.* 2011).

Anticipating a growth of a further three billion middle-class consumers by
2030, the issue of risks, shortages and price changes in the global supply of food
and other resources was identified as being of key importance. The McKinsey
report linked the deterioration of the environment to the growth in resource
consumption, and recognised the enduring fact that many of the world's population do not have their basic needs for energy, food and water adequately met.
Increasing supply and resource productivity could meet the projected global
demand, the report stated, but this would probably be insufficient to prevent
global warming rising above the two degrees centigrade that is currently anticipated by scientists, or to alleviate the resource poverty affecting many people.

Significant new public and private investments in renewables, energy efficient
buildings and radical changes in costs and price mechanisms would be needed
too. Global government subsidies of up to US$1trillion would provide a disin-
centive to the more productive use of resources as currently does the failure to
price production externalities such as carbon emissions which for McKinsey
ought to be at least $30 a tonne. From McKinsey's free market perspective,
removing agriculture, energy, and water subsidies and putting a price of US$30
per tonne on carbon emissions is required. Without clear pricing and consistent
and stable policy regimes produced by the world's governments, investors in such
important and necessary areas as renewable energy will demand unrealistically
high returns in order to compensate for the high perceived and actual risks.
Throughout the McKinsey report are the overriding aims to maintain and
improve return on private sector capital investment, creating conditions and
possibilities for competitive advantage and managing business risks, including
that of regulation, in a more sophisticated manner. Profit remains the name of
the game even if this also means ensuring developing countries benefit the
commercial activities of the multinational extractive industries and that environmental clean-up becomes a condition of their 'social license' to operate. The
Resource Revolution report concludes by stating that societies must enhance their
long-term resilience in the face of the resource challenges outlined. Public
awareness of resource related risks need to be raised among both consumers and
businesses and social protections schemes need to be developed to mitigate the
impact of these economic risks on poor people.

These issues can be effectively distilled into the questions asked some years
earlier by Elinor Ostrom (1990) in her book *Governing the Commons*, when she
explored who is best placed to effectively protect and equitably share common-
pool resources. For Ostrom, and for Molly Scott Cato, the solution lies with an
institutional arrangement that supports and enables collective self-governance.
For McKinsey, the answer is that responsibility should lie with the corporations
and the markets aided and abetted where appropriate by government. Given all

this, it seems unlikely that free market neoliberal policies can, or will want to, deliver the equity, equality and sustainable development advocated by environmentalists and others. The McKinsey analysis is far more measured and accommodating of the rapaciousness of advanced capitalism as seen by Sassen and Harvey. Thus, it needs to be emphasised that for McKinsey and for the business and political leaders at Davos, 'resilience' does not infer the end of capitalism or the end of neoliberalism or for that matter the end of economic austerity, but it does clearly recognise that some changes and accommodations are required.

This became clearer at the Davos gathering the following year, where the theme for the global economic and political elites was 'Resilient Dynamism', or 'How to Get the Global Economy Back on to a Path of Stable Growth and Higher Employment' (World Economic Forum 2013). Aditya Chakrabortty, economics leader writer for *The Guardian*, noted that in true Davos style the term would make equal sense the other way around. More seriously though, with a basic entrance fee of £45,000 and a special fee of £98,500 for those leaders who intend to participate in the all-important private sessions, the World Economic Forum is essentially a body that virtually from its inception in 1971 says one thing publicly but works relentlessly behind the scenes to maintain the dominance of global neoliberalism (Chakrabortty 2013; Lapham 1998).

For Molly Scott Cato this notion of necessary change is possibly the most important connotation of the term 'resilience'. It opens up a crack and offers an opportunity for transformations that may just possibly have consequences unintended by the global CEOs gathering at their exclusive and extremely expensive Swiss resort venue.

> The reason I like the concept of resilience is that it implies that change is inevitable. So, I think we need to have a theory as to how we respond to that change. Critical changes are inevitable now for various reasons to do with what we've done to the environment and the way the economy is. Resilience is a positive way of framing responses to critical and potentially disruptive change. You don't go back to exactly the same shape you were in before which is why the engineering definition is so useful but you adjust your shape, metaphorically, so that the new shape is better.
>
> (Scott Cato 2012)

Engineers often use the term 'robustness', which has connotations of a designed resilience. That is, there is an assumption of a bounded uncertainty with known ranges and kinds of disturbances or shocks the system may encounter. For engineers, the question asked is how much something will take before it breaks and for green economic and political thinkers like Molly Scott Cato, the overarching pursuit of short term profit invariably makes economic systems, whether at regional or global levels, far more brittle, vulnerable and unhealthy than they ought to be. Similarly, the resilience of a local food system is one defined by being aware of its vulnerability and dependence on nature. This is turn requires the system to act on this awareness to create some security by recognising, rather than denying, limits and by creating a flexible and adaptive management process that may, according to other market orientated criteria, be deemed inefficient.

A local system of food co-operatives, allotments, productive gardens, fair trade shops and farmers markets offers a security, adaptiveness and flexibility especially important in a period of food price volatility brought on by climate change, energy price rises and the globalisation of food supply. In addition, local co-operative food system helps to reconnect people to the land, to values of co-operation and sharing rather than private profit, to the bioregion and the local environment (Beecher *et al.* 2012; Scott Cato 2012). Such a system can be a basis for wider transition and social learning, as will be discussed in Chapter 6.

Jonathon Porritt has been a leading figure in the British sustainability movement for many years. He was an early member of the Ecology Party in the 1970s, later renamed as the Green Party, and director of Friends of the Earth in the 1980s. He is a co-founder of the global sustainability organisation Forum for the Future, and former chair of the now defunct UK Sustainable Development Commission, established by Tony Blair's New Labour government. Resilience is an important concept for Porritt, but he feels that it should not supersede the concept of sustainability as an overarching way of understanding and initiating those policy and practical actions required to deal with our current problems. For Jonathon Porritt, sustainability and sustainable development both remain as important philosophical goals.

Unfortunately, the 'alternative' Green New Deal (Green New Deal Group 2008) that was developed following the financial crisis of 2007–2008 with its call for an ecologically conscientious economics and a renewed participatory democracy had little purchase on the public imagination or the internal debates of politicians.

> All sorts of people love the concept of resilience, but seem reluctant to confront a critical paradox that now loams larger and larger: one of the most resilient systems on show today is contemporary capitalism itself!
>
> This is a system that seems to be able to cope with limitless shocks, black swans and all the destabilising consequences of the way in which it operates. Unbelievably, there is still a consensus around the world that this is a system that can still deliver the goods in terms of meeting people's needs and aspirations. You don't hear even a hint of the need to pursue a new paradigm now in the speeches of world leaders.
>
> For me, this is a remarkable demonstration of what high-level, geopolitical resilience looks like: hanging on to a system that is demonstrably failing at every turn. I'm not sure that's the kind of resilience that its advocates have in mind.
>
> (Porritt 2012)

There are increasing numbers of business 'gurus' or 'change agents' that use nature as their business model by promoting holistic and systems thinking, biomimicry, and resilient and pioneering entrepreneurs who are able to conjure success out of chaos. Fast Company calls this new wunderkind 'Generation Flux' (Safian 2012), and Giles Hutchins (2012), author of the pithy modular business toolkit, *The Nature of Business: Redesigning for Resilience*, stresses that sustainability is the only way to do good business. There needs to be more sharing between internal and external stakeholders, greater trust and a mutual understanding of each other's values and objectives.

Resilience, adaptation and responsiveness are the key terms in the Hutchins lexicon, around which all businesses and business mentalities must and can be redesigned. He presents successful case studies from the likes of General Electric, Coca-Cola, Nike, Unilever, Apple, Tata and Virgin, but clearly does not wish to dwell on their other less sustainably laudable achievements or the wider cultural and ecological contradictions where growth and capital accumulation continue to be business's order of the day (Prudham 2009).

New greener airlines and space tourism are now all part of the mix. Sustainability practitioners know that economic growth cannot continue as it is but how to achieve prosperity without growth has not yet commanded anything like a consensus which is why, for Porritt, so many business leaders are open to ideas of change. Many recognise the current paradigm is not working and is bad for business and society. It is therefore possible for sustainability organisations to work with business, and within a business orientated frame of reference, to initiate some progressive reforms. There are two ways in which this can be done:

> The first is directly related to the concept of resilience at the level of the individual firm. At a time of increased unpredictability and discontinuities within the system (most particularly discontinuities in the supply chain), you don't have to work very hard to demonstrate why good management equals protection against potential disruption. When they're thinking through supply chain issues, in terms of both relationships and finance, they can begin to see what resilient strategies look like – diversification of suppliers, elimination of high risk aspects of that supply chain, ferocious pursuit of efficiency on energy, raw materials and water.
>
> All of these things make a great deal of sense to a well-managed company: they can see it makes a short term difference because it doesn't cost them anything, and for the long-term, it makes them less vulnerable to potential disruption.
>
> The second thing has more to do with the general analysis of corporate sustainability at societal scale. It is incredibly difficult for business to thrive in an environment that is increasingly being disrupted by the social and economic factors we see multiplying all around us. Against that kind of backdrop, the argument that business should be a 'force for good' in terms of addressing these challenges is not a hard sell. How else will the conditions for company growth and sustainable markets be maintained?
>
> (Porritt 2012)

Being a force for good and playing a progressive part in economic and social recovery is something that resonates soundly with the iconic status and almost mystical aura business and business leaders are accorded by the media, politicians and educational managers. Much of this assumed progressive activity tends to fall under the corporate social responsibility (CSR) rubric, as Porritt suggests, but as Banerjee (2008) argues, a great deal of the corporate rhetoric around citizenship and responsibility is defined by quite narrow business interests that are not always directly of benefit to businesses' many stakeholders. Those people, groups and organisations who may not toe the corporate line are frequently marginalised, as many local communities and victims of corporate malfeasance frequently testify.

Indeed, much research has indicated that where environmental strategies are concerned, once the 'low-hanging fruit' and cost savings and efficiency increases have been made, further environmental improvements requiring considerably more investment are undertaken with reluctance if at all. The key factor determining CSR and environmental improvements is shareholder value and it is more than interesting to note that shareholder value together with the remuneration of chief executives also tends to be linked to the size and number of layoffs a company makes. Additionally, it is rare that social opprobrium induced by unsustainable or unethical business practices has a long term effect. Nestlé has survived and prospered very well as nearly two generations that have grown up since the baby milk scandal first became of global public concern. Only in August 2012, after fifty years, did the drugs company Grünenthal apologise for the serious birth defects, deaths and other sufferings the Thalidomide drug caused. Although compensation had previously been paid, some class action lawsuits seeking compensation are still in the courts and likely to remain so for some time to come. Additionally, Union Carbide still has not made a satisfactory settlement thirty years after the Bhopal disaster, and similar tales can be told of Exxon, Shell, Nike and many others. British American Tobacco, whose product is known to be lethal and addictive, has won many corporate responsibility and sustainability awards while the World Business Council for Sustainable Development reiterates that the markets can be a positive element in the sustainable development process and the construction of a low carbon economy. As the Council's Vision 2050 confidently states, there are genuine business opportunities in becoming more sustainable, and these should not be considered as being optional or simply ethical alternatives:

> The transformation ahead represents vast opportunities in a broad range of business segments as the global challenges of growth, urbanisation, scarcity and environmental change become the key strategic drivers for business in the coming decade. In natural resources, health and education alone, the broad order of magnitude of some of these could be around US$0.5–1.5 trillion per annum in 2020, rising to between US$3–10 trillion per annum in 2050 at today's prices, which is around 1.5–4.5 per cent of world GDP in 2050.
>
> (WBCSD 2010: iv)

This clearly shows that much of the sustainable development discourse can easily incorporate neoliberal values, sometimes without knowing it, and sometimes in the belief that in doing so sustainability advocates are being pragmatic, wise and realistic. No organisation, however, will publicly support unsustainable practices, although arguments for delay or moderation may cloak themselves with arguments relating to economic necessity, competitiveness, cost and, of course, jobs, jobs and more jobs.

Ecological problems are at the root of many of the world's deep economic problems and certainly are extremely serious in many parts of the global South, often impairing the South's ability to repay its debts to its Northern creditors. Ironically, as Harvey (1996) notes, it is this impaired capacity to pay that has perhaps prompted the interest of the World Bank and other international agencies in socio-ecological and sustainability projects. 'What is then evident', Harvey writes, 'is that all debate about ecoscarcity, natural limits, overpopulation, and sustainability is a debate about the preservation of a particular social order rather than a debate about the preservation of nature per se' (Harvey 1996: 148). For the World Bank (2009), adaptation and resilience are about future proofing economic growth and development, certainly in sub-Saharan Africa but undoubtedly elsewhere too, against the effects of climate change and other risk impacts. Given this, the sustainability and sustainable development discourse can even serve to reinforce the mechanistic root metaphors that shape the world views integral to the capitalist mode of production and reproduce the military type metaphors that pervade business, education and indeed some sustainability and conservation practices – strategy, tactics, competition, cohorts, targets, logistics, field, operations, and so on (Audebrand 2010).

For Keith Budden, who has worked in the broader field of sustainable development for over twenty years as an NGO worker primarily in east and west Africa, and more recently in the public sector as head of sustainability at Birmingham's Strategic Partnership Council and in the private sector as strategic partnership manager with the energy company E.ON in the UK, dealing with the existing social and economic structures have remained a constant:

> From my experience of working in developing countries, it is absolutely clear that for people and places to get an improved quality of life, managing their localised environment over the long term sustainably is absolutely critical and that has to be done in a way that creates work and employment and deals with existing social and economic structures.
>
> (Budden 2012)

Budden believes that over the years both the language and principle values of sustainability and sustainable development have changed:

> In some ways what was a left-of-centre holistic and sustainable way of thinking has been taken over by the World Business Council for Sustainable Development, has become a mainstream tool and has been misused. The key

conceptual challenge is in relation to 'trade-offs' or balance. In order to create jobs we can balance this against environmental damage or social disruption. Thus, creating a balanced triple bottom line. I don't think the idea of 'trade-offs' was ever there in Brundtland, but has been developed largely by a traditional business community on the basis that they can be perceived to be sustainable without altering the fundamentals of their business model. I think the business community and some of their acolytes in academia, consulting and in NGO's have supported this idea of a balance with a view that if business are spending a bit more on corporate social responsibility and reporting their impact then that this is success. This success can only be achieved by funding, employing or sponsoring these academic, NGO or consulting organisations. However, this approach can prevent business evaluating the core principles of their business model.

(Budden 2012)

Each organisation typically approaches sustainable development and resilience from its own specific concerns and aims. For the NGO and conservation community, climate change has clearly increased in importance as it as for businesses at least in terms of reducing costs, carbon footprints, and developing its commitment to being 'responsible'. There is, however, still a long way to go as sustainability does not yet determine 'the what' and 'the how' of business activity, wealth creation and resource use.

I think some of the NGO community has tried to remain focused on the key underlying issues but maybe have missed the opportunity of communicating it fully. The language has changed and has become mainstream. The dominant focus on climate change has also not helped. The view that what matters is carbon reduction without considering the environmental or social impact can lead to some very unsustainable decisions...From a business perspective, the challenge is how do we get away from a corporate social responsibility being part of the marketing or health and safety function. How many businesses put sustainability at the heart of their corporate strategy team and work directly with the CEO and board? I think we are still a long way off from sustainable development being the best way to do business.

(Budden 2012)

This is not the complete picture as some companies do take corporate responsibility very seriously, even if they do, obliquely in a way, challenge the dominance, and legitimacy, of market values and the market economy. These companies tend to subscribe to the notion that a market economy does not necessarily mean there has to be a (globalised) market society.

The large employee-owned engineering consultancy Mott MacDonald (MM) is one such organisation. One in seven of its 14,000 staff are shareholders, its corporate style is collegial and, being cash-positive, MM claims to be largely free from the influence of external shareholders and financial institutions. Its public commitment to sustainable development is pronounced particularly in its infra-structure developments in the global South, its renewable energy, water and resource management activities, its health care and education projects, and in its use of smart new media technologies throughout the world. Sustainability is part of MM's organisation culture, clearly evident in its internal operations as well as public relations (Mott MacDonald n.d.).

Dr Anne Kerr is the practice leader for environment and sustainability in Asia Pacific and Australasia for MM, and believes great strides have been taken in terms of global appreciation of matters relating to sustainability and sustainable development in recent years. However, there remains a lack of appreciation at government, political, business and community levels of the extent of the chal-lenges facing existing and future communities. Many people are now aware of the 'energy crisis' and more are becoming aware of the 'water crisis', but connection between the water, energy and food crises facing us are not widely recognised.

The three essentials are referred to by Kerr as the 'trilemma' for future society, are intrinsically interlinked. It is profoundly worrying that few decision makers recognise these as being related to and as important as poverty alleviation and the global food crisis and food security. There is a lack of holistic understanding and a failure to acknowledge the real cost of resources such as water, which may be heavily subsidised or even free. Once the costs have been monetised, she argues, their holistic importance becomes obvious and compelling to all.

Many economists would agree, and some have started to put a price, or value, on the environment as a whole. In a seminal article in *Nature*, the American ecological economist Robert Costanza and colleagues (Costanza *et al.* 1997) esti-mated the economic value of the planet's ecological resources and services were in the region of US$33trillion annually. They warned that this estimate must be considered to be at the minimum level and that natural capital stocks and ecosys-tems services were likely to become increasingly stressed and far more scarce in the future. These ecosystems services and natural resources had conventionally been perceived as being inexhaustible as well as free were now most probably approaching irreversible critical thresholds an as this occurs their value could increase markedly perhaps towards infinity. Kerr clearly recognises these argu-ments seeing both the concept and practice of resilience as an important and well established element in her own field of civil engineering. For Kerr, 'resilience' is possibly less amenable to dispute and argumentation that the more discursive and disputed concept of sustainability 'because to many people it means different things' (Kerr 2012).

In addition, another major problem emerging from the economic recession, Kerr argues, is the lack of Government leadership and the basic inadequacy of public and private sector investment in infrastructure developments which will build up further issues for the future.

> Taking the example of water supply pipelines in many post war urban envi-ronments, they are reaching the end of design life. Losses due to leakage can be as high as 40–45 per cent, and hence a vast amount of water is wasted.

Energy is also wasted as a result, where energy is required for treatment of potable water, and for conveying water across cities and communities. If the repairs are left for another five or ten years you have a massive potential regarding the increase in the number of bursts and so forth. We are actually costing ourselves dearly by not doing the repair and renovation work early on. Similar challenges exist for other infrastructure. Somewhere of the order of 80 per cent of bridges in the United States will reach the end of their design life in the next decade. This does not mean they are unable to be used, but repair and maintenance costs will increase, replacements may be needed, and budgets will be strained.

While Governments should take a very strong lead in providing and maintaining assets and infrastructure, we cannot merely wait and rely on Governments to act. The business communities have a role to play in finding creative ways of raising finance to provide for our infrastructure. If we focused more on utilising resources in an integrated manner, and took cognizance and acted on the trilemma to society, as well as maintaining and repairing infrastructure in a timely manner, we would be in a better position to accommodate the resilience people are expecting for our planet in the next thirty years.

(Kerr 2012)

Sustainability, work and employment

Jobs and productivity are invariably conjoined in the public discourse on economic development and recovery, the resilience of people and social and economic systems. But the relentless drive for increased productivity often means, as it has meant consistently in recent decades, work intensification, short term and insecure employment, under and unemployment, low wages and forms of labour exploitation that would have been very familiar to the author of *Capital* and the author of *Hard Times*. Work and the nature of work have until recently attracted little attention from sustainability advocates and practitioners.

Things are changing, though. In recent decades economic recoveries have been largely jobless and the private sector, particularly in the new hi-tech knowledge industries have not created the level of paid employment that the era of industrial growth produced in the decades immediately following the conclusion of World War Two (Rifkin 2000; Aronowitz and DiFazio 2010). There is a very strong likelihood that full employment will never return but that work will retain its significance as an ideological and disciplinary construct. The Marxist economist Harry Cleaver maintains (Cleaver 2000: 82) that capitalism is 'a social system based on the imposition of work through the commodity form' and the glorification of work as an essential ethical imperative, a key to a person's individuality and humanity, remains a fundamental foundation of contemporary capitalist social relations (Weeks 2005).

Even before the 2008 economic crisis wage growth were stagnating and the proportion of people on low pay increasing. As the International Labour Office (2010) reported:

Redistribution from wages to profits and from median-wage earners to high wage earners reduced aggregate demand by transferring income from individuals with a high propensity to spend to people who save more. Before the crisis, some countries were able to maintain household consumption through increased indebtedness, while other countries based their economic growth mainly on exports.

Figure 4.1 Fishing for jobs: advice and guidance for job seekers, Birmingham, UK
Source: John Blewitt

In the three years following the onset of the latest global economic crisis, 27 million jobs have been lost, with global unemployment likely to remain at 6 per cent for the foreseeable future. Global youth unemployment is also high, at 12.7 per cent, and the employment to population ratio is the lowest it has been for over twenty years. In 2011, 1.52 billion workers were in vulnerable employment with the number of working poor also continuing to grow steadily. The International Labour Office (2012) states:

> to generate sustainable growth while maintaining social cohesion, the world must rise to the urgent challenge of creating 600 million productive jobs over the next decade, which would still leave 900 million workers living with their families below the US$2 a day poverty line, largely in developing countries.

In fact a new labouring class has recently been identified: 'the precariat', which comprises not only those workers with low skills and qualifications but increasingly highly educated professional workers, particularly those in the creative industries, whose work patterns are often bulimic and just as unhealthy (Gill and Pratt 2008). Many part-time, low-paid, agency and essentially insecure outworkers fall in to this precariat class, and can be found virtually everywhere, but particularly in the US, Italy, Spain and increasingly the UK.

In South Korea 60 per cent of all workers are in insecure casual jobs, many in the high-tech sectors, and in India perhaps up to 80 per cent of the formal labour force is outside 'formal' employment (Standing 2009). Precariousness is nothing new to capitalism and the post-war lull in precariaty was probably just an aberration and certainly should never have been regarded as a never ending norm. Work in the market society is a commodity and, as Antonio Negri argues, labour is now deterritorialised and dispersed with the whole of the society now at the service of profit. 'Capital has insinuated itself everywhere, and everywhere attempts to acquire the power to coordinate, commandeer and recuperate value' (Negri 1989: 116).

The worker is now totally socialised, and in order to grow and to control labour, capital has to, and in large part does, control and manage knowledge, science and communication. The worker is now no longer apart from the labour process. She or he is an intimate part of it. Many companies use techniques of psychological profiling and other tools from the business consultant's magic box to ensure prospective employees will fit in, will be suitable, and will invest their personalities and souls in the work. The reward is not so much security or even wages but a presumed sense of identification and 'ownership'. Indeed, with stagnant and insecure wages combined with cuts to welfare benefits, health, pensions and other forms of public expenditure, the social income for many people in the global North has markedly declined.

The resilience of neoliberal market capitalism seems to lie in having succeeded in fashioning a new worker subjectivity in large part based on the development, again particularly in the global North, of 'immaterial labour' that is, labour that produces the cultural and informational content of a commodity. It is around immateriality, Maurizio Lazzarato (1996) suggests, that the quality and quantity of labour is organised. 'Work has become defined as the capacity to activate and manage productive co-operation' with participative management technologies creating new subjectivities and processes (Lazzarato 1996: 135).

Thus, control resides with the subject and within the communicative process at work such as the good citizenship awards, the 'we want to hear your views' communiqués which lasts only so long as the labour is required. Hyper-exploitation is the actually existing experience of the new intellectual proletarian and this extends far beyond the workplace for it is the various ideologies of consumption and consumerism, articulated by the advertising and marketing industries, that ensure that the ever changing nature of consumer needs, tastes, images and wants maintain and reproduce the social relations that capital requires. Lazzarato notes that prior to manufacture, a good or service has to be sold. The consumer, the ideological subject, actively intervenes in the production process:

If production today is directly the production of a social relation, then the 'raw material' of immaterial labor is subjectivity and the 'ideological' environment in which this subjectivity lives and reproduces. The production of subjectivity ceases to be only an instrument of social control (for the reproduction of mercantile relationships) and becomes directly productive, because the goal of our post-industrial society is to construct the consumer/communicator – and to construct it as 'active.'...The fact that immaterial labor produces subjectivity and economic value at the same time demonstrates how capitalist production has invaded our lives and has broken down all the oppositions among economy, power, and knowledge.

(Lazzarato 1996: 143)

These forms of life are essentially innovative and they are a product of the relation between the producer and consumer. Creativity in productivity resides in the dialectical relationship between these forms of life, the values they produce and in the activities of the subjects that constitute them. This offers possibilities for an alternative because, as Lazzarato and Negri argue, the capitalist entrepreneur is no longer the main, or perhaps even the sole, source of innovation. For many sustainability advocates, 'consumerism often acts as a substitute for real engagement with the world' (Newman and Jennings 2008: 116). Consumerism is therefore not just about the overconsumption of material resources but the waste of human creativity and the degradation of work. Sustainable economic and industrial reform could liberate the creativity of individual workers and their communities.

This rather heady theory has much to commend it, and the notion of precariousness and the reappearance of what was once quite commonplace – casualisation – is something that resonates widely with many people's experience of work and everyday life throughout the world. Although there may be some benefits, especially for those members of the precariat who are able to command highly paid contracts for work they enjoy doing, the vast majority of those who fall into this category still experience a perennial economic and ontological insecurity. For some commentators, 'precariaty' could possibly be made more acceptable by introducing a form of guaranteed basic income, an assured individual and collective voice in the public debate on the economy and the collective negotiation of worker entitlements many of which have been eroded in recent years (Standing 2008).

The idea of a guaranteed minimum or citizens' income is not new and is perhaps even more necessary when one considers that many of the new jobs that green economists and supporters of a Green New Deal say could be produced will themselves be short-term, part-time and precarious. Advocates argue that a citizen's income could easily be introduced on a universal basis leading to a degree of social and economic justice and security. It would also fashion a more resilient society and more resilient individuals.

Molly Scott Cato sees a citizen's income as establishing a green commitment to autonomy, a demonstrable way green economics can alter conventional social relations. It could be funded, at least in part, through a new system of eco taxation which would include taxing common resources such as the land.[1] It would be fair, and possibly offset any further drift towards social division and political reaction, for according to Standing (2011) the precariat are the new dangerous class. Being permanently temporary, invariably without employee benefits, without access to even a denuded social income, frequently vulnerable to being undercut or replaced by (legal or illegal) migrant labour, the precariat are likely to become increasingly responsive to the rhetoric of neo-fascist populist politicians who play on their fears and anxieties.

A progressive political strategy and social justice for the precariat must involve a more equitable control over the key assets of quality time, quality space, knowledge and financial capital. Income redistribution in favour of the poor and vulnerable rather than the rich and super rich is absolutely essential. But more needs to be done. For some members of this class, what is needed is also an enhanced and carefully nurtured personal resilience. What should be sought are a wide range of schemes, advice, guidance, 'how to' manuals and occasionally company-sponsored personal training schemes (usually in order to improve performance), cognitive coaching as well as introductions to alternative beliefs systems.

Chris Johnstone, author of *Find Your Power* and the *Happiness Training Plan* and consultant on the psychology of resilience believes the individual has to be immersed in a philosophy of deep ecology – a far cry from the competitive and possessive individualism of neoliberal market economics and the military metaphors discussed by Audebrand (2010) but similar advice and turns of phrase, are not so uncommon in the more mainstream world of business consultancy where green is becoming a new management fashion. However, although the growing interest in individual psychological resilience may be yet another ideological mask, it is certainly an element of the new worker subjectivity, the experiential reality of precarious and immaterial labour and the system of post-industrial capitalism.

Despite all the entreaties to work, to find meaning and value in work and to be blamed personally if one does not have it or succeed at it, meaning per se is indeed something that should be valued in and for itself. Work contributes to the overall happiness of a person's life but it should not become a burden through self-exploitation or by being consumed by what is in essence actually quite meaningless and unproductive. Where there is exploitation there is also considerable social inequality, ill health and unhappiness and this is by no means simply contingent, an accident or a coincidence. It is a systemic effect of the way the capitalist economy operates. As the nineteenth-century artist, craftsman, businessman, writer and ethical socialist William Morris wrote in *Useful Work versus Useless Toil*, 'wealth is what nature gives us and what a reasonable man can make out of the gifts of Nature for his reasonable use' (Morris [1885] 1962: 121).

Morris saw what was at fault was not the individual person but the whole system of industrial capitalism. What leads to alienation at work and in society is a lack of autonomy, an inability to exercise one's creative potential in a system that only sees value in terms of what can be realised in market terms (Schwartz

1982; Schumacher 1980; Gorz 1999). What is crucial 'is the development of people's autonomy irrespective of companies' need for it' (Gorz 1999: 74).

The French sociologist and philosopher André Gorz (1999: 77) argues for an agreed time-based multi-activity society which 'must impose itself by virtue of the aspirations by which the autonomous and 'rich individualities', which companies need, transcend their productive function and become irreducible to that function'. The socialised worker, immaterial labour and the inevitability of productive co-operation, where communication, innovation and knowledge creates value, provides a basis to develop the human potential that has 'the capacity to break the sclerotic systems within which late capitalism has imprisoned us, and create the conditions necessary for a new mode of production' (Negri 1989: 79).

For Negri, Weeks, Cleaver and other radical autonomist theorists, any strategy that can transcend the current crisis and the damning limitations of the present system needs to entail 'the refusal to work' which has both negative and generative elements. First, the establishment of a universal guaranteed minimum (citizen's) income will sever the ideological connection between paid (exploitative) work and capitalism; and secondly, this refusal presupposes and emancipates the immense productive power, potential and accumulated social knowledge existing within society itself. This 'going beyond work' is not just a liberation from alienating work but an affirmation of new creative possibilities, new social relations of work and of everyday life. As Molly Scott Cato argues there is a real need now for educators, intellectuals and others involved in radical social movements, Green parties and other bodies to help people reframe the way they see the world. With others who are either members of, or closely associated with, the UK Green Party, Molly Scott Cato helped established the Green House think tank, for this purpose:

> What we are trying to do is a linked focused project based on generating public discussion and new forms of knowledge and understanding. It's saying that when you propose to people a citizen's income they are likely to see you as nuts. You have to change the way they see the world so that it becomes, 'Oh yeah, that's a good idea'. It's a project for reframing the way opinion formers frame the world and that has a lot of aspects to it. One of them is being more confident in the way you present yourself, refusing to be seen as fringe, but in building structures and networks...and trying to have some influence on this adaptation of capitalism that is taking place...At the moment we accept that workers have created value in businesses and it all belongs to Bill Gates. We need to raise questions that go beyond saying that workers can buy shares in the company but address fundamental issues like the ownership and control of business. The commons is a good way of framing our understanding of the environment particularly when resources are scarce. It raises questions as to who owns it [the environment] and how much of it.
>
> (Scott Cato 2012)

New business models can be and indeed are being developed. There are virtual TV safaris and profit sharing with all stakeholders. Co-operation and co-operative enterprises have a long and noble history too, and in various guises have survived the onslaught of neoliberal economics, war and political upheaval though not without some cost (Flecha and Santa Cruz 2011).

The Australian corporate governance specialist Shann Turnbull has long argued that private corporations are inherently undemocratic and that what needs to replace them is more localised control, stakeholder councils and co-operative enterprises (Turnbull 1997). Radical spaces for change (Kohn 2003) and for 'the social liberation of the producer' (Negri 1999: 79) have occurred in the past and are being formed today and may well do so in the future. Any notion that market-driven resilience will solve the world's ecological problems of resource depletion, catastrophic climate change and profligate use of fossil fuels is an absurd denial of eco-system principles and basic logic. Appropriate, inter-mediate and humane technologies, offering control, satisfaction and environmental sustenance are, and have been, available for many years though they do perhaps need to be rediscovered and re-articulated for this digital century. If 'resilience' is to play a part in this process of change it will also need to assure us that this other world is indeed possible and can come about before it is too late.

5 Regenerative and resilient eco-cities

Towards eco-cities

It is unnecessary to rehearse the arguments why cities are fundamental to a sustainable future as it is apparent that the bulk of the world's populations live in them and tremendous quantities of material and energy resources are consumed for and by them. Around 90 per cent of urban growth occurs in developing countries, and by 2025 China alone will probably have added 350 million people to its urban population. In 1979, 18 per cent of Chinese were urban dwellers, but following rapid economic development and urbanisation, by 2015 over 50 per cent of the Chinese population will reside in cities (Baeumler *et al.* 2012).

With economic development likely to continue, increasing amounts of resources will be used and carbon emissions generated, so it is imperative that old, new and future urban settlements be more ecologically responsible. Currently, urban ecological footprints are huge and need to be drastically reduced. Local economies need to be reshaped, transport systems modified and urban professional and public learning re-conceived (Rees and Wackernagel 1996; Satterthwaite 1997; Newman 2006; Kenworthy 2006).

Cities consume in the region of 60–80 per cent of the world's energy production. It is no wonder that in recent years there has been tremendous interest in eco-cities. The urbanist, sustainability advocate and founder of the non-profit organisation Urban Ecology, Richard Register, believes that we must rebuild cities in balance with nature. An eco-city is therefore an urban area that in its design and functioning is informed by a range of connected ecological principles and practices including assiduous recycling, ecological restoration, mixed use communities, decent and affordable housing; and, establishing and maintaining maximum biodiversity, transport and communication privileging access and proximity rather than car dependency, exceptionally efficient use of energy and materials, social and environmental justice, urban agriculture and horticulture, community based economic development, bioregional awareness and have compact and complex three dimensional forms similar to natural living organisms (Register 2006).

Climate change, traffic congestion and the general growth of environmental awareness among professional bodies, businesses, governments, scientists, urban planners, educators and the general public have ensured that the idea of a sustainable city has become a key element of most visions for a sustainable future. Creativity and innovation emerging directly from our developing understanding of sustainable ecosystems and bioregions in urban and architectural design are fundamental. This ecosystem perspective is essentially inclusive seeing humans as elements of local socio-ecological systems, relationships and processes that enable and support life in all its various forms. The concepts and practices of eco-social partnerships and co-operations receive considerable emphasis in this way of thinking, an approach quite distant from the aggressive competitive instincts of neoliberal ideologies. As Mark Roseland writes:

> Building eco-cities requires access to decision-making processes to ensure that economic and political institution promote activities that are ecologically sustainable and socially just. It requires that these institutions respect our needs as whole beings and citizens, not just as producers, consumers and voters. It requires attention issues of social equity and livability, and to truly democratic decision making processes that ensure the full participation of all.
>
> (Roseland 1997: 12)

Figure 5.1 Sustainable transportation: bicycles at Karslruhe, Germany
Source: John Blewitt

Figure 5.2 Sustainable transportation: bus mural, The Hague Netherlands
Source: John Blewitt

In 2002 an international charette was organised to identify and explore the major components of sustainable urbanism and the Ten Melbourne Principles that emerged were later adopted and endorsed at the Johannesburg Earth Summit later in that year. For Newman and Jennings (2008), these ten principles are the main ingredients of a sustainable urban future which includes the need to have a clear vision, the capacity to achieve economic and social security, the recognition of the intrinsic value of biodiversity, minimal ecological footprints, modelling the urban development of ecosystems, developing a distinctive sense of and commitment to place, empowerment and participation, partnership working, sustainable production and consumption, and good and transparent governance (UNEP/IETC 2002).

A sustainable city, though, can never be complete or finished. It will always be in the process of becoming, of continuing to make progress towards sustainability goals and visions that are in themselves ultimately ethical ones. Even though systems thinking, the science of ecology and sustainability, certainly presents a particular worldview, the values underpinning and informing sustainability also encompass issues of social and environmental justice, democratic empowerment and participation, human and other species wellbeing. Creating sustainability is therefore dependent on creating a sustainability culture. As Jeb Brugmann writes:

Progressive transformation is values-driven. People and institutions only align their private strategies and instrumental uses of the city to a common strategy because the ends create a more compelling value for them. Achieving strategic alignment in the urban free-for-all is nearly impossible if local practices of urbanism do not offer a value proposition that relates to the underlying culture of a good part of the city. This cultural dimension of cities is perhaps to most subtle aspect of urban strategy.

(Brugmann 2009: 234)

The importance of learning in the development of these sustainability cultures cannot be over-emphasised. Information has to be reliable and comparable, statistics meaningful and accurate and feelings and experiences acknowledged as fundamental for people and other non-human animals inhabit cities not abstracts or management plans.

The World Bank's Eco2 Cities Program, launched in 2009, aims to enhance the wellbeing of citizens and society by fully harnessing the benefit of ecosystems, facilitating those structure changes necessary for a transition to a low carbon economy and by emphasising the importance of integrated urban planning and management (Suzuki *et al.* 2010). For the World Bank, an Eco2 City is also an economic city, as its guidance states:

An Eco2 City builds on the synergy and interdependence of ecological and economic sustainability. Innovative cities in both the developed and the developing world have demonstrated that they can economically enhance their resource efficiency (realising the same value from a much smaller and renewable resource base), while simultaneously decreasing harmful pollution and unnecessary waste. By doing so, they have improved the quality of life of their citizens, enhanced their economic competitiveness and resilience, strengthened their fiscal capacity, and created a system of sustainability. Such cities are more likely to survive shocks, attract businesses, manage costs, and prosper

...An Eco2 City represents a second generation of eco-city. Instead of focusing on ecological performance alone and good practices in different sectors, it encourages cities to adopt a holistic framework for analysis. Eco2 City also embraces a highly participatory process for managing change at all levels of decision making bodies and across all sectors.

(Moffat *et al.* 2012: 7)

This practical and scalable operational support connects to a variety of important drivers including the use of green buildings to reduce greenhouse gas emissions and the use of Information and Communication Technologies – that is, 'smart technologies' – to more efficiently manage and operate the cities themselves. New eco-cities are being built in many parts of the world including the Middle East, Malaysia, Singapore, Korea and most significantly in China where sustainable city building has become a major industrial enterprise. It is doubtful whether these eco-cities are directly replicable in other parts of the world but clear lessons can be learnt in terms of the development and application of new green technologies, the need for clear visions and objectives, the organisation and contracting of public-private sector partnerships, the need for flexibility and adaptation as socio economic conditions and technologies change, the relevance of community engagement and recognising the importance of local knowledge, secure financing and investment and robust governance and management systems (Joss 2011). Many of these current and proposed eco-city developments are hugely ambitious and occurring in political environments that are not always known for their commitment to democracy and human rights. Some new eco-city projects have also been stalled (Dongtan in China) or in various ways scaled back (Masdar in Abu Dhabi). However, eco-city initiatives are also occurring in India, Japan, Germany, South Africa, Canada, Brazil, New Zealand, Sweden, the United States and many other places. Some of these are fill-in or retro-fitting projects rather than shiny new cities, and they also often go by other names such as solar city, carbon-neutral city, zero-energy city, Oekostadt, eco-municipality, sustainable city or Transition Town.

After the 1959 revolution in Cuba an extensive 12–15 kilometre green belt was established around Havana, which incorporated small farmers in the new economic programmes that also included the development of ponds, water reservoirs, small towns, public parks and Zoological and Botanic Gardens (Nevárez 1999). Since 1990, Havana, like other urban areas in Cuba, has increased its resilience and self-reliance by dedicating considerable areas to organic horticulture and urban agriculture.

There are many eco-city developments in China, with names such as Dongtan, Guangming, Changxing, Rizhao, MenTouGou, Tangshan, Wanzhuang and Tianjin becoming increasingly familiar to urbanists and sustainability practitioners throughout the world (Joss 2010; Joss *et al.* 2011). For Fan and Qi (2010) the key issue for China given the continuing priorities of economic growth is whether ecological constraints can be respected and an increase in social inequality avoided. Most large cities are equivalent in size to small regions and provinces and a city's administrative unit includes both an urbanised core and extensive rural areas including any smaller towns.

For example, Chongqing at one time had an administrative area of 82,300 km² and in 2006 a residential population of 32 million. Urumqi, on the other hand, is relatively small, with a population of 2 million but composed of 47 ethnic groups, and the city is struggling with a legacy of massive industrial pollution. Many cities have high volumes of migrant workers who experience low income, low status and low living standards. Fan and Qi found that between 2003 and 2006 despite extensive economic growth many Chinese cities did not increase their equity ratings and some became generally more unequal. Urban air quality and general environmental degradation have accompanied rapid urbanisation and industrialisation.

Even China's most sustainable city, Guangzhou, has worse ambient air quality than exists in most cities in advanced countries. There are inevitably huge regional differences and with cities and city-regions varying in size, wealth and economic profile generalisations are hard to sustain. Chinese authorities are taking both sustainability and economic development very seriously, but rapid urban growth, weak planning and regulatory regimes may also make many Chinese cities highly vulnerable to natural disasters and climate change. It has been estimated that about 70 per cent of China, including 80 per cent of its agricultural and industrial and about 50 per cent of its people, are at risk. It is likely that the country will suffer increased vulnerability to more frequent and intense rainfalls and floods especially in the southwest, and although typhoons may decrease in number, they too are like to become more intense and damaging.

China also has to confront increasing problems of water scarcity with existing arid areas likely to experience desertification. In addition, around 130 million people who live in the coastal cities are vulnerable to rises in sea level and this is additional to other potentially desperate consequences of climate change such as food shortages, the spread of respiratory and water-borne diseases, population displacement and political conflicts over scarce resources (Procee and Brecht 2012). Inevitably, because large numbers of people live and work in cities and physical and economic assets are concentrated within them, risks of considerable damage and loss of life are very real. Many cities find themselves located in areas that currently amplify their risks and vulnerabilities and even the sites of some new eco-cities have not been selected with as much care as perhaps they should have. Eco-cities will undoubtedly have to be resilient but it will not be until the latter part of the third decade of the 21st century that the full costs and benefits of eco-cities will be clearly apparent.

In India, the eco-city concept represents a fresh approach to human settlement development. Surjan and Shaw (2008) draw various lessons from its application in terms of addressing urban social and ecological vulnerabilities and thereby contributing an already extensive amount of work on urban risk reduction. Community-based initiatives such as those occurring in the 1,000-year-old coastal city of Puri indicate that local communities have a great deal to offer contemporary eco-city developments and in creating disaster resilient eco-communities. However, economic development based on encouraging tourism has transformed residential areas and expanded commercial activities exerting increased pressures on the fragile urban eco-systems. Low-lying areas and wetlands have been built upon, and hotels and guesthouses discharge waste water directly into the sea, causing skin diseases and other ailments.

Being in Orissa, Puri is also subjected to violent tropical cyclones. Various planning proposals and projects have concentrated on infrastructure solutions but a resilient eco-city cannot be created by just upgrading existing or even developing new facilities such as an ecocar park alone. Local communities in their everyday lives, routines, achievement and beliefs also exhibit ecologically sensitive and resilient capabilities and this collective wisdom needs to be valued and harvested rather than threatened and compromised by economic development and growth. Surjan and Shaw noted that the cohesive ancient community of Sahis in Puri represent a robust community bonding nurtured through many generations. Citizens discuss local problems and issues among themselves and try to search for acceptable solutions through mutual co-operation. The mutual trust among the people is further harnessed by the spirit of working together for community religious or environmental concerns. There exists a very potent sense of belonging to the place, which is exemplified by the preservation of the neighborhood heritage identity, water harvesting elements, gardens, open spaces, etc.

(Surjan and Shaw 2008: 260)

The Jagaghar community maintains self-owned environmentally friendly recreational facilities that demonstrate considerable understanding of the need to conserve water, flora and fauna. Their religious beliefs link a spiritual concern with sustainability science. Surjana and Shaw also discuss community-based solid waste management schemes, which include door-to-door waste segregation and collection schemes, raise awareness and knowledge, engage tourists and nurture sustainable partnership and consensus building. Many cities will be confronting increased risk and vulnerabilities so the need to combine disaster resilient capacities with eco-city infrastructure and sustainable lifestyles are of paramount importance. Engaging local citizens in decision-making will undoubtedly increase their understanding of risk vulnerabilities and sustainability and may encourage them to become more sustainably proactive.

Increasing numbers of cities annually compete to become known as the 'greenest city' as the eco-city idea becomes increasingly common, practically implemented, and to an extent, globally mainstreamed. A small number of global corporations are involved who, together with the city and other governmental authorities, are keen to exploit the cultural branding potential of sustainable urban developments. Thus, Destiny in Florida is marketed as 'America's first eco-sustainable city' and Black Sea Gardens in Bulgaria as 'the world's first carbon-neutral luxury resort'.

Curitiba in Brazil is often presented as a model eco-city with its former mayor Jaime Lerner, environmental economist Lester Brown and others at the forefront of Curitiba global media promotion. The city has consistently been branded an exemplar of sustainable modernity and indeed in terms of city planning, local economic development, transport and, to a degree, social inclusion, Curitiba is a real success. However, the city planners, economic and political elites have treated the city as an island and its success has been at the expense of other municipalities where poverty stubbornly persists. Lerner and his colleagues have used planning as a major political intervention tool to solve both the city's physical and collective social problems. However, as Joseli Macedo concludes:

As long as Curitiba is surrounded by poverty, it cannot be held as a model of successful planning nor called a 'social capital'. Until there are no families settling in riparian areas within the water supply watersheds of metropolitan Curitiba, it cannot be dubbed 'the ecological capital.' As with most urban areas in Latin America, Curitiba will continue to grow, and so will the need for adequate shelter, affordable transportation, employment, education and health care.

(Macedo 2004: 548)

In the first decade of the twenty-first century, car-manufacturing industries have relocated to Curitiba, contributing to a rise in car ownership in the city.

Visions and master plans have been and remain a key element of eco-city and sustainability thinking, but their realisation inevitably means having to confront and overcome foreseeable and unforeseeable problems. Apart from specialist expertise realising visions and co-ordinating projects at whatever scale but certainly at city-region level requires the capacity and capability to see the whole, to understand multiple views and perspectives, professional and disciplinary viewpoints and how they relate to each other. For Stephen McKenna, head of town planning at Mott MacDonald, the people who are able (or at least should be able) to see this bigger picture are, perhaps unsurprisingly, town planners who can review sustainability and resilience in all its various aspects (public space, construction, energy, etc.). Importantly, McKenna makes a distinction between a place succeeding and a place being resilient. Success depends on a number of factors, but there is a temporal factor at work in McKenna's understanding of a resilient city:

> If a place is to survive, that is what you might call urban resilience. A city like London has the planning capacity and stakeholder resources to manage its critical infrastructure to try to ensure it will be there in 100 years' time? Will it be the same sort of place or will it be very different? Will it have had to lose a huge part of its identity and character just to survive? These are more difficult questions. A resilient place, I would say, manages to remain a place that offers opportunity for its people and a chance to progress. London is a success story yet will it be resilient looking ahead to these wider issues in another 100 years?
>
> In a developing and urbanising country you might see a very different pattern. There are some cities that will risk being overwhelmed. For instance, Jakarta has 18 million people but the infrastructure is probably only good enough for two or three millions. Half a million people entering it every year combined with threats such as sea level rising mean that the city is at risk like numerous other cities round the planet.
>
> When I look at resilience, I therefore think in part of the long term. When I think of successful places I may think twenty perhaps, thirty years. If a place like Calcutta say is resilient then it will have to be able to cater for all of its diverse communities, adapt to the challenges of global warming, its water infrastructure... It may be successful in the interim by functioning as major economic hub within a massive hinterland but longer term the issues are growing. We are talking about double the urban area on this planet in the next thirty to forty years. There's going to be three billion more urban

dwelling people and a vast rise in consumption of resources associated with that. Resilience at the mega city scale may prove to be rather different a characteristic of our future planning than sustainable development. The latter cannot easily be achieved in an era of unplanned massive urban growth which will challenge the life support systems that we depend upon. Art the smaller scale cities have been able to offset their environmental impacts through complex relationships between the public and private sectors but at the mega scale the ability to perform these actions may become irreconcilable.

(McKenna 2012)

Resilience in sustainable development therefore encompasses continuity and change or perhaps rather continuity in change.

Technology and infrastructure

Much of the discourse around eco-cities and other sustainable developments have focused on the contribution of new, or sometimes 'appropriate' technologies. Joss (2010) noted that around 75 per cent of the eco-cities he had included in his global survey of eco-cities emphasised technological innovations with the majority focusing on energy technologies including renewables.

Other technological innovations focused on waste to energy management, transport and water management. Less than 25 per cent seemed to take a more holistic approach with genuine attempts to integrate technology with social and cultural elements of urban living. Some cities, particularly in Japan, do place a special emphasis on civic engagement and community involvement, albeit from a top-down perspective, and a few, such as Auroville in India, emphasise 'bottom-up' community engagement processes.

The technological and smart city is frequently presented by business and government as a major means to empower citizens but these policy prescriptions are invariably top down in conception and practice. Promoted by companies such as IBM, Hitachi or Cisco, or local and national governments in Korea, Japan, China and the UK, they inevitably involve a considerable financial and ideological investment in the capital value of the technology. Smart cities are primarily cities for business development. The Hitachi smart city concept has three elements:

- Adding intelligence to urban infrastructure and creating value by reducing carbon footprints and increasing businesses return on investment.
- Fusing control, generation and distribution of information particularly regarding utility (water and energy) an transport infrastructures.
- Giving cities their own sensory nervous systems that can improve the lived experience of urban living by increasing safety (surveillance) and traffic flow.

(Khono et al. 2011)

Many universities work closely with technology companies and, unsurprisingly, frequently reproduce the idea that technology, albeit combined with other necessary processes that relate to ecological modernisation can lead to workable mitigating solutions or a delay in the onset of irreversible ecological damage and/or urban failure. There are also plenty examples of geo-engineering projects, biotechnology innovations, vertical farms and other infrastructure developments that seem to almost uncritically privilege the role of technology while perhaps evading significant ethical concerns (Ahmed and Stein 2004: Clarke 2005; Jackson and Salzman 2010). There are also many critics not least those who remain convinced by E. F. Schumacher's advocacy of intermediate technology and practical action (Schumacher 1974). Anne Kerr, of the engineering giant Mott MacDonald, explains:

> I think we can be over reliant on the belief that technology can fix everything for us while forgetting about the fundamentals. First principles of engineering and good planning are fundamentally important, as indeed is sophisticated technology, but we must not forget 'common sense' and sense checks and fundamental understanding of what is required. When planning developments and considering resilience for future generations, the value of detailed planning cannot be overstressed.
>
> (Kerr 2012)

For Joss (2010), the strong technology focus is probably a result of the recent mainstreaming of eco-cities with their strong engagement with climate change and urbanisation/economic development policy frameworks. These may have diluted some of the original ideas and concepts particularly as they pertain to social justice, civic empowerment and local democracy. However, whether or not eco-cities will deliver the necessary sustainability outcomes will partly depend on socio-technological innovation, but also on their political and socio-economic governance and social benefit. In many ways, the newly constructed eco-cities are laboratories for knowledge generation and transfer or spaces where new technologies and innovation processes can be shaped, tested, evaluated and perhaps replicated. However, where replication is concerned, Anne Kerr advises caution:

> It must always be remembered that no solution fits all. You cannot take China's solutions for Eco-cites and transpose these to Manchester or Barcelona. However it is important to remember that there are always lessons to be learned and solutions to be considered. Many eco-cities have failed or remain on the drawing board through lack of consideration and integration of performance indicators at the early stage of development. For example many solutions are proposed at concept stage, which appear to be extremely 'sustainable' until they are costed, often later in the planning process. These features are then removed from plans and the tenet of the eco-city vanishes. Or in some cases the developments become eco-enclaves and places for only a certain class of people. These are not good examples of

eco-cities as economics and social aspects are overlooked. Sustainable cities must be able to survive many generations . . . and fulfil society's expectation of a 'city'.

(Kerr 2012)

Zhang *et al.*(2013) have noted that wider green strategies, such as BioRegional's One Planet Living (see pages 90–5), are not valued as highly as strategies for low carbon technologies. Fundamentally important sustainability principles are frequently not fully considered or thoroughly implemented meaning low-carbon commitments are frequently a skin-deep 'hype concept' used for marketing purposes by property developers who fail to create an integrated sustainable urban system involving energy, transport, waste and water management.

The other elements of any meaningful green strategy that seems to get left behind in implementation are 'natural habitats and wildlife' and 'equity and fair trade'. Establishing low-carbon communities provides opportunities and avenues for improving public awareness and education, encouraging participation and 'ownership'. Sustainable infrastructure developments however do involve, and inevitably generate a great deal of cross-sector, cross-disciplinary and inter-professional working.

Peter Head, a civil and structural engineer by background, former head of global planning of the consulting company Arup, is one of the leading promot-ers of sustainability in construction and engineering. He toured the globe with the well-received and influential presentation (and Brunel lecture) 'Entering the Ecological Age' (Head 2008), and was closely associated with the currently stalled but highly innovative eco-city project of Dongtan. A major and continu-ing interest throughout his career has been to connect intensive research to practical infrastructure outcomes in an effective, efficient and fast manner. As founder of the Ecological Sequestration Trust and as a leading member in the global World Futures Council think tank, Peter Head is more concerned to immediately address the problems the world is facing and the need to find resilient outcomes regarding energy, water and food rather than engage in philo-sophical exposition of sustainability. The idea that we need to make the world a better, or at least no worse a place, for the generations who come after us is a strong motivating factor in his work. The overriding aim for Head is to help create a more secure local and global future and improve people's quality of life. Clearly a very ambitious and important aim and key to this is ensuring that inter-disciplinary and inter-professional co-operation can successfully occur.

The Ecological Sequestration Trust is a participant in the United Nations Global Compact which is a global network bringing together businesses and other bodies to mainstream the Compact's ten universally accepted principles relating to labour, human rights, the environment and anti-corruption. An important area of work relates to carbon capture and storage (i.e. geo- and eco-sequestration). New renewable energy technologies are absolutely essential but for the moment the world, still being a heavy user of fossil fuels, needs to prevent the carbon emitted from entering the atmosphere.

The problem for Head is that current technological solutions are complex, expensive and so far inadequate. Attention has also been heavily concentrated on what is familiar or at least seems. So the idea has emerged in the public energy debate that clean coal is a possibility and nuclear power can be a saviour. They tend to be viewed as stop gaps, temporary solutions, but will most likely continue for a very long time. An alternative solution is bio- or ecological sequestration which prioritises biological carbon capture and storage through deliberate measures relating to forest protection and management, afforestation, soil improvement through the addition of biochar and also by restoring ocean vegetation.

Unfortunately, there seems to be less interest in this, even though some countries, including China, complement their economic, industrial and urban developments with massive ecological projects such as tree planting to arrest desertification and deforestation. Because insufficient attention has been paid to ecologically sensitive areas, hydrological, pedological and landscape factors, by no means all afforestation schemes have been successful (Cao *et al.* 2011), but with 40 billion trees being planted since 1981 there has been gradual improvements in some areas as well as a modest impact on mitigating the effects of increased carbon emissions.

Bio-sequestration is therefore beneficial to both human society and the environment for it is a proven way of absorbing carbon, offers clear opportunities for nurturing biodiversity, preventing soil erosion, potentially enhancing food production and in some areas rural poverty by reducing the need for rural dwellers to seek work in the cities (Girardet and Mendonca 2009). This type work and visioning requires the establishment of conditions for a structured collaboration among professional groups, researchers in universities and corporations and politicians; developing and sharing knowledge of capacity building tools and accelerating the development and where possible scaling up the development of integrated low carbon technologies. Peter Head recalls that structured collaboration is sometimes easier to suggest than to do.

> I could see everyone struggling to make something happen. Even in China they were not really implementing the plans that were on the table. We tested how we would get collaborative working before we started the Ecological Sequestration Trust, we set up the Institute for Sustainability in London which in a way was a test house for the trust. Everybody was saying that you can't implement this. Individual universities were not really able to integrate things because of the institutional barriers within the organisation. We invited a whole raft of universities to bring their topics into the Institute in a range of different disciplines. We invited the finance community to engage, we invited the world's leading companies to engage and the public sector and focused on some demonstration projects the largest of which is east of London. The Institute for Sustainability has now been running for about four years and it has a throughput of around £15–20 million projects per year, with most of the funding coming from Europe, and its focus is very much on implementation.
>
> (Head 2012)

The projects relate to developing resource-efficient buildings, transport and logistics, sustainable infrastructure and a 'total community retrofit'. Working with the Bromley by Bow Centre, the London Borough of Tower Hamlets, Poplar HARCA (Housing and Regeneration Community Association) and the not-for-profit ALMO (Arms Length Management Organisation), Tower Hamlets Homes is concentrated on an area of about 5 km², over twice the size of the Olympic Park, and includes around 20,000 dwellings. The Institute's aim is to ensure that local people are central to the planning, design, delivery and management of the total retrofit programme which includes local economic development, job creation, creation of local community amenity, green supply chains, remanufacturing and up-cycling, building retrofits, waste to energy plants, community based renewable energy, water efficiency, green space, and sustainable cultural and behaviour change. Although much of the work of the institute and the Trust may seem to concentrate on technological solutions, Peter Head is wary of those who believe technology can fix everything. He feels the hi-tech, high rise solutions to urban food production is an interesting concept worth investigating but other form of urban horticulture are more important for empowering communities, nurturing local businesses and the local economy. Food growing in the city can be, and often is, a very human social activity that most cities need more of.

> Too many people think technology is the solution. It is very important and we probably have got most of the technologies we need, so we don't need a lot of new ones. The idea that we should keep on inventing new ones rather than implementing the ones we have is a bit of a distraction in my view. I think we should really put much more effort on changing things on the ground by integrating existing technologies into integrated infrastructure and living systems such as land use which actually make a factor three or four difference in resource productivity. Therefore we are very focused on working with the community and providing tools for them to understand and see the changes that are coming. We use art and culture to stimulate behaviour change and a way of engaging communities.
>
> (Head 2012)

In addition, governance structures and processes, integrated legal systems thinking, new business models and financial systems involving the major banks that can enable this total change to happen quickly are of supreme importance for without them the conditions of possibility may not be created. For Peter Head there is no one preferred approach. Different bioregions will require a different combination of tools, models and approaches appropriate and attuned to its own peculiar issues and contexts. Solutions need to be culturally sensitive and people need to be persuaded and involved. If they don't understand or for whatever seem resistant then sustainability projects will not work. Consequently, Head strongly believes in the power of dialogue, of going deeper into the issues, in explaining, rationalising, of communicating in such a fashion that the connections, the whole picture, emerges ensuring that people can learn and understand. All this, of course may take time, and time is something that many sustainability practitioners see as being in short supply for although the long range issues like climate change are presented as a problem for governments, international agencies and large corporations, these issues do often palpably feed back into everyday life experience.

Creating regenerative cities

For Herbert Girardet – author, film-maker, urbanist, and adviser to city governments and the United Nations – we live in an age in which the majority of people are urban citizens and the coexistence of cities and the ecosystems on which they depend requires urgent examination. In this context, he sees major new opportunities for city governments to expand their remit. He believes there is perhaps less of the short-termism in urban governance than exists in national politics or in business operations and forecasts.

That also applies to urban populations. Many families have lived in one city for generations and, because of that, they wish to see their living place to have a viable future. The American urbanist Lewis Mumford recognised that the continuity of human settlements were important to the health and wellbeing of not just individuals in the present but to generations that came after and to the world as a whole. His long view places the immediate and the now, together with the technologies we produce that remake us, in their proper temporal, ecological and cultural context (Mumford 1934, 1938, 1961). This perspective is central to understanding not just the future of cities but the whole sustainability project itself.

For Girardet, too, the possibilities of making a direct and positive impact at the social, spatial and ecological levels of the city offers greater possibilities than seeking change at either the national, international or the individual, levels. Similar to Jeb Brugmann, Herbert Girardet sees the world today as essentially a multitude of city-systems embedded in the world's ecosystems. Urban sustainability, or regenerative urbanism as he sees it, requires a clear understanding that the nature of urban metabolisms, of the interaction of social with ecological urban systems, and this key to all our futures (Girardet 1996).

Although city governments are necessarily concerned with day-to-day operational matters, Herbert Girardet's work with some city authorities, such as the Greater London Authority, and particularly Adelaide (where he was employed as a 'thinker in residence' during 2003), is testimony to the fact that city governments and urban dwellers can make a significant difference. In his report, *Creating a Sustainable Adelaide* (Girardet 2004), he advocated that the city draw on its natural and human resources in a culturally and ecologically sensitive manner by progressively 'solarising' and 'localising' its energy and food systems, by exploiting solar energy (the region's most abundant resource), by creating new solar industries and making buildings more energy efficient, by ensuring the city deals with the perennial problems of water scarcity water and by creating a zero-waste system.

Green architecture projects would be created. Native tree-planting schemes would act as carbon sinks, and urban transit options would encourage residents to use their cars less. Through these actions the report estimated that up to 9,000 new white and green collar jobs could be created for a population of some 1.2 million people and the benefits of sustainability would become clear to all. *Creating a Sustainable Adelaide* also placed considerable emphasis on creating a culture of sustainability through:

- actively linking with the international community and using Adelaide's expertise in sustainability as a resource;
- ensuring that sustainability issues are strongly addressed in the education system and through community based meetings and events;
- encouraging the press and broadcasting media to report imaginatively on sustainability initiatives; and
- ensuring that all citizens have a clear understanding of their environment and so help foster sustainable development.

In this way Adelaide could become a sustainable or even a regenerative city. In *Green Urbanism Down Under*, Timothy Beatley (2009) identifies Adelaide as one of the most sustainably progressive cities in Australia, a country which nationally has not developed an especially green reputation. Girardet is now starting to undertake similar work in the Bristol city-region in the southwest of England.

The ideas developed for Arup's Dongtan project in China have been very influential on a project in the Arabian Gulf region: the Masdar eco-city development in the desert of Abu Dhabi. Masdar will eventually cost in the region of US$22 billion and will be a working and living environment for about 50,000 people. Its original completion date was 2016 but it now seems that this will put back to 2020. Much of the thinking behind and current promotion of the project has addressed the price of carbon and the ways in which Masdar can both implement low carbon living and also develop technologies that can be scaled up, adapted and applied elsewhere in the Middle East and further afield (Nader 2009).

As well as being a city, Masdar is in effect a research and development business with the likes of Siemens and MIT deeply engaged. Solar energy is perhaps not surprisingly a key component of Masdar's energy mix but there are problems: sandstorms, which are a significant feature of this desert region, can lead to a serious degradation in the functioning of photovoltaic panels. For example, in August 2009, the amount of suspended dust in the air was calculated as between 1,500 and 2,000 parts per million, which is more than 10 times higher than usual. As a result, the Masdar solar plant functioned at about 40 per cent below its actual capacity (Rose 2009), and it took a week to clean away the sand.

In addition, being in the desert inevitably means securing a regular supply of fresh water. Exploitation of local aquifers caused the ground water to become saltwater intrusion and overexploitation caused the groundwater to become saline. Water supply throughout the region is now mainly from desalination of sea water. Fifteen desalination plants operate as part of the Gulf Cooperation Council on the Arabian Gulf and adverse environmental effects such as releasing gases, hot brine, treatment chemicals and other trace elements together with a negative impact on marine life has been recorded (Kumetat 2009). The leftover water concentrate that is discharged into the sea has a salinity level at least twice as high as sea water.

There is also a problem with energy use: Masdar's desalinated water is currently the most carbon intensive clean water in the world (Stanton 2010) although as Trieb (2007) points out, the use of solar thermal plants to power seawater desalination by either electricity alone or in a combined generation system with process steam does offer some new opportunities. There is no denying that water management is a real problem that detracts from the sustainability credentials of the Masdar project and its long term resilience.

Apart from desalinisation and rigorous processes of environmental impact assessment and monitoring, then, Masdar and the Gulf states as a whole will need to develop and implement equally rigorous processes of water conversation and recycling (Mezher *et al.* 2011). Undoubtedly, learning and change has certainly been a significant element of the project from the start. The original idea put forward by Norman Foster and colleagues was that the city would be built on two rectangular or square concrete platforms. On the first would be located the city's services, sewage and so on, and on the second a couple of metres above would be the city proper. It proved too expensive, and the design was rethought. As Herbert Girardet says:

> Concepts are great things but when reality comes into the picture they invariably change. Masdar is an example of that. Certainly to conceptualise, for instance, how much surface area would be need to produce renewable solar energy, what would happen to its waste, what sort of building materials would be required are useful but relatively theoretical exercises. The idea of building eco-cities, particularly in places where there is still rapid urban growth, is important. The Masdar concepts are being applied in toned down ways in other projects in Abu Dhabi. Dubai, which is an insanely unsustainable city, is also beginning to have second thoughts about the next phases of its urban land use and resource management.
>
> (Girardet 2012)

Learning has also been an important part of Herbert Girardet's career journey too. Having embraced the concept of sustainable development when it was conceptualised by the Brundtland Commission, publicised by the 1992 Rio Earth Summit and endlessly argued over, defined and redefined, used and misused in the years since, Girardet is now convinced that there is a need to go beyond sustaining what we have. 'Regenerative development' is the term he is currently working with believing the notion of 'regenerative cities' is far more meaningful, positive and active than either 'sustainable' or 'resilient cities'. In a paper published by the World Futures Council, Herbert Girardet (2010: 15) outlined his ideas on regenerative cities arguing that 'policy makers, the commercial sector and the general public need to jointly develop a much clearer understanding of how cities can develop a restorative relationship to the natural environment on which they ultimately depend.' Sustainable development is too passive a concept, perhaps even rather boring, he says. However:

> coming up with the concept of regenerative development is also fraught because it means ignoring some of the impact of our lives. A lot of what we do is destructive. Some people prefer not to talk about recycling but down-cycling because you cannot put something back to the same quality it was before. People are also talking about up-cycling, turning rags into something like dresses but that is taking only very little out of the waste stream...We have to do everything possible to give back to ecosystems, restoring soils, composting in cities...In Adelaide this happening in amazing ways – some 170,000 tonnes of organic waste being turned into compost and being put back onto peri-urban farm land. There is also very large-scale reforestation on the edge of the city, Adelaide, partly to stem soil erosion and partly to absorb carbon dioxide. Perhaps these are examples of regenerative urban development that go beyond the more passive concept of sustainable development.
>
> (Girardet 2012)

Allied with sustainable development, resilience, for Herbert Girardet, is a rather passive term too but still quite useful. Like other terms, ideas, concepts, movements, projects and theories, 'resilience' does help to move the discussion forward often creating the conditions for further dialogue. For Girardet though, moving on has a more creative and dynamic connotations – more a sense of looking at and engaging actively with the future. In his own evaluation of regenerative Adelaide, Girardet writes:

> Creating not just sustainable but environmentally regenerative cities is a challenge that urban politicians, administrators, and educators have so far rarely had to deal with. However, there are major benefits: the awareness is growing that integrated, restorative planning and management of cities presents major new opportunities for reviving regional economies and creating new businesses and job opportunities.
>
> The remarkable changes that have occurred in Adelaide in recent years were brought about by a combination of policy measures and vigorous public participation. Urban communities harbor a huge variety of talents and experiences that are essential for giving substance to the democratic process. In an age of resource depletion and climate change democracy needs new content. I would submit that regenerative, integrated urban systems thinking can bring people together in the understanding that the whole is greater than the sum of its parts.
>
> (Girardet 2012: 53)

Indeed, the regenerative concept is slowly emerging in other, albeit closely related, areas of sustainability practice. Ray Cole has written about regenerative building design arguing that sustainable architecture needs to be re-conceptualised to imagine, formulate and enable other contexts to emerge thereby privileging such things as community participation and engaging more sensitively with place to ensure social, economic and ecological health can flourish. A number of design tools are now available that make regenerative design not only a conceptual but a practical reality and some large architectural practices, such as Perkins+Wills in Canada and the United States, are pioneering this approach in both small and large scale projects.

There is more – regenerative design thinking is also about changing mindsets by shaping, encouraging and facilitating the adoption of ecological world views (Mang and Reed 2012). Regenerative design and the notion of regenerative cities both integrate human and ecological systems in theory and practice at local and global level recognising that the vectors of global change are profound at an individual human and micro level too. Rebirth or renaissance is quite possible, quite feasible. For built environment specialist Chrisna du Plessis:

> the regenerative sustainability paradigm represents a shift to the holistic living systems worldview held by many…as a necessary point of departure for engaging with the problems of sustainability. This paradigm attempts to address the dysfunctional human–nature relationship by entering into a co-creative partnership with nature. It aims to restore and regenerate the global socio-ecological system through a set of localised ecological design and engineering practices rooted in the context and its socio-ecological narratives.
>
> (Du Plessis 2012: 19)

In many ways regenerative thinking has been a growing element informing a number of practical approaches to the building of sustainable communities. The term 'regenerative' might not be used all that frequently and like 'resilience' may remain latent but possibly something that is immediately recognised when discussed explicitly. The concept of One Planet Living might be considered in this context.

One Planet Living

The One Planet Living (OPL) concept is most closely associated with BioRegional, a UK-based social enterprise, co-founded by Sue Riddlestone and Pooran Desai in the 1990s and now employing around thirty-eight people internationally. The organisation frequently works in partnership with a wide range of public, private and third sector bodies to initiate and implement practical actions that seek to secure sustainability solutions at both local and global level. Its ten OPL principles emerged from the various projects BioRegional has initiated since its inception.

Box 5.1 The ten One Planet Living principles

- *Zero carbon:* Enabling access to energy, making buildings more energy efficient and delivering all energy with renewable technologies.
- *Zero waste:* Reducing waste, reusing where possible, creating products and employment through recycling and ultimately sending zero waste to landfill.
- *Sustainable transport:* Encouraging low carbon modes of transport and public transport, reducing the need to travel, ensuring a good range of local facilities within walking and cycling distance.
- *Sustainable materials:* Using sustainable and healthy products, such as those with low embodied energy, sourced locally, made from renewable or waste resources.
- *Local and sustainable food:* Sustainable and humane agriculture and farming, access to nutritious low impact, local, seasonal and organic diets and reducing food waste.
- *Sustainable water:* Access to safe drinking water and sanitation. Using water more efficiently in farming, buildings and in the products we buy. Designing to avoid local flooding and water course pollution.
- *Land and wildlife:* Protecting and restoring existing biodiversity and natural habitats through appropriate land use and integration into the built environment.
- *Culture and community:* Protecting and restoring existing biodiversity and natural habitats through appropriate land use and integration into the built environment.
- *Equity and local economy:* Creating strong, diverse local economies that meet peoples' needs and support fair employment and international fair trade.
- *Health and happiness:* Promote good health and wellbeing through access to healthcare. Encourage active, sociable, meaningful lives to promote good health and wellbeing.

Source: BioRegional (n.d.)

These ten principles represent both a vision of a sustainable future and a template for fashioning more sustainable lifestyles. They inform BioRegional's ecovillage/residential developments, of which the most well known is probably BedZed, the low-carbon sustainable residential development in south London designed by green architect Bill Dunster in association with the housing charity the Peabody Trust. Other projects have included One Brighton on the south coast of England and One Riverside in the northeast of England. BioRegional is also involved in similar projects in China (a 5,000 eco-home development, Jinshan, in Guangzhou), Australia (a 22 hectare mixed commercial and residential development in Sydney), California, Washington state (USA) and Montreal (Canada).

The concept of One Planet Living was applied in the planning and visioning of the London 2012 Olympic and ParaOlympic Games (BioRegional/WWF 2005). BioRegional worked closely with the Olympic bid team to make the games the 'greenest ever'. The organisation proposed to do this by:

- maximising the re-use of construction materials and minimising embodied carbon during the building phase;
- undertaking a carbon footprint study of the media broadcast centre and international press centre, which helped to reduce their embodied carbon from a predicted 130,000 to 65,000 tonnes; and
- in co-operation with the WWF, acting as a critical friend to the London Legacy Development Corporation through providing formal comments on the Olympic Park Legacy Masterplan Framework, in order to attempt to ensure consistency between the legacy and the initial sustainability vision.

BioRegional also made a significant contribution to the Rio+20 summit through their promotion of One Planet Living. Although the Summit's outcome may have been disappointing to many, there are nevertheless, for BioRegional, good grounds for optimism as all the ingredients for a more sustainable future can be found in the concluding Outcome Document. For Sue Riddlestone the work of BioRegional should not be categorised as simply concerned with the environment:

> The social and the economic are coming together seamlessly with the environmental particularly given the backdrop of the current crisis. I wince a bit, sometimes, when people say we're an environmental charity. I say we're an entrepreneurial charity... implementing solutions for sustainability. That's what we need. We started with the economy. That was the BioRegional ethos and it is almost like we're coming back full circle. Carbon reduction is important but it feels like it's more joined up, more holistic now.
>
> (Riddlestone 2012)

BedZed is an iconic, instantly recognizable residential community – a sustainability design with glass, wood and coloured funnels for ventilation, loudly proclaiming something different, something ecological. The site encompasses around 100 homes, and includes space for business and community facilities including a small special school. Completed in 2002, energy use in the homes is about 60 per cent less than in conventional residences of a similar size, and with a biomass energy plant and off-site renewable energy production likely to come on-stream in the near future the aim is for BedZed to be carbon-neutral.

The unfamiliar design certainly gained the project a significant degree of publicity but the residential developments that have been constructed around it conform to the more conventional image of a suburban residential development.

Figure 5.3 BedZed eco home development, south London
Source: John Blewitt

However, sustainability is not simply about the design of the buildings, but also about the way people live, shop, travel, work, eat, dispose of their 'waste' and so on. In the ecovillage's first year, BioRegional employed a 'green lifestyles officer' to help and advise residents on developing a One Planet lifestyle, and at this early stage much of the officer's work revolved around education, training and other community development activities. The aim was clearly to move way beyond the idea that designing and constructing a green building, or a collection of green buildings, will create an environmentally sustainable social environment or will lead to generate by itself other similar activities, project lifestyle changes, green business developments and the like.

The architect, BioRegional and the Peabody Trust make no claims that BedZed has been an unqualified success, but a great deal has been learned from it that has informed later developments. In the words of geographer James Evans (2011: 231), this is where resilience happens for 'in the experimental city, sustainable test settlements like BedZed are literally embedded in the urban fabric as truth spots in their own right'.

In BioRegional's seven-year evaluation report on the project evidence was presented that design does contribute to nurturing more pro-environmental behaviours, 'we have found that it is important to make it easy and convenient for people to take sustainable actions and difficult for them to take unsustainable ones' (BioRegional 2009: 6). For example, it was important to the BedZed designers that the dominance of the car ought to be tackled head on. This meant that road and parking spaces were situated at the edge of the community, and pedestrianised areas were created for its centre. However, practical problems with this design have arisen for residents when they need to go grocery shopping, for BedZed is located in a fairly suburban area with a relative paucity of local stores and amenities. Given this, BedZed may perhaps be viewed as an iconic island of sustainability, a design adventure in a culture that is not too keen on looking, being or seeming to be that different. However, this is not the whole picture.

> On balance the BedZed design has been good but you have to show sustainability in many many ways. With the One Brighton project that our spin out development venture did with Quintain and Crest Nicholson looks like a regular block of flats which was all within the normal range of build costs. It was sold on green lifestyles and convenience but it has all the same features as BedZed. It just looks normal. It hasn't had as much publicity but then BedZed was a little bit of its time. In the homes around BedZed, which look like any normal suburb, we're doing a lot of neighbourhood planning and retrofitting. You can't see the difference but retrofitting is much better than starting from scratch.
>
> (Riddlestone 2012)

The later One Brighton development is also basically car-free. It has its own biomass boiler and includes green lifestyle features such as rooftop allotments, a composter, organic vegetable delivery box and a communal sky garden. OPL is part of the physical and social fabric, clearly showing what can be done, but the issues our unsustainable world faces are immense, and however valuable these initiatives are in themselves, there is yet more that needs to be done.

Perhaps this 'more' is not so much about establishing the conditions for resilience as such but, as Herbert Girardet argues, establishing the conditions for regeneration and renewal. This involves developing local distinctiveness and commitment to place, using and renewing existing infrastructure and other assets as well as, and perhaps even more than building new eco cities in the desert.

For Sue Riddlestone, everyone involved in the sustainability field has been on a very long journey. She likens the world economic system as like a 'barbaric Godzilla' which has not properly evolved or matured. A lot has been learned since the early days of Agenda 21 in the 1990s and much of this has been significant and profound: 'we almost have all the tools in the toolbox to be sustainable' she said adding that the concept of resilience is one of those tools but one that is not used very frequently or extensively. When the term is used it is rarely questioned or examined for there seems to be a generally accepted common sense understanding that allows it to float by.

I use it [resilience]. People don't say 'what do you mean?' They just take it in. They talk about creating more 'resilient communities'. In a way it's another word for sustainability, but not exactly. I tend to use it as something that is locality based...in terms of making our area resilient rather than making our life resilient. I use it in terms of not being wasteful, being resource efficient and therefore you don't have to spend so much money, that we have access to the things we need locally...that we can live on less money so we don't have to worry about losing our job or that our job is not well paid. And, that we can live well, we know who our neighbours are, we have a sense of community and can rely on people...Resilience is a bit like hunkering down in a crazy world. It could be seen as negative as I think it is quite inward looking. Being safe.

(Riddlestone 2012)

Of course, we need to be safe, but we also need to play safe with our common future, and this will certainly entail changes that are profound, radical, and perhaps even a little intimidating. Doing and being different often is.

6   Risks, transition and an ecology of circumstances

The risk society

The corollary of risk and vulnerability, whether induced by 'natural' or 'anthro-pogenic' factors, is increasingly seen as resilience. So we have resilient, individuals, resilient communities, resilient cities, resilient businesses, resilient governments, resilient nations, resilient economies and of course a resilient planet. There is nothing, it seems, on heaven or earth that cannot be in some way resilient. Indeed, when confronting our vulnerabilities in the face of actual and potential (natural) disasters brought on by changes to the Earth's climate, resilience is frequently associated with the concepts of adaptation and learning.

For geographer Mark Pelling (2011), adaptation includes both the capacity to adapt and the actions that realise adaptive aims and intentions. Adaptivity is both a component of vulnerability and its opposite as it tends to decline as vulnerability increases. Consequently, resilience has a multifaceted character. It is diverse, and in practice, quite fragmented particularly when analysed in contexts of risk and disaster management. Resilience can be difficult to measure and to operationalise for the impacts themselves have multiple causes and are not always easy to identify:

> The processes and pressures determining resilience for a unit of assessment change with spatial, temporal and social scale – a community may be resilient to climate change associated with hurricane risk (through early warning and evacuation, for example) but less resilient to the long-term inflections of climate change with the local and global economy.
>
> (Pelling 2011: 43)

There are other complications too. Actual and potential risks may be denied by certain groups and individuals, businesses, communities and governments mean-ing that a certain resistance to the idea let alone the practical actions required for resilience are basically ignored.

On the other hand, risks may be acknowledged but only partially so, leading to piecemeal and inadequate responses. Policies and actions may just address the symptoms rather than the deep causes of the problems that need dealing with.

There may be arguments and discussions that delay or even derail effective action. Caution may be advised when caution is really a means of ensuring gradual and incremental change fails to challenge vested interests, established ways of doing things or looking at the world. Interventions may be piecemeal, fragmented and unconnected rather than integrated and holistic (Upton and Ibrahim 2012).

However, those groups and individuals, social and political systems that are open to tackling the deep causes, confronting and challenging established interests, habits and routines, are invariably the most flexible and adaptive and best placed to positively engage with risks, uncertainties and vulnerabilities. Inclusivity of lay and expert, the great and the not-so-great, seems to be a key factor in enabling this adaptability and flexibility to emerge politically and socially, to gain acceptance and legitimacy and a purchase on the minds, feelings and expectations of those affected.

Nevertheless, adaptability to change often involves making choices and these choices are almost inevitably framed by economic (cost) and ethical (value) factors. Change and adaptation often involves new and additional expenditures rather than a reallocation of existing expenditures influencing discussions over the intrinsic or extrinsic value of doing something rather than nothing at all. So resilience, adaptability and sustainable development ultimately have to engage with the realities, or otherwise, of negotiation, conflict mediation, dialogue and social learning.

Yet top-down solutions and individualistic values tend to erode capacities such as these, and may not necessarily nurture environmental sustainability (Fazey *et al.* 2010). Thus, as Pelling (2011: 50–51) argues, 'transformative adaptation will at a minimum include a critical reflection on existing institutions and practices working at the levels of transition and resilience'. Behind all of this may be the ideological assumption that resilience is actually about protecting a desired way of life or in assuring, future-proofing, the conditions for securing and maintaining human wellbeing and ecological sustainability as presently constituted. Thus, it is quite possible for resilience, understood as adaptation, to be culpable in sustaining practices that are unjust, conflicting and discriminatory. The key questions for sustainability practitioners in debating and attempting to operationalise the notion of resilience must be: who benefits? And to what degree? As Evans (2011) writes, resilience has become a significant element in a pseudo-scientific discourse that exerts considerable influence on the way things supposedly should and are being done.

For some years now, as the German theorist Ulrich Beck has written, we have been living in a risk society. The failure of modernism, of our techno-rationality, has rendered Westernised capitalist society purblind. The concept of resilience especially when combined with a stress on self-limitation, prevention, adaptation and mitigation, provides a kind philosophical lifeboat. 'The utopia of the risk society is that everyone should be *spared* from poisoning', writes Beck (1992: 49). In accepting a world that is constantly in flux the idea of resilience seems to promote a passive acceptance of change. Periodic crises are presumed to be inevitable systems related occurrences. There is thus an inherent tendency for the risk society to become a scapegoat society with displaced thought and action becoming increasingly common. Environmentalists become doomsters, sometimes even seeing themselves as such; and, scientists, business leaders and entrepreneurs become the saviours. So resilience needs to be framed politically and socially, as a property of social collectivities and of purposive learning.

Evans develops this further:

> Rather than question the all-too-human causes of crises (whether of the climatic or economic variety), resilience emphasises the need for individuals, communities or cities to simply get on with adapting to them. This tendency to naturalise crises resonates with neoliberal discourses of capitalism...which preclude political debate concerning the wider causes and desirability of change.
>
> (Evans 2011: 224)

New values and new ideas must be able to see the light of day and not be marginalised because of their inconvenient truths or because doing something differently is more politically threatening than doing nothing at all. Sustainable development, adaptation and transformation, rests on the ability to conceive and realise alternatives, to experiment, to resolve disputes and to manage not only environmental and other risks but a whole host of other factors too. The French existentialist Jean-Paul Sartre finished his play *No Exit* with the famous line, 'hell is other people'; that is, other people frustrate our own desires and intentions. In a less theatrical context, as Keen *et al.* (2005: 11) a significant fact that complicates our understanding of human-ecological systems 'is the capricious behaviour of humans themselves'.

Humans certainly have the capacity to learn, but they do not always respond to the same event, issue, or crisis in the same way. Humans react differently and greatly across time and space, culture, value, knowledge and emotional states. For Wals *et al.* (2009) social learning is a means of coming together, of sharing, much like a jazz ensemble. They argue that it is basically a process by which people are stimulated and enabled to reflect upon implicit assumptions and frames of reference which can facilitate the development of new forms of knowledge and ways of knowing, new perspectives and new actions. Social learning also requires a degree of self-organisation and this may emerge gradually rather than swiftly but whatever the case the capacity for this to occur has to be present somewhere. It may be nurtured by an external body – a state agency, NGO, business – but nothing will come if nothing is there in the first place. However, as Pelling (2011) remarks it is not possible to measure this capacity, or capability, for self-organisation solely from existing organisational forms. Existing organisations might impede or restrict the capacity for self-organisation but to overcome this, a degree of political will as well as improvised ensemble learning may be necessary.

Sustainability and social learning is undoubtedly complementary and mutually constitutive and its object is necessarily concrete and real rather than abstract or detached. Urban inhabitants learn how to manage, prepare, respond to and restore their social, built and ecological environments after earthquakes, riots, war, economic collapse, technological breakdown, political incompetence, corruption and now increasingly the consequences of climate change. Vale and Campanella (2005) show how various cities have recovered, have been rebuilt and have experienced regeneration after all manner of devastating disturbances. Social and urban systems, local communities and individuals, governments and businesses have not always been resilient and learning has not always been effective let alone social, sustainable or inspired.

Interestingly, jazz and the other cultural heritage of New Orleans were significant inspirational factors in the human resilience that emerged following Hurricane Katrina and the appalling failings of the city and federal administrations in the aftermath of the hurricane's impact on the city-region.

Vale and Campanella's conclusions are salutary and suggestive. Resilience is often referred to as the capacity to 'bounce back' but people let alone cities are not rubber balls and a disaster is not a flat plane from which the angle and direction of a rebound can be predicted, calculated or measured with assurance. Models, templates, toolkits, ten point plans are in effect little more than heuristics and there are no, or at least few, short cuts, quick fixes or simple technical solutions. Recovery or transformation often takes years, sometimes decades. It is complex, intensely human and intensely political. Vale and Capenalla focus on (system) specifics, asking who recovers – which aspects of the city recovers, and how?

The extent, pace and direction of recovery can be charted in general terms, but what matters are the variations and what drives these variations at different times, in different spaces and places, and among different peoples, cultures and societies. Eliciting common messages or generalised recommendations therefore is extremely difficult, and perhaps even counter-productive, although management structures, frameworks and particularly human stories of recovery, of previous experiences, of past learning and past reflections can be psychologically reassuring and helpful. Given this, Vale and Campanella identify and elaborate upon ten axioms of resilience from they create important of narratives of inclusivity, place, learning, opportunity and optimism. Thus urban resilience, like other adjectival resiliences, is socially constructed and essentially interpretative frameworks will in the future invariably be further adapted, changed and improvised upon according to circumstance, context, learning and reflexive action.

Approaching resilience and sustainability

For Keith Budden (2012), who has experience of working in a senior sustainability role for both Birmingham City Council, the biggest local authority in the UK outside London, and the international energy company E.ON, there are familiar challenges, issues and problems that are common to big organisations whatever the sector:

> The biggest lessons for me have actually been the similarities between Birmingham City Council and working for E.ON. Everybody said, 'it will be very different working for the private sector'. But the main similarity is that they are large, complicated siloed organisations both running many parallel programmes often with contradictory incentives and targets. My role has always been to cut through the confusion, integrate targets and help people to think differently. Sustainable development provides a framework that makes it so much easier to deliver joined up outcomes. In my experience at the city council and at E.ON most people are very keen to do this and find the concept of Sustainable Development helpful. The key is to build collaborative leadership at a senior level and thus provide the space for managers to join up across business silos.
>
> (Budden 2012)

His experience was very different in the voluntary sector, where working on small projects often meant feeling that progress was frustratingly slow, inconsequential or plain non-existent. He recalled how Shell, working in Nigeria in the aftermath of the execution of Ken Saro-Wiwa, made a concerted effort to redirect their community investments away from infrastructure developments that had little relevance to local people. He helped develop and deliver an NGO-led programme that was more socially and culturally sensitive, and was based on a process of community planning, empowerment and organisation. As for the concept of resilience, Keith Budden (2012) believes the term has been used and operationalised for some time within the field of international development where it had frequently been articulated with other concepts such as sustainability to infer a the ability of a community to cope with sudden change such as crop failure or civil unrest. On the other hand, the concept of sustainability still remains relatively unfamiliar especially within the institutional carapace of major public and private institutions in the UK and other parts of the developed world. When 'resilience' appears it most frequently does so in a security context such as terrorism or associated forms of violence but more recently in discussions on the economy or the environment.

> From a public sector view [in the UK] it means how to deal with the bomb or flood. There is a resilience partnership in Birmingham and they are interested in short-term disaster management, whatever that might be. They are slightly interested in climate change but more interested in bombs or train cashes or when climate change and sustainability is concerned, in terms of a flood. From an E.ON perspective it is, 'will power stations cope with a hotter summer? What happens if there is a major problem with gas supplies or we have to shut a power plant down for whatever reason?' It is very much emergency-based. It is not really based on how an organisation responds to long term change.
>
> (Budden 2012)

Figure 6.1 E.ON at Eco Build Conference, London, 2012
Source: John Blewitt

As a security specialist working at the University of Haifa in Israel, Rachel
Suissa's interest in resilience is very much to do with the preventative connotations of the term and the versatility of its potential meanings which can extend
to an almost medical notion of immunity and resistance to challenges and threats
(Suissa 2012). Although this is not exactly a part of Keith Budden's (2012) experience or understanding a prevalent sense of risk is, and these risks, and
expectations of future risks, are growing as economic troubles reverberate in
other spheres. As public expenditure cuts bite deeper into public services and as
the economy continues to falter the need to integrate environmental, community, citizen and organisational resilience becomes increasingly prevalent in a
public discourse requiring practical action at a variety of spatial scales and in a
variety socio-political and economic spheres to articulate what this thinking
differently actually means. Social learning is part of this, but social learning
seems, at first glance, to be somewhat different from sustainability learning
particularly as expressed within a discourse of adaptation and environmental
management. Tàbara and Pahl-Wostl write:

> sustainability learning relates to learning to develop the capacity to manage
> options for the adaptation of human societies to the limits and changing
> conditions that are imposed by their own socio-ecological systems.

Sustainability learning entails becoming increasingly aware of the limits and of the unintended negative consequences of collective action upon life-support systems and being capable of anticipating and managing those effects. It also requires overcoming many cultural dualistic perceptions that are still embedded in the way humans interpret their coevolutionary connections with the larger ecosystems and with other agents. To a large extent, sustainability learning can be understood as a search for a collective truth that, although it will necessarily be contextual, will not be totally random. In this regard, learning is a search for truth that can be applied to learning about socio-ecological systems.

(Tàbara and Pahl-Wostl 2007)

For Phil Beardmore whose long experience of working in the voluntary sector, community development and environmental movement in Birmingham this sustainability and social learning is integrally related to setting up new co-operative business models, social and eco enterprises, establishing opportunities and spaces for formal and informal learning, for advocacy, political lobbying, community liaison and urban regeneration. At any one time Phil Beardmore may be working on five or more projects simultaneously which often, but do not necessarily, overlap. Having left Groundwork UK in 2010, his freelance work has enabled him to broaden his experience and understanding of urban community based social and sustainability initiatives. When concentrating on energy and climate change issues he has learnt great deal from reflecting deeply and critically on his own experience as an activist and change agent. He has concluded that economic rationality, or even a moral concern for the environment, may neither be necessary or sufficient for humans to change their behaviours.

What I can see changing is that energy efficiency and climate change is being seen more as an economic good than as a social good. You are beginning to see a market economy in it even though there is still market failure. A lot of people who care about the environment see it as a moral issue: 'Wind turbines should be built and homes should be insulated because it is the right thing to do.' So the economic perspective is a fundamental challenge to their mind-set . . . Up until recently I believed that most people are rational. Because they believe in an ideal or a product they believe that idea is rational, so everyone else will want it. I assumed that everybody would want to save energy because they will rationalise either in terms of the environment or in terms of want-ing to save money, but they don't even if it is clearly in their financial self-interest. I began to realise there was a psychological dimension and I have become increasingly interested in the psychology of environmental behaviour and the way the human mind actually works, which is very differ-ent from the way economic textbooks would have us believe. My role now is to convince others that this is the way to go, to abandon the idea that people will do the right thing because it is the rational thing to do.

(Beardmore 2012)

Phil Beardmore's (2012) approach to the psychology of environmental behaviour is strongly influenced by the work of Chris Rose (Rose *et al.* 2007; Rose 2011) on the psychographic mapping of value modes, and the report from the UK Department for Environment, Food and Rural Affairs (Defra), *A Framework for Pro-environmental Behaviours* (Defra 2008), which uses a range of social marketing methodologies to identify seven population segments categorised by their varying degrees of willingness and ability to act. These range from being a *positive green*, which roughly equates to 18 per cent of the UK population and signified by the comment 'I think it's important that I do as much as I can to limit my impact on the environment', to being *honestly disengaged*, also about 18 per cent of the population, and captured in the statement 'maybe there'll be an environmental disaster, maybe not. Makes no difference to me, I'm just living life the way I want to.'

The Defra report also outlined twelve headline behaviour goals, reduced from an original thirty, and these include using more efficient vehicles, cutting down on short haul flights, using water more responsibly in the home, installing domestic insulation, eating more food that is locally in season, wasting less (food), recycling more and adopting a low impact diet. Accompanying this are tools, checklists of actions and principles by which organisations and individuals may strive to encourage more pro-environmental behaviour in their businesses and communities.

There are, of course, many other potential frameworks, tools and guidance strategies that claim to help bridge the value action gap or perhaps simply change behaviour allowing pro-environmental value sets to develop through force of habit and gradual social and cultural familiarity. Andrew Darnton and Martin Kirk (2011) were commissioned by Oxfam and the Department for International Development to explore ways in which the UK public could be effectively engaged with the problems of global poverty through articulating and mobilising a common set of 'bigger than self-values' latent within the wider society. Influenced by the work particularly of psychologist George Lakoff (2004, 2008, 2010) and others, Darnton and Kirk (2011: 8–9) argue that 'a frames approach has the potential to transform everything about an organisation and its practices' but probably understate the situation when they suggest that rebalancing the dominant values of a society is 'potentially a formidable task'.

What they do believe is less formidable but quite possible is that transformational change can be affected by reinforcing or enhancing the level of significance of those positive values and deep frames already used by people. Ultimately, 'we see change as a process of reflective practice, pursued through deliberation and debate' (Darnton and Kirk 2011: 9).

Cognitive psychologist George Lakoff (2004) has made a distinction between deep frames and surface frames whereby the former tend to represent whole worldviews and so connect to value systems and are therefore more foundational and invariably more abstract than surface frames, which refer basically to simple meanings and what may be recognised as dictionary definitions. Frames engage with the complexity of the world, are in conversation with it, and as such, are perhaps more resilient in the face of criticism and perhaps evidence than values. However, it is this resilience that offers pro-environmental activists and sustainability practitioners opportunities to activate values like dignity, justice and so on, that may otherwise remain abstract or hard to operationalise. Research in the field of environmental behaviour is becoming increasingly rich and although environmental self-identity is also clearly important in many ways it is sometimes difficult to discern or predict how one type of behaviour, or indeed attitude, may catalyse other related attitudes and behaviours (Thomashow 2002; Whitmarsh and O'Neill 2010).

Pro-environmental behaviour change tools and strategies are often accompanied by surveillance and monitoring devices, penalties and reprimands, rewards and incentives, which effectively constitute of another form of socialised discipline and social subjectivity that is more about control than learning or ethical conduct (Hargreaves 2010). Although all this is of great interest, Barr *et al.* (2011) caution that when dealing with enormous issues such as climate change, additional levels of complexity and complication are attached to theories, policies and practices aimed at encouraging pro-environmental behaviour change among citizens and consumers. The perceived value of pro-environmental actions may be, almost certainly is, in conflict with existing forms and frames of material consumerism, work and everyday life. Simply driving more responsibly may simply not be enough when there are two or more cars in the garage and your neighbour also has two cars. What is important here is certainly working and learning together, mobilising those deep frames but also localising both knowledge and learning even if the issues themselves are genuinely global in scope and significance.

> I think the consumer society has made people less resilient because a lot of skills have been lost because we have so many machines to do things. People are less resilient both as individuals and as communities and people are less able to cope with any kind of adversity... There is not enough shared learning. It's about mindsets rather than technological innovations. We need to learn from each other. I recently worked on a Sustainability West Midlands low-carbon economy programme. The approach we developed was crowd sourcing existing knowledge, but also packaging it up for people in a crowd sourced way. So what used to happen with the Energy Saving Trust Green Communities programme is that you would get five communities apply for support for the same thing and you'd send a consultant to each of them for five days. What we do with the Sustainability West Midlands programme is that we get those five communities together and we deliver some consultancy time to them and achieve better outcomes because it is shared learning. You can spend all day reading reports and articles but it means nothing to the people out there. They need to see their neighbours do something so they will then do it. We do need to localise the way we learn from things... and that takes resources.
>
> (Beardmore 2012)

Sustainability consultant and author of *How Local Resilience Creates Sustainable Societies*, Philip Monaghan (Monaghan 2012) believes that there is an absence of any universal values that may serve to bring people together for the common good. There is a lack of clarity and consistency with the term resilience partly due to private sector influence which relates it to economic profitability, consumer materialism or urban development.

To counteract this influence some sustainability practitioners have promoted a happiness index, but there is a problem here. Social inequality may be seen, measured and evaluated as a cause of unhappiness but then, Philip Monaghan argues, so might being stuck in traffic and being stuck in traffic may literally, as well as figuratively, be a close to home issue. Climate change and social inequality are more abstract but they too need to be brought closer to home, made real and concrete in terms of directly comprehensible human social experience and ethical beliefs in right and wrong. Thus values again, particularly when clustered in the form of worldviews or perspectives, often come to the fore as more significant than 'the facts', of which people can have too many.

Values can be shared across a variety of cultures, generations, spaces and places. Thus the set of values, or frames, around community, autonomy, fairness, friendship and family can create a context favourable to bringing people together co-operatively, collaboratively and collectively. Like Darnton and Kirk (2011) and like Tom Crompton (2010) whose WWF report *Common Cause* argued that a common interest frame can successfully promote what is valued inherently for itself rather than what it may produce, Philip Monaghan (2012) argues that we can make big things happen if we really want to but we must have the courage and vision to do so.

> There is still a failure in sustainable development and resiliency to get the narrative right. I have been involved in [urban] regeneration and the term resiliency was used to some extent but it was to do with risk and risk management. The term is used in different ways in different disciplines but it has been taken over by the accountants and risk managers and it is more around mitigation than transforming, learning and so on. There is also a danger to how people respond to the word – I should say how people respond to the word in English. It's almost like the boxer Rocky: how much punishment can you take and still stand up at the end of it? That's not a particularly attractive destination and it is now being contextualised by the current financial crisis – how can we make it through this rather than changing the system.
>
> (Monaghan 2012)

In his professional consultancy work with city officials resilience is beginning to take on a wider environmental meaning but interpretations vary according to official and to location. Low carbon retrofitting may be a priority in one urban area and dealing with water shortage or water scarcity in another. Persistence over time, sustainability and survival, is recognised as involving a degree of transformation and change which may be enabled by new technologies for eco-efficiency and urban economic development. Sometimes one change does lead to another but not necessarily in an intentional or planned way.

> My experience is it is learning through errors or shocks to the system, which is part of resiliency anyway, and then people saying what is the business management thinking around this and people will either come to complexity or systems theory. I think there is a number of organisations trying to develop the language such as ICLEI which has had a long running annual conference and related research called Resilient Cities and it is always hosted by the city of Bonn. That's bringing together thinking around resilience starting with climate-related resilience and now it's just resilience. Resilience is now beyond risk as it is about evolving, involving, transformation and learning. It is about establishing a community of practice of city leaders...One of the ways in which the city connects to the individual is through the smart city concept which is like an electronic brain which is supposed to reveal unhelpful choice to individuals or to guide them in a helpful way. There's also an emotional–social contract around negotiated rights and responsibilities. the city of Philadelphia believes it can halve its $4 billion storm water management bill over twenty years by decentralising management as well as centrally through better planning, porous surfaces...Through tax rate relief and grants they are allowing individual households, community groups, small businesses to get water butts and invest in green things and the reason why that is happening is because it is about self-help, self-reliance, self-interest, self-determination. It makes the place look better, so it's good for them and their neighbours.
>
> (Monaghan 2012)

Smart cities and hybrid social spaces

The smart city vision has increasingly engaged urban policy makers and sustainability practitioners, although the concept itself is really a theme from which many variations can be produced, including anything from a cybo-technical utopia to a neoliberal urban fantasy to an environmentally conscientious learning community (Hollands 2008). However, as Mitchell and Townsend (2005) write, the globally networked world is certainly not one that is self-regulating or a host to libertarian harmony. 'Smart' has become more a marketing and propaganda tool for urban 'boosterism' than a serious academic tool of analysis and evaluation. Nonetheless, 'smart' is irrevocably associated with technology particularly new media technology. In 2009 the European Union issued a *Green Digital Charter* (NICE 2009), building on an earlier report identifying the complex relationship between Information and Communication Technology (ICT) and energy efficiency (European Commission DG INFSO 2008). The Charter promotes smart cities, smart grids and many other ICT enabled solutions that can reduce the environmental impact of urban areas and even of ICT itself given that these digital technologies are heavy users of energy, are created out of increasingly precious rare earth metals and other toxic substances (Maxwell and Miller 2012).

There are clear vulnerabilities and risks involved with ubiquitous computing and complex digital telecommunications infrastructure ranging from cyberterrorism, hacktivism and the propagation of viruses through code replication to the inadvertent loss or corruption of important data and information. From a risk management perspective it is assumed cities will quickly be able to mobilise regenerative resources in times of crisis if their digital operating networks remain robust. From a perspective that is looking to promote social and sustainable learning, civic engagement and participation digital connectivity and the emergence of hybrid spaces and places that interface on different social worlds has significant potential to facilitate transformative learning and progressive change.

One such hybrid space is the public library which in a number of cities are being refreshed architecturally and philosophically in line with the city's smart digital and sustainability agenda. New major public libraries in Birmingham and Worcester in the UK, Seattle in the United States, Helsinki in Finland, Amsterdam in the Netherlands and Aarhus in Denmark have not only been built (or are currently in the process of being built) to impressive green standards but continue to offer spaces and opportunities for the whole city and not just a section of it. They offer possibilities for wide social, economic and environmental regeneration and democratic renewal. For example, the Vallila Library in Helsinki has its own environmental policy, modelled on that of the city, and exhibits six ecologically aware qualities encompassing image, circulation, sustainability, leadership, design and public space:

> A green library projects a clear, ecologically aware image. Such thinking is visible in everything the library does. An 'eco label' is a good way to show that the library operates in an environmentally conscious way.
>
> Circulation and recycling are the watchwords of a green library. A green library works as a platform for sharing things both material and immaterial. Books and knowledge, tools for work and thought.
>
> Conservation of resources and energy is of vital importance. A green library strives for sustainability in everything from acquisition to waste management.
>
> Working as an advocate of green values and sustainability is natural to libraries. A green library is an opinion leader that breathes influence and respect.
>
> Design and green design are aimed to both last and please. A green library aims to only have items of quality. Durability, not disposability.
>
> In any modern city non-commercial public space is a luxury. A green library offers free space for work and culture. A shared living room for customer that helps build the society.
>
> (Vallila Library n.d.)

For Michael Dudley (2013), public libraries have the capacity to give a city resilience and a city-system its identity. Francine Houben, the leading architect within Mecanoo in the Netherlands which has built a number of sustainable buildings, including public (the Library of Birmingham) and university libraries (the Technical University in Delft), offered the following observations:

> It is about creating space, identity and coherence and ensuring that people love the building. Most of Mecanoo's buildings are organic in conception so you have a total package. It should also be beautiful. Beauty is a part of sustainability, I believe. The Library of Birmingham will be BREEAM Excellent but it also has to do the concept or sequence of rotundas that allow a journey or voyage through the building, has spaces that will be used for many different events throughout the century and, of course, with the green roofs, so many grey roofs in Birmingham, will give Centenary Square [where the Library is located] a more pleasant identity.
>
> (Houben 2012)

It is still possible to create physical, digital and hybrid places and spaces that are both public and free, where groups and individuals can learn a new self-respect, assert and refashion their group or individual identities, articulate the values of

Figure 6.2 The library of Birmingham – the biggest public library in Europe under construction in 2012, UK

Source: John Blewitt

co-operation and civic virtue, and, as Evans and Boyte (1986: 17) state, 'act with dignity, independence and vision'. By their very nature libraries are places of informal and formal learning, information, research, leisure, communication. Some of these newly redesigned public libraries are perhaps prefiguring the emergence of new heterotopic spaces that are green and socially inclusive (Blewitt and Gambles 2010; Blewitt 2012, 2013), and may even be creating a mobilising power defined by cultural values that may help fashion deep value frames conducive to pro-sustainable, transformative social and political change.

As Polletta (1999: 20) writes, 'what is crucial is the set of beliefs, values and symbols institutionalised in a particular setting'. Libraries are networks and networked, they are places where sharing occurs, that lends and enables borrowing, reuse and recycling, and where environmental sustainability and co-operation is, or can be, enacted. As Mattern (2007) concludes in her design study of new libraries in the United States, they are transitional institutions located in the public sphere but touch the private, they are both physical and digital real and virtual and in many ways are icons of transparency. The library is its contents, its people, its activities, its city and its city's culture offering multiple ways of learning and knowing with values that are both timeless and evolving and ideals that find expression in both built and organisational form.

In his book *Native to Nowhere*, Timothy Beatley (2004: 268) shows that sharing institutions are central to developing community and 'our sense of and commitment to place'. Many will stock books that are not necessarily of principle commercial value and many offer sharing services that extent to tools, toys and people. It offers multiple pedagogies including social and sustainability learning, deep and surface framing. These are not so much big claims but too often unannounced ones. For Francine Houben, working across disciplinary, professional and community boundaries and recognising that technology is just part of solution is most important:

> Maybe some things are becoming too technical. I also like the idea that sometings are simple – back to basics. Two or three weeks ago in Holland a mobile telephone network provider was burned down. People found that they're mobile phones didn't work anymore. It was one big day for they were out for a whole week. The back to basics ... It was a very pleasant way to live. People think of resilience in times of crisis but its more than that. It's fun. You feel independent. You feel democratic. It is not a negative thing.
>
> (Houben 2012)

Transition towns

Resilience is at the heart of the Transition movement, which started life in the Republic of Ireland in the small town of Kinsale in 2005 under the leadership, guidance and inspiration of permaculturalist Rob Hopkins, who has since moved to Totnes, in the southwest of England. Rob Hopkins has further developed the Transition movement and concept in Totnes and the movement has spread to countless cities, towns and villages in the United Kingdom, continental Europe, the United States and elsewhere. Thirty-four countries now host Transition initiatives.

For Hopkins, permaculture holds the key to developing a more sustainable world although the concept of resilience was not something that figured much in Hopkins' education or his work as a permaculturalist. He remembered that the first time he really took notice of the idea was when he read Thomas Homer-Dixon's *The Upside of Down* (Homer-Dixon 2006), which was about the time he started to write his own book *The Transition Handbook: From Oil Dependency to Local Resilience* (Hopkins 2008). However, although the concept is used far more frequently than it used to be, Hopkins recognises that it remains fairly marginal. For Rob Hopkins there is a danger exists that it could go the same way as 'sustainable development', requiring 'thousands and thousands of books arguing about what it means and what it doesn't mean . . . but to me it seems much clearer'. He continues:

> I go out and do a lot of talks to communities, and when you talk about peak oil, and it's that question of 'what would your community look like if oil cost $200 a barrel? How are you going to manage your basic functions?' . . . that automatically can lead people into thinking about resilience even if they don't call it resilience.
>
> (Hopkins 2012)

The Transition idea has certainly caught on, because perhaps of the growing interest in the need for resilience, and also because Hopkins's innovative ideas makes sense. Change has spread rhizomatically with individual transition communities each articulating a need to fit in with their bioregional, cultural and historical contexts while ensuring each learns from the other in a larger Transition network. This makes for efficient but sensitive use of human and digital modes of communication and social connection. The Transition in Action website produced by Transition town Totnes (http://totnesedap.org.uk) is replete with stories marrying the past with the present and future, stories relating to work, local food growing, heating and lighting the home and community, transport, farming, shopping and so on. There is a certain nostalgia about these stories that run contrary to the harder edged political discourses, self-help handbooks and management prescriptions taking also resilience as their central theme. For instance, one narrative recollection refers to a certain Mr Hoopell, who was the town's lamplighter:

> He used to go round on a pushbike until about 1948. He'd go round at night, had a chain on them with a pilot light, and he would just go and, with a hook like a boat hook, pull the chain and put the street lights on. He'd come around first thing in the morning and turn them out. The whole town was gas-lit.
>
> (Totnes EDAP n.d)

The point is to understand context, to recognise that innovation and technology needs to be appropriate not necessarily either high-tech or low-tech, complex or simple, but appropriate – human scale.

For Hopkins and others making up the Transition movement there are two major issues which we all need to confront. One is climate change and the other, probably more important or immediate, is that of peak oil. Both act as a frame for discussions of survival as much as change (Barry and Quilley 2009). The fact that our modern advanced technological economies, cultures and lifestyles are fuelled mainly by fossil fuels, especially oil, is a problem not only because converting it to energy produces greenhouse gas emissions but also because it is quickly running out. The world has already reached the stage where oil production has peaked in terms of quantity extracted and cost. Future oil extraction will be more difficult, more expensive, more risky and more damaging to the environment (Roberts 2005; Heinberg 2011). The filtering of oil from the tar sands of Alberta, Canada, is immensely controversial, costly and inefficient but issues of energy and political security and consistent failures to envisage a future without or with considerably less oil has eluded political and economic decision-makers, business and media elites (often one and the same) and the general public in most if not all countries of the world.

The Transition movement consequently values, and has sought to develop, alternatives which include the introduction of local currencies, reskilling, local food production and, of course, the design and implementation of localised energy descent plans that will wean towns, families and businesses off their addiction to oil, preparing them for the inevitable post-carbon future (Hopkins 2008). In doing this climate change and peak oil act as mobilising device and a way of envisioning a possible future which can involve those who are not necessarily ardent supporters of the green movement.

> In Totnes, over the last couple of years we have had a very interesting process of shifting the dialogue, for there are lots of people who may not necessarily agree with climate change or peak oil but see Transition as something interesting. So peak oil and climate is still the foundation but the shift is focusing on about creating a new economy for the town and the whole idea of community resilience being about economic development and how do we revive our town's economic fortunes through transition, by creating a culture of social enterprise. It's incredible the number of people who come out of the woodwork and the whole thing shifts. I no longer make it my life's work to try to convince people that climate change or peak oil is not rubbish ... It is about co-operation. There's a big ethical debate about 'should we carry on as we are or be more co-operative?'. That's the direction the Transition movement is moving.
>
> (Hopkins 2012)

Transition will take different forms in different places although the overarching aim is to restore resilience and ecological responsibility to a culture that has been carelessly and mindlessly destructive during the age of abundance and affluence. Increasingly, promoters of Transition stress economic factors. Our planet and society cannot afford continual economic growth and indeed growth may not actually occur. Economies may just decline until a steady state is reached. Japan has been since the 1990s a post-growth or largely no growth economy and Japanese society has not collapsed. 'Renewed prosperity will come in a large part from diverse, vibrant and robust local economies. The best response we can make to our economic instability is to shift our support to an economy based on social justice, resilience and protection of the biosphere. Nothing else makes sense.

(Transition Network n.d.)

Community resilience is now largely understood as economic development. Despite criticisms of the movement failing to adequately address the broader issue of political power, vested financial interests and economic inequality, the movement does offer a fresh perspective on community self-reliance, resilience, environmental responsibility and respect for others. Indeed, *The Transition Handbook* is aptly subtitled 'From Oil Dependency to Local Resilience', offering heuristic guidance to communities of various descriptions about to how to embark on this change process (Hopkins 2008). The free edit version of the book was published on the Internet under a creative commons copyright and included an accompanying wiki, networked face to face and online meetings. Although it had to be taken down because of some copyright issues the movement has developed its use of social media as a means of ensuring geographically spread groups and individuals are able to remain co-operative, collaborative and dynamic. Significantly, there is a reluctance to prescribe a set or series of standardised steps, procedures and actions for transition. However, although Hopkins offered his own 'twelve steps to transition', he provided only a rough charcoal drawing rather than a finely etched engraving of the transition process:

[The steps] don't take you from A–Z, rather from A–C, which is as far as we've got with this model so far. These steps don't necessarily follow each other logically in the order they are set out here; every Transition initiative weaves a different way through the Steps, as you will see. These Twelve Steps are still evolving, in part shaped by your experience of using them. There may end up being as few as six or more than fifty!

(Hopkins 2008: 98)

In fact the steps have now turned into 'ingredients' which are roughly divided into five stages and include visioning, awareness raising, forming working groups, creating an inner space, celebrating, celebrating failure, storytelling, education, personal resilience, pausing for reflection, energy descent plans, social enterprise and entrepreneurship, intermediate technologies, community ownership of assets, strategic thinking, pro-environmental policies and financial investment for transition (Hopkins 2011). Transition is, for Rob Hopkins, an experiment, perhaps a journey, without a guarantee that it will definitely work but something that must be undertaken.

For Scott Cato and Hillier (2010: 878), Transition initiatives are not so much opting out of the mainstream, but really attempting to change it from within by thinking and acting differently or 'transversally and embracing more eco-sustainable ways of living to reorient the objectives of material and immaterial production'. This involves fashioning new subjectivities and a liberated political action that sees little hope in actually existing political democracies and conventional politicians.

Although *The Transition Handbook* did become the fifth most popular book choice of British members of parliament during the summer recess 2009 (Bunting 2009), the movement itself is not a serious formal challenge to the dominant economic ideology and political arrangements, and is somewhat tangential to mainstream electoral green politics. Whether the small changes, the micro-political actions, occurring in Totnes and elsewhere will lead to consequences similar to the flapping of a butterfly's wings is yet to be seen. Perhaps Transition is creating new radical social or transformative hybrid spaces that may prefigure or at least generate further spaces and actions that are both more resilient and more sustainable than those that presently dominate our social and economic environments (Harvey 2000; Langley and Mellor 2002).

> So long as community and environmental groups refuse to engage with the idea they need to become the new economy, and it's not just the case of hoping Tesco will go away or campaign against Tesco, but it is the argument that we need to be the change we want to see. Transition has largely operated under the radar and from the outset of Transition people would tell us 'if this starts to get anywhere, they won't let you' and that somehow those shadowy forces will mass against Transition...That hasn't happened yet and we have gone an enormously long way without something like that happening but in the long term we have to be aware that we will rub up against some vested interests. Interestingly, Bath and West Community Energy Company which emerged from Transition Bath are working with Scottish and Southern Energy who actually invested £1m in them to help them get started and develop a model which they wouldn't have otherwise been able to do. The money enabled them to develop a share option offering 4 per cent a year on investment rather than as usual with community share option giving a return if and when it is viable. They raised £750,000 in shares in three weeks It gave people a degree of confidence and security to move their pension over into it which revolutionised the whole thing.
>
> (Hopkins 2012)

The Transition movement is about dealing with current or future emergencies and initiating slow but systemic change. From the perspective of resilience, Transition is about what happens before a crisis hits. It is about building capacity, cultivating dispositions, habits, routines and values, and creating the conditions for creativity, adaptability and the overcoming of the learned help-lessness technologically advanced and oil-dependent consumer societies produce. It cannot therefore rely on community action and local empowerment alone but as green political theorist John Barry (2012) suggests, although living in a truly sustainable society means more than simply greening the existing one, Transition does help produce collective narratives of change, self-understanding and radical hope. Transition has to engage and interact with radical changes operating at other spatial scales and in a democratic sphere that exceeds that of the local and the immediate. It is necessary to do more than play community as Ash Amin (2005) has argued in his analyses of other approaches to community regeneration and urban development. However, for Hopkins, the Transition movement is the 'ultimate Trojan horse', ushering possibilities that have only been partially imagined but inform and perhaps give the movement its ultimate value in that it is something that creates moments 'when you feel part of some-thing and we are so used to feeling that we are not part of something anymore, atomised and isolated' (Hopkins 2012) and if Transition is going to happen it has got to happen in the next fifteen years – a far shorter period than the agricultural and industrial revolutions.

Local food: incredibly edible

The growing, distribution and sharing of food locally is a significant element of the Transition movement and has become increasingly important in urban areas as citizens, local politicians and policy makers acknowledge the close intercon-nections between health and wellbeing, social interaction, good nutrition, community, exercise, biodiversity and food safety and security. Local food grow-ing and through that reconnecting with nature can be extremely important for developing a sense of place, a sense of locality and distinctiveness in a world which seems increasingly homogenised and global.

For bio-regionalist Robert L. Thayer (2003: 71) it is an element for generat-ing a 'life-place culture', fulfilment, an embrace of nature, 'lifelong learning in and about one's place' and an opportunity 'to experience membership in a community including plants and animals as well as other humans'. As well as this, public concerns have mounted over the carbon footprint of importing unseasonable produce and the fearsome power of agribusiness that has created monocultures in many parts of the world and has projected the spurious argu-ments that genetic modification will not only feed the hungry world with its expanding and increasingly hungry cities. There are also issues relating to (un)fair trade and the dominance and double edged convenience of the (out of town) supermarket (Blythman 2004).

Above all, perhaps, it is personal and community health that has come to domi-nate the public, professional and academic discourse on food and nutrition. As some Western nations have increased in wealth and social inequality so has stress, mental illness, poor health and obesity. The McLibel trial and Franny Armstrong's careful presentation of the issues in her documentary *McLibel* (2005), or Morgan

Spurlock's tragi-comic take on fast food in *Supersize Me* (2004), or Robert Kenner's frightening expose of the industry that is food, animals and vegetables, in *Food Inc* (2009), or popular non-fiction books like Eric Schlosser's *Fast Food Nation* (2002), Felicity Lawrence's *Not on the Label* (2004) or Carolyn Steel's *Hungry City* (2009), have all drilled deep down into public awareness. The inescapable veracity and academic legitimacy of such studies as Wilkinson and Pickett's *The Spirit Level* (Wilkinson and Pickett 2010) has successfully connected social and environmental sustainability with a sustainability learning and public pedagogy.

The growing recognition that the social and sociability is being lost at work, at play and at home is now palpable, and is a possible reason why cookery and dinner party programmes such as *Masterchef* or *Come Dine With Me*, as well as gardening programmes, are becoming staple fare on prime-time television in the UK and the US. Carl Honore's *In Praise of Slow* (2004) may have been initially perceived as something for a bourgeois gourmet or those who are rich in both time and money, but a few years later this does not seem to be the case. Local food festivals and food exhibitions worldwide have helped developed a public understanding of the possibilities and benefits of growing food locally in cities, peri-urban and rural areas.

The travelling Carrot City exhibition, for example, has toured Canada, the United States, Britain, France and Germany. It is based on research and development work at Ryerson University, Toronto, which has demonstrated how design can facilitate the development of local food systems by fostering social relationships through formal and informal urban horticulture. Projects such as the edible schoolyard and roof space farms have been combined with design initiatives promoting effective growing, such as composters, planters, solar bubble greenhouses and the like.

A visually impressive book has been written by the curators of the Carrot City exhibition detailing how urban planning and sustainable architecture can include local food production as a fundamental requirement of city design. Community gardens, greenhouses located under raised highways, food plots replacing manicured lawns, green walls, and productive green roof gardens on schools and residential apartments blocks are presented as practical and feasible propositions (Gorgolewski *et al.* 2011). Anthropologists have demonstrated that the preparing, sharing and consumption of food has important implications for our sense of common identity, fairness, belonging and equality. Although local food growing or family or communal consumption may not be a matter of survival as it once was, human sociability remains of primary psychological and epidemiological significance.

The cultivation of vegetables on allotments, in domestic and community gardens, urban farms, public spaces or unused or derelict land is increasingly commonplace. Often initiated in times of crisis community vegetable gardens are also attractive to those who wish to use organic methods. Urban food justice movements, urban agriculture programmes and various forms of sustainable and self-sufficient local food systems frequently nurture strong civic values, dietary improvements and paid employment in the local economy.

Unfortunately, insecurity of tenure is often a considerable obstacle to establishing and maintaining urban food growing plots throughout the world (Levkoe 2006; Boone and Modarres 2006; Dixon *et al.* 2007). In rust belt cities like Detroit in the USA urban horticulture and agriculture is revitalising what is left of the city. Nearly 2,000 newly created food gardens have been created in London since 2008, when a Capital Growth fund was established by the mayor to encourage groups and individuals to establish new growing spaces – edible gardens within the city. A grant of up to £350 is available on application, and an annual Grow for Gold competition is run by the Capital Growth organisers which have spaces in a diverse range of places including schools, a prison, on roofs, in skips, on canal banks and housing estates.

Some spaces host social enterprises and beekeeping, providing opportunities for skills development and horticultural learning. The success stories of Edible Hackney in east London made the UK national press with an article in *The Guardian* (Platt 2011), reporting how some estate residents have colonised the open space surrounding their flats to cultivate a wide variety of fruit and vegetables. A local collective called Growing Communities operate a veg box scheme and in the Dalston area of the borough a design partnership is attempting to turn a shop into a farm. In 2010 a local beekeeper and PhD student at the University of Brighton, Mikey Tomkins, created an interactive digital map of what an edible Hackney might look like complete with walking tours and a web-based audio commentary.

Paul Clarke, a Professor of Education at St Mary's in London and an employee of Mott MacDonald the engineering consultancy, has been instrumental in developing the 'edible' town concept first in Todmorden on the Yorkshire–Lancashire border and now in many other places too. The success of the project, initially conceived as a bottom up community project was co-opted by local politicians who have seemingly steered it away from its original purpose and intention. As a result Paul Clarke joined forces with a few other like-minded people and established another local food-based project by the name of Pop-Up-Farm, which in many ways is a simple version of permaculture.

> What we have been interested in with Pop-Up-Farm, all along, is how do you get some basic ideas about sustainability out to large numbers of people. We call it 'flat pack sustainability'. It's sort of Fordism for another time. We have a website because we want to connect people together, accessible to everybody, and we challenge people through different initiatives that take place such as in Burnley with regards food and growing. The network of schools that are involved have some land and are growing some stuff but we've said to them why don't you look at the yield on some of this and bring together forty different school sites as a communal growing space, a diverse farming space. Look at it systematically rather than a scattered group of little random activities and start to develop an accumulated knowledge base around sustainability, energy, food, water and waste in terms of strategies people can adopt in their own settings, relatively easily applied with

modifications and then build up a network round this in the region and through the website to people in other parts of the world.

(Clarke 2012)

The Pop-Up-Foundation project, a not-for-profit social enterprise, now includes Ugandan school children experimenting with solar instead of wood burning ovens. This improves human health and also encourages groups and individuals to arrest the process of deforestation. Other Ugandan children grow coffee because it is a high cash crop with the intention that they will eventually sell the coffee to the schools in Burnley who are also part of the network. It is already being sold to masses of fans at Burnley Football Club and any financial surplus generated in return to Uganda and as well as helping to finance local initiatives closer to home Urban food growing can therefore take many different approaches and related activities but whose coherence is framed by the deep frames and values that motivate them and which they themselves express.

Allotments and food gardens are sometimes referred to as a 'green gym', but it is also about claiming a right to the city, transforming a way of life and perhaps widening those fractures within the domineering culture of consumer material-ism and resource extravagance. Allotments are replete with reused materials, practices of recycling and self-management and enable the retelling of a past, whether they relate to historic or recent urban migrations of wartime 'dig for victory' campaigns, that become refashioned into a contemporary narratives of resilience, sustainability and autonomy (Crouch and Parker 2003). In their sensi-tive account of the history of allotments in Britain and continental Europe, Crouch and Ward (1997: 25) articulate a structure of feeling that is clearly appar-ent in the Transition movement and other community based sustainability initiatives:

> A basis for human relationships is enhanced where there is not an institu-tionalised separation of the people – and such a separation is not possible in the field of things grown or made at home. However, it is not all altruism. Giving and sharing are underpinned by a feeling of inclusion in the commu-nity, awareness of the importance, socially, culturally and economically, of one's involvement in the community, a stake in the relationship that may be reciprocated. On this scale, having the right to give, to choose to give and to exchange freely, forms an important bond between people. It is especially welcome in communities that feel themselves ineligible for the benefits available to wider society, and excluded from relationships within that society.

All this is a long way from the technological vision of biologist Dickson Despommier (2011), who has vigorously promoted the idea of technologically advanced vertical farms, massive schemes for hydro and aeroponic agriculture in urban areas but the search for resilience in sustainable development will undoubtedly take different forms in different places. For Paul Clarke this type of

Figure 6.3 Handsworth Allotments, Birmingham UK: local food growing, local
          resilience
Source: John Blewitt

technological approach is probably inevitable to some extent given the need to
feed a swiftly increasing global population but it does not address the problem of
urban dwellers losing touch with nature:

> As we move towards an urban culture we've lost that sensibility to what the
> natural support systems actually are and why they are so important. Unless
> we can reintroduce that into urban spaces I think we will just perpetuate the
> problem really. And that's why Pop-Up-Farm focuses a lot on growing and
> tries to get kids particularly to reappraise the environment they have around
> them. An audit of land, water and energy similar to what occurs in the build-
> ing trade . . . It's not part of the current [school] curriculum except perhaps in
> Geography but I think kids need this stuff ingrained at an earlier age and
> which goes right through their school life.
>
> (Clarke 2012)

Parents are also involved for each school has a wooden shed, known as the 'plot-
ting shed', donated by the supermarket chain Asda, which has become the
community hub for the project. The children together with those parents who
wish to get involved are tasked with making the shed a self-standing sustainable

building. Some sheds are used as coffee shops, while others are used to promote farm produce. Some people have plans to construct temporary straw bale extensions to the sheds. The inter-generational learning involved here is extremely important in nourishing a connected to place and to each other.

Paul Clarke (2012), though, wants to go further by connecting the work being done with school level children to the research undertaken at the University and to the construction and development projects of Mott MacDonald. He uses the information, knowledge and examples of practical sustainability actions emerging from this network in a wide variety of public education settings extending beyond the seminar rooms at St Mary's or the virtual spaces of the Internet. The information and case studies enable learners to connect the local with the global and to learn from experiences and initiatives they would otherwise remain ignorant or fail to see the relevance of.

Mott MacDonald currently has a contract with the government of Mauritius to develop policies and practices that can become a lifelong learning resource about how the country's precious biodiversity is the key to its future economic and sustainable wellbeing. For Paul Clarke (2012), whether the projects are taking place in Uganda, Mauritius or Burnley, what is important is their long term survival – their survival and resilience.

> One of the reasons we adopted a lot of the concepts around permaculture in our [Pop-Up] programme was because of the need for sustainability. We were interested in integrated systems, the way smaller scale technologies might give people more confidence to experiment and build their own localised resilience. We talk about Pop-Up-Farm not as a project but as a way of thinking and a way of doing. The hand, heart and mind are embedded in the programme. People have to think about the challenge and be able to act on it. In our society it is too easy to think we can buy a solution to these problems.
>
> (Clarke 2012)

These place-based (but connected) initiatives and experiments are where resilience in sustainable development happens. It is where learning takes place and where certain localities within the city may become, as Evans (2011: 232) writes 'truth hotspots' that dissolve the boundaries between formal and informal learning, knowledge makers and knowledge users, urban citizens and the technologies of governance and power. The city is thereby transformed in an ecology of circumstances enabling and stimulating various performative innovations and deinstitutionalised participatory engagements.

An example of this may be viewed in Faith Morgan's short documentary *The Power of Community* (2006), which shows how Cuba managed to survive the loss of financial and other support following the collapse of the Soviet Union, and has become such a truth hotspot. By going organic and converting as much available land to agriculture and horticulture as possible Cuba has been an inspiration to many sustainability advocates because here it is clear that agri-business is not necessarily the answer to feeding the city and certainly not to empowering communities. During 1996, Havana's urban farms provided the city's urban population with 8,500 tonnes of agricultural produce, many millions of flowers, 7.5 million eggs and 3,650 tonnes of meat. The 'popular gardens' may not meet all the food or nutritional needs of the country, but much of the harvested food is shared between the family, childcare centres, hospitals and other community members. Some is sold in small food markets. A number of traditional crops have been revitalised, and generally, it seems, Cubans are also healthier and thinner than they once were:

> In addition to increased food security, urban gardens have also helped to empower many individuals and communities. They have renewed solidarity and purpose within neighborhoods, sustaining morale during the ongoing economic crisis. The popular gardens have helped to build community pride; they clean up vacant urban spaces that had once been local dumps, replacing these eyesores with greenery. To some people, the gardens also serve as a source of leisure, exercise, and relaxation.
>
> (Altieri *et al.* 1999: 139)

There is certainly something to be said for a 'back to basics' approach, although the Special Period, as Fidel Castro termed time following end of Soviet support, also saw some considerable hardship and hunger, as the public food distribution system for a while effectively collapsed (Anon 2008).

7 Education and conservation

Building social resilience

The people factor

Resilience is not the successor of sustainability but a 'synergiser' that can enhance the effectiveness of sustainability efforts, argues Dave Newport (2013) from the University of Colorado–Boulder. He challenges Andew Zolli's (2012) notion of resilience as an alternative to sustainability. Zolli's 2012 opinion piece in the *New York Times* frames resilience as a people-facing, community development process which engages the 'victims' of sustainability in a variety of responses from constructing flood dikes to community building to counselling services. Dave Newport is critical of Zolli's pragmatic and damage control approach: 'Nobody gets out of bed inspired by damage control', he argues (Newport 2013: 1). Despite his reservations, Newport recognises the value-addedness of resilience:

> The resilience frame speaks not just to how buildings weather storms but to how people weather them, too. Here, psychologists, sociologists and neuroscientists are uncovering a wide array of factors that make you more or less resilient than the person next to you: the reach of your social networks, the quality of your close relationships, your access to resources, your genes and health, your beliefs and habits of mind.
>
> (Newport 2013: 1)

Newport concludes that resilience needs sustainability as much as sustainability needs resilience. The sustainability advantage comes from its future facing and envisioning components which go beyond a 'band aid' approach offering people inspiration, hope and the dream of alternative futures. Resilience grounds these visions and offering practical change strategies which can help rebuild our people and planet relationships. Both Newport and Zolli agree, however, that social learning and education (both as a process and system) underpin any prospect of improving our life chances and sustaining life on earth.

Education a panacea?

The Rio+20 Sustainable Development Dialogues, a key platform that informed the outcomes of the 2012 Summit, captured the sentiment that sustainable development cannot be attained without education. The dialogues asked stakeholders to select key actions for the future: three of the ten priority actions voted on (out of a total of 100) relate to education (Chasek 2012). Those negotiating the key outcomes document agreed and endorsed education and learning as a key implementation measure in *The Future We Want* (United Nations 2012). Pamela Puntenney (2013), UN education caucus co-chair of the UN Commission on Sustainable Development, reminds us that this Rio+20 document was the first official UN summit negotiated text to formally acknowledge the role of higher education for sustainable development and its criticality in shaping the future of the world. Education, and the people related-processes such as learning, capacity building, training and public awareness, have a strong presence across documents released by the UN Commission for Sustainable Development, including all 40 chapters of Agenda 21 and the three conventions on biodiversity, climate change and desertification that were negotiated in the 1992 Rio summit (Hopkins 2012). Previous to Rio+20, however, education had been framed mostly, around improving access to primary education and loosely on influencing attitudes and behaviours. The recent pronouncements acknowledge that social change for sustainability will require not just new knowledge and professional responses but new ways of thinking and working; for the first time attention is drawn to further and higher education.

Figure 7.1 Rio+20 higher education side event: Daniella Tilbury chairing the event
Source: Ingrid Mulà

Educators and proponents of sustainable development, such as Stephen Sterling (2011, 2013) and Daniella Tilbury (1995, 2011a, 2013), believe that education is both part of the problem and part of the solution to sustainable development. These authors see education as reproducing unquestionably exploitative behaviours and social patterns rather than generating alternative pathways through education. This view is echoed in the Rio+20 People's Treaty in Higher Education for Sustainable Development (Copernicus Alliance and Treaty Circle 2012), which was developed by leading higher education bodies to influence the UN summit outcomes. The treaty is supported with over 90 signatories from higher education organisations, agencies and groups from across the globe, is persuasive in its argument that if (higher) education is to play a transformative role in our societies and assist in the construction of a more sustainable world, it must first transform itself.

The treaty's authors acknowledge that the sector has a long history of engaging with the generation of knowledge and shaping social and scientific paradigms that influence everyday life. However, these paradigms, as David Orr (2004) poignantly advises, are those that underpin current mindsets and practices that exploit people and planet. This argument resonates deeply with many commentators across cultural divides (see, for example, Fadeeva and Mochizuki 2010; Alvares and Faruqi 2012), who are critical of education practices and systems which promote unsustainable relationships.

It is within this context, and with a reminder of what is at stake for people and planet, that Daniella Tilbury (2013) argues that a global rebooting of education is required. Her argument is that more than knowledge of sustainability or commitment to it is needed to transform higher education. The turnaround moment will come when we have the leaders capable of deep and systemic change across our schools, colleges and universities (Scott *et al.* 2012). Until then, our students will leave the education system without the understanding, commitment or capability to resolve sustainable development tensions or create more positive futures.

Education for conservation and sustainable development

The authoritative voices in the international conservation movement, including IUCN, WWF and UNEP, have long understood the potential power of education in shaping worldviews. These organisations have a history of engaging with education, learning and capacity building and of leading programmes that seek to build social contexts for conservation. The reach and diversity of WWF's work in this area was captured in the late 1990s by a strategic review of WWF education programmes which sought to assess the value of these initiatives and capture the outputs, outcomes and impact of this work (Fien *et al.* 1999). The study reviewed:

- Vintsy School Clubs for Nature in Madagascar;
- the education components of integrated conservation and development programmes (ICDPs);

- targeted faith groups in Tanzania;
- greening schools initiatives in Malaysia;
- national park and community education programmes in Venezuela;
- nature study groups in Colombia;
- capacity-building programmes for conservation staff across the Mediterranean;
- curriculum development and creation of regional education centres in China;
- the Threatened Species Network of educators in Australia;
- the education and capacity of local action groups in Spain; and
- learning programmes offered at the Mai Po Marshes Wildlife Centre in Hong Kong, among others.

These projects were chosen as examples of good conservation practice across the WWF network and reflect a time when donor and aid agency funds were directed towards environmental education efforts. Education was seen, by a handful of WWF national and programme offices, as important for building social context and responses to conservation and the broader goals of sustainable development. The evaluation documented and confirmed the effectiveness of education programmes based on sound educational practice and the value of these programmes to meeting conservation targets.

Looking beyond these flagship programmes, several of the key informants interviewed for this book believe that conservation groups (such as WWF) have not always understood learning processes or the premise that education systems and models need reorienting to address sustainable development concerns. For example, the proposed environmental education model produced by WWF Malaysia (Boon 2012) makes scant reference to the destruction of the forest, the controversies surrounding the palm oil industry or its impact on species loss (particularly the orang-utan): instead the learning is focused on appreciating human's place in the natural ecosystem.

Ann Finlayson, who headed WWF's Education Unit and acted as Sustainable Development Commissioner for Education in the UK, reflects on her own learning journey within the conservation movement and experience of promoting sound educational practice. She recalls how, early on in her career, she was inducted by the conservation movement into outdoor education and into assumptions that providing opportunities for learners to experience the natural environments was critical to the attainment of conservation goals. Her experience taught her otherwise:

> Many did genuinely believe that these outdoor environmental experiences would turn children into environmentalists . . . the reality is that children did enjoy their day out – they love field trips as they differ from their everyday classroom experience. To some extent there was cognitive dissonance as they were taken out of their comfort zones and challenged to learn in a different way but the learning was not deep and did not shape or change mindsets.
>
> (Finlayson 2013)

It was this experience that drove her to work at a more strategic education level and to learn about the power of pedagogy. Roel van Raaij (2012), a senior policy civil servant to the Dutch government with a long history of engagement with conservation education, shared a similar experience. His view of education and its contribution to conservation evolved over time, as he reflected on lack of impact of many initiatives that sought to draw the human experience closer to nature.

The belief that experiencing the environment first hand is an essential component of engaging people in conservation has its roots in the work of Steve Van Matre (1978, 1988) and his experiential outdoor learning activities. Arjen Wals (2010), a UNESCO chair in education for sustainable development and respected environmental educationist, explains that these education efforts were informed by behaviourist socio-psychology models that assumed a linear causality between experiencing the environment first hand and pro-environmental behaviours. In his inaugural lecture, he pointed to experience, as well as research studies, that show that people's environmental behaviours are far too complex and contextual to be captured by a simple causal model (Wals 2010).

Kartikeya Sarabhai, the founder director of the Centre for Environment Education (CEE) and vice-chair of the Indian National Commission of IUCN, agrees. His experience has taught him that learning is about liberation not manipulation of behaviours. David Norman, from WWF UK, also questions the linearity of these assumptions and draws a parallel with today's conservation efforts associated with climate change, that encourage people to take small and painless pro-environmental behaviours without challenging mind-sets. Underpinning these strategies, he argues, is an incorrect assumption that people will be ushered 'onto a virtuous escalator to ever more significant behaviour change' (Norman 2008: 2). In a 2008 WWF report entitled 'Weathercocks and Signposts', he concludes that the environmental movement must reflect carefully on its people engagement strategies if it is to remain relevant, given that experience and research studies[1] have shown that behaviour-change approaches have been found wanting.

Arjen Wals (2010) points to the ways that funding levels for education, from government and conservation organisations, have fluctuated over time, as the limited impact of these nature-centred behaviour change practices on conservation targets has been assessed. Indeed, Ann Finlayson (2013) recognises that there is a place for understanding and discovering natural environment and how we relate to nature. She acknowledges how this perspective of education (which dominated WWF International education efforts form the 1980s and the pro-environmental behaviour work which followed) resulted in the closure of the WWF International education programme, as it became increasingly difficult to justify expenditure on initiatives that had limited short- or medium-term impact.[2]

Surprisingly, these models of education have been the subject of renewed attention as the social marketing promise appeals to donors and conservation agencies return to romantic notions that nature education, particularly in early years, underpins environmental commitment. The latter continues to be at the heart of many WWF education activities, such as natural art competitions, nature school clubs and development of resources which bring natural environments to the classroom. The WWF UK and SKY 'I Love Amazon Week' education initiative, launched in 2012, is one such example:

> Schools who want to go on an exciting journey of discovery to learn about the wonders of the rainforest are being encouraged to get involved in a new project. I Love Amazon Week is a free initiative that gives pupils aged 7–11 the opportunity to explore the Amazon rainforest through a fantastic range of flexible curriculum-based resources.
>
> (WWF 2013)

Ann Finlayson (2013) reflects on the way that WWF had learnt other education related lessons over the years and had come to terms with the fact that communicating the science behind conservation was not enough to influence people. 'Although studies were identifying WWF as the most respected conservation NGO, they were not being listened to', she explains. It was a tough learning experience, Ann recalls, as many senior managers struggled to acknowledge that education was not an advocacy tool or fund-raising campaign but needed to be underpinned by sound educational models and approaches, such as appreciative inquiry and competency-based learning. Ann believes that only a handful of WWF colleagues went beyond the didactic and learner-deficient models that underpinned conservation education. The WWF South Africa's School Water Action Projects (SWAP) is an example of an initiative that connected students to their physical environments but through an appreciative inquiry approach that built students' ability to identify, as well as respond to, quality of life, socio-cultural and environment issues in their locality (Tilbury 1999d).

In the midst of a wave of the positivist approaches to conservation education that Ann Finlayson identifies, a few examples of socially critical learning can be found. WWF Brazil's 'Muda o Mundo, Raimundo! (Change the World, Raimundo!) ran from 1995 until 2000 and left a legacy that was still palpable in 2012.[3] The programme took on the dual challenge of confronting education systems (and models) which confine teachers to unsustainable curriculum practices, at one level and at another level, of developing pedagogical approaches[4] that enable learners to question existing social practices and work towards more sustainable futures. Various programme evaluations, undertaken during the life of the Raimundo project, documented positive changes in the school system, the learning experience of students but also in the local communities where the students lived.

The project was underpinned by a key multiplier concept that extended the project reach to Brasilia, Parana, Pernambuco, Maranhao, Rio de Janiero, Rondonia and Sao Paolo. WWF effectively partnered with the Ministry of Education, the Brazilian Institute for Environment and Renewable Resources, the Robert Marinho Foundation, UNESCO and several Brazilian NGOs. It supported school teams and individual teachers through regional hubs, professional development, networking and mentoring opportunities, while also encouraging initiatives to reach out beyond the walls of the schools (Tilbury 1999a). The notion of, or need for, resilience was never articulated through the programme. Equally, one would need to look long and hard to find any links to resilience in its framing or learning strategies. Nevertheless, 'Raimundo', as it is affectionately known by stakeholders, remains today as one of the most successful education partnerships and programmes led by WWF.

Another conservation education programme worthy of attention is the Environmental Education Initiative for China (EEIC) that began in 1997. This ambitious initiative, facilitated by WWF China, also recognised the power of education systems as well as the need to reorient them towards sustainable development. EEIC, which ran for over two decades, changed education from within and focused efforts on the professional development of teachers, resource developers and university educators who could catalyse change across the system. It was innovative in that it went beyond the schools clubs, nature competitions and awareness raising campaigns which dominated conservation education practice at the time, to engage education and educators in a deep assessment of existing teaching practices and how curriculum and pedagogical innovation[5] could make a contribution to more positive futures.

The programme recognised that it was not simply a question of adding new concepts to the curriculum or centring education around issues such as the protection of China's pandas or other indigenous species. Instead, it sought to develop an understanding of the social context and development practices which were threatening biodiversity and quality of life in China, as well as potential responses and actions.[6] The legacy of the programme continues today thanks to the spheres of influence established in key provinces. The universities that were at the centre of these spheres of influences (Beijing Normal University, East China Normal University, Shanghai and South West Normal University, Kunming) act as catalysts for sustainable development in education and the local communities that they serve. Partnerships with the Ministry for Basic Education, leading NGOs and China's official textbook writers enabled an ecological and sustained approach to educational change (Tilbury 1999b).

Five years after the work of these innovative programmes was captured by the WWF review, the UN Decade of Education for Sustainable Development was launched. The DESD, as it is commonly referred to, explicitly acknowledged the need to reorient education systems and to renew pedagogical approaches (UNESCO 2005) used in formal and non-formal learning environments. Pedagogical innovation was taking under a variety of labels such as environmental education, conservation education, learning for sustainability, education for sustainable development, but this occurred mostly outside of the formal structures of schooling (For example, 'It's a Living Thing' Professional Development Programme for Conservation Professionals, NSW Australia). Midway through the DESD, UNESCO commissioned an expert review which recognised critical thinking, values clarification, futures thinking, cultural learning and participatory

Figure 7.2 Pedagogical innovation in education: 'Its a Living Thing' professional
        development programme for professionals engaged in conservation
        management, New South Wales, Australia

Source: Daniella Tilbury

engagement as important learning processes for the attainment of sustainable
development (Tilbury 2011). These were key components of the WWF China
and WWF Brazil education programmes that had been successful in building
social contexts for sustainable development. The concept and vocabulary of
resilience was still absent from this work.

The DESD international implementation scheme of 2005 brought to the
attention of many policy makers (and donors) the need to support education and
learning for sustainability outside of formal education. As Arjen Wals (2010)
points out:

> The search for sustainability cannot be limited to classrooms, the corporate
> boardroom, a local environmental education center, a regional government
> authority, etc. Instead, learning in the context of sustainability requires
> 'hybridity' and synergy between multiple actors in society and the blurring
> of formal, non-formal and informal education. Opportunities for this type of
> learning expand with an increased permeability between units, disciplines,
> generations, cultures, institutions, sectors and so on.
>
> (Wals 2010: 2)

The IUCN has a long tradition of supporting work across these boundaries. It endorses education for sustainability but often does not refer to it in these terms, choosing instead to identify itself with communication, social engagement or learning processes. Grazia Borrini-Feyerabend's seminal book *Beyond Fences: Seeking Social Sustainability in Conservation* (International Union for the Conservation of Nature 1997) built upon the best of IUCN's work in this area. She documented how participatory learning pedagogies needed to be present in community development, national park and nature reserves contexts. It reframed conservation education and engagement practice in ways that empowered people to learn and act for conservation. This book was released at time when communities were still being fenced out of protected areas (see Chapter 3).

In the early 2000s, it was the IUCN Commission on Education and Communication (CEC) that played an influential role in reshaping conservation education through promoting critical reflective practice, futures and systemic thinking and other participatory pedagogies. IUCN CEC acted as a network of innovation bridging the experiences of its 800 members whose reach spanned the globe. It promoted innovative conservation models that were people-centred and took conservation educators and environmental professionals along a journey signposted by key gatherings and resources.

IUCN CEC's two-day event at Johannesburg entitled Engaging People in Sustainability marked a key milestone along this journey; this oversubscribed event provided a snapshot of the level of interest and degree of influence that IUCN CEC was commanding at the time. The essence of this event was captured in an IUCN CEC publication that went out of print within two months of release (Tilbury and Wortman 2004).[7] Pamela Puntenney recalls the energy at this event as well as IUCN CEC's ability to convene policy dialogues and influence negotiations relating to communication, education and public awareness articles in the Convention on Biological Diversity, Convention on Desertification and Convention on Climate Change.

Whilst IUCN was turning its attention to influencing the pedagogical approaches of educators and international policy instruments relevant to education, UNEP was focusing its efforts on the training of conservation professionals. UNEP also has a long tradition of investing in education, training and community development through its Environmental Education and Training Unit (EETU) – and it has also shifted tactics over the years (Pradhan 2013). Currently activities are organised around six priority thematic areas, with climate change; resource efficiency and environmental governance taking centre stage. Its latest flagship programme, the Global Universities Partnership on Environmental Sustainability (GUPES), seeks to scale up the successes of the Mainstreaming Environment and Sustainability in African Universities (MESA) programme (Box 7.1). Although there are no publicly available independent evaluations of the programme, MESA is well regarded by stakeholders who believe it has left a positive legacy across various higher education and stakeholder communities. The initial work in Africa was later modelled in the Mainstreaming Environment and Sustainability in the Caribbean Universities (MESCA) and

---

Box 7.1 The Global Universities Partnership on Environment and
Sustainability

GUPES seeks:

- To provide a strategic platform for the mainstreaming of environment
  and sustainability concerns into university systems across the world,
  and to facilitate inter-university networking on sustainability issues
  with emphasis on South–South and North–South tertiary partnerships.
- To build, through university education systems, a professional capacity
  and leadership needed for the prevention of and responses to environmental issues, risks and associated sustainable development
  challenges.
- To contribute to revitalising the global higher education system and
  enabling it to address current sustainable development challenges with
  emphasis on UNEP's six thematic priorities.
- To contribute to the knowledge generation within UNEP's six priority
  thematic areas and other contemporary environmental and sustainability issues, risks and challenges.
- To optimise development opportunities provided by ecosystem services in a sustainable manner in line with the principles of 'Green
  Economy' and in the context of sustainable development.
- To help prepare the world for the projected impacts of global climate
  change, disasters and conflicts, harmful substances and hazardous
  wastes, as well as to assist in reversing and mitigating these and other
  negative environmental and sustainability trends.

Source: Adapted from UNEP (2011)

---

the Asia-Pacific Regional University Consortium (RUC) initiatives which also
count on grassroots support and have set the context for a global platform of
higher education for sustainable development (Pradhan 2013).

Resilience and education

The Rio+20 platform confirmed that the resilience discourse is now strong across
WWF, UNEP and IUCN strategic arenas. However, concepts or capabilities associated with resilience have yet to make their way into the educational work of
these organisations. Mitch Thomashow (2012), a leading author and higher education professional, observes that resilience is linked to being creative, reflective and
imaginative. Education for resilience, he believes, goes beyond the knowledge and
awareness of what is around you and focuses on the competences and confidence

of the individual. Others interviewed for this book, such as Roel Van Raaij (2012), Kartikeya Sarabhai (2013) and Morgan Williams (2012), agree and see a critical, reflective, but also confident and positive outlook as vital ingredients.[8] Approaches to learning for resilience start at where the individual or community is and build capability and positive outlook – avoiding the doom and gloom scenarios often associated with climate change and risk management initiatives.[9]

Along similar lines, Berkeley-based educational researcher Joel Brown and his colleagues (2000) believe that resilience education, and resilience in education, is worthy of significant and substantial development. These researchers see the need to 'weave positives' into educational practice and to learn to connect. They call for resilience work to:

- shift its focus from identifying risk-factors (mostly in relation to young people at risk) to identifying capabilities, attitudes and experiences which have contributed to (their) resilience; and
- move towards a holistic view of people (and communities) that focuses on interest and strength development rather than problem-focused and modelled on deficit view of the learner.

Ann Finlayson (2013), Mahesh Pradhan (2013), Roel van Raaij (2012) and Kartikeya Sarabhai (2013) spoke in similar terms when defining learning for resilience and the shifts required in existing educational practice.

Lyn Worsley, a clinical psychologist with a background in nursing, youth work and education, based in New South Wales, Australia has sieved through research findings and identified common qualities among individuals who are able to 'bungee jump' through their pitfalls and keep thriving' (Worsley 2013: 1). Worsley draws on this research in her practical resilience building strategies that are captured in her Resilience Doughnut (see Box 7.2).

She has adapted the Resilience Doughnut model for application as an organisational development tool that can build a culture of resilience, which assists staff to 'bounce forward' from professional challenges. The doughnut, Worsley believes, enables staff to have a clear focus on the personal purpose and meaning they have for their work, in order to cope with stress and plan for the future. She offers organisations thematic support in the areas of:

- *leading for integrity* (which develops the capabilities of future leaders);
- *personal and professional resilience* (which helps teams to cope with major organisational change);
- *pursuit of happiness* (which helps teams to develop resilient characteristics associated with happiness); and
- *bouncing forward from life's challenges* (which supports growth through adversity in the work setting and/or personal life).

How tools such as these could be adopted and adapted by conservation and sustainable development practitioners remains to be seen. It is also perhaps more

Box 7.2 Resilience Doughnut

The Resilience Doughnut combines educational strategies, participatory pedagogies and creative resources to build a sense of hope and optimism and thus strengthen an individuals, community and/or organisation ability to be resilient.

Lyn Worsley's Resilience Doughnut is composed of two parts:

1   The hole in the middle of the Resilience Doughnut represents a person's core beliefs, that are strengthened as they build the tools and resources they need to be resilient in the world. These beliefs are concerned with three areas:
     • their awareness of those who support them (who I have)
     • how they view themselves (who I am)
     • the degree of confidence they have in their own abilities (what I can do)
     Worsley points to research that documents how people who have strong positive beliefs in each of these areas are more likely to be resilient.

2   The doughnut ring is divided into seven sections representing an external factor in the person's life which influences their ability to be resilient. These seven factors each have the potential to enhance the positive beliefs within the person and thus to help the individual to develop resilience. The seven factors are:
     • *The parent factor:* characteristics of strong and effective parenting.
     • *The skill factor:* evidence of self-competence.
     • *The family and identity factor:* where family identity and connectedness is evident.
     • *The education factor:* experience of connections and relationships during the learning process.
     • *The peer factor:* where social and moral development is enhanced through interactions with peers.
     • *The community factor:* where the morals and values of the local community are transferred and the young person is supported.
     • *The money factor:* where the young person develops the ability to give as well as take from society through employment and purposeful spending.
     Worsley's work is based on the findings of various research projects. These documented that resilient individuals had only some, and not all, of these seven factors featuring in their life experience. Their ability to focus on the factors that were strong in their lives was, she argues, a key aspect of their resilient mindset.

Source: Resilience Doughnut (n.d.)

than a little unfortunate that the doughnut is not really a credible symbol of vitality or for that matter sustainability but is, in the practice of everyday life, frequently associated with overindulgence, obesity and unhealthy living.

The World Economic Forum convened in January 2013 and located social resilience and dynamism at the heart of discussions associated with raising standards of living and quality of life. Delegates sought strategies for embedding resilience within our social systems to assist the economic recovery. Few would dispute that learning for resilience is an essential ingredient of programmes that seek to improve the security and quality of lives as well as protect natural resources, environments and biodiversity. However, the interviews conducted for this book suggest it is difficult to define what form this added component would take or how its presence would be felt. As Keith Wheeler (2012) explains, arguments for its place across conservation and sustainable development are well rehearsed but scalable examples of how this can be done are hard to find. There are however, a few clues to what resilience can bring to education systems and learning practice.

Education for sustainable development brought a critical edge to environmental education practice,[10] encouraging learners to question deeply, learn to connect as well as envision alternative futures. Learning for resilience brings with it a new twist, favouring sociological and psychological approaches, which, if added to the social-critical, systemic and envisioning frames of education for sustainable,[11] may lead to more significant societal (and not just individual) change for sustainability. Dave Newport (2013) sees the synergies as they apply to higher education:

> Thus by folding resilience techniques we make sustainability better. By focusing our campuses on adapting to the new climate realities, we make our campuses better. This means we work on adaptation plans that include disaster planning not just low flow toilets. It means we talk to our leadership about investments in durable assets like renewables that are immune from impending resource shortages – and pay better anyway. It means integrating skills-based content into sustainability curriculum such as learning to weatherize low-income homes in local neighbourhoods to build resilience – and sustainability – in our communities. Resilience is not the antidote to sustainability; it's an additive.
>
> (Newport 2013: 1)

In other words, an integrated model would promote an education that questions social assumptions and efforts that to do not take into account the wellbeing of people and planet. It would also build communities that can understand, learn and adapt to change, and develop more future-facing, socially just and sustainable societies.

Roel van Raaij (2012) reminds us that the challenge for education in the context of sustainability development is to be more influential in mainstream policy agendas. The challenge, he argues, is not just to reorient our education systems or improve the reach and effectiveness of our education programmes but to embed education into our global and national frameworks; token references to the importance of education in international declarations and outcome documents is not enough.

Looking ahead, Anda Adams (2012) from the Center for Universal Education at the Brookings Institution identifies seven global frames where education needs to be a meaningful ingredient, if sustainable development is to be attained:

- ending absolute poverty;
- equity and inclusion;
- economic growth and jobs;
- getting to zero;
- global minimum entitlements;
- sustainable development; and
- wellbeing and quality of life.

These post-2015 policy platforms and the dialogues that inform their articulation may well hold the key to the building of resilient communities and societies. This new sustainable development framework will not so much replace the aims and ambitions of the Millennium Development Goals, but strategically reframe and enhance them:

> How people in different contexts around the world can be better governed and can live more prosperous, peaceful and fulfilling lives depends upon ensuring widespread opportunities for quality education and learning. As the world continues to debate the [Sustainable Development] goals and means of global development over the next three years, the requisite knowledge and skills that individuals need in order to improve their own lives and the communities around them should be a central consideration to define the global development agenda for the next generation.
>
> (Adams 2012: 23)

8 Resilience, sustainability and the utopian future

Metaphors we live by

Resilience is sometimes used as a variable and sometimes as an outcome, and occasionally both simultaneously. Resilience is also a term that is frequently used as metaphor, and the role metaphor has in shaping understanding of what sustainable development might actually mean in the practice and culture of everyday life is something that systems thinkers do not always seem to be aware of. When applied to people, to human communities, resilience invariably stands for health, survival, adaptation. A human being as a self-organising system is an abstraction rather than a description or even analysis of a lived experience. Consequently, for psychologists Fran Norris and her co-authors (Norris *et al.* 2008), human and community resilience must be understood in their own terms, free from the inherited meanings from the physical sciences. A collection of resilient individuals does not constitute a resilient community, for resilience is essentially a process of becoming and a capacity for adaptation. Resilience, understood in this way, is about recognising, learning, creating and interacting. The concept's value, like that of sustainability, is the degree to which it can act heuristically, as a motivator and inspiration for thinking differently and of doing things that can revolutionise the world and the way we engage with it. So whether resilience is an abstraction or a metaphor, its aptness must, loosely following Lakoff and Johnson (1999), address the following:

- whether it plays a constructive role in structuring experience;
- whether it has non metaphorical entailments; and
- whether it aids understanding and learning.

It will also need to prove that social and environmental justice is at its heart and the test case here will be whether all the tools, technologies, discourses, policies, strategies, technique, technology, research frameworks, campaigning, and so on, will create a positive difference for those who are most in need. That is, for those without a home, without a livelihood, without good health and without either social respect or even self-worth. Technocratic control and bureaucratic ratio-nalisation separate and isolate the various elements of the social and cultural world. They disconnect them from original contexts and only tend to emphasise their significance in relation to the bureaucratic system of management plans and strategies rather than with the wider society as a whole.

Health and wellbeing, for example, cannot be divorced from other areas of social and community life and the concept of resilience, even if it is not used explicitly can, with its systems and ecological resonance, possibly help break down conceptual, governance, and other fragmenting and disabling silos. In their study of resilience and aboriginal communities Lawrence Kirmayer and his co-authors conclude:

> Resilience depends on complex interactions within systems, including physiological and psychological processes within an individual and social, economic and political interactions between individuals and their environment, or between a community and the surrounding ecosystem and the larger society. As a result, resilience can only be understood by considering systems in their ecological and social context.
>
> In the case of communities, resilience is determined both by dynamics and by structural issues influencing access to resources, political organisation and collective efficacy.
>
> (Kirmayer *et al.* 2009: 102)

The Big Issue

Resilience is undoubtedly a big issue, and it is from *The Big Issue*, a magazine supporting the homeless published in four continents, that many lessons about resilience may be learnt. Homelessness is a serious problem in most developed and developing countries, although the incidence and extent of the phenomena is not always accurately reflected in official statistics. What is clear, though, according to the UK charity Crisis, is that since 2010 homelessness and sleeping rough is increasing.

It is clearly a problem growing in importance because at one level it is an indicator that something quite fundamental is awry with the social, economic and political arrangements of a society, and at a personal level it is invariably a harsh, debilitating, destructive and fatal experience for those directly concerned. Relationship breakdowns, domestic abuse, substance misuse, unemployment and leaving what Erving Goffman (1968) referred to as 'total' institutions such as the army, hospital, prison, asylum, etc., are frequently cited by homeless people as major turning points in their lives (Smith *et al.* 2008). The sight of people sheltering in doorways, living in cardboard boxes under railway arches or under bridges, and begging (panhandling) is complemented by the knowledge that among the homeless, not least in the wealthy countries of Europe and the North America, drug abuse, violence, prostitution, drunkenness, physical and mental deterioration are commonplace.

The illnesses homeless people are prone to are numerous, including cold injury, tuberculosis, dermatological disease, nutritional deficiencies, sleep

Figure 8.1 Homeless people sheltering in Birmingham Peace Gardens
Source: John Blewitt

deprivation, depression and other mental illnesses, alcoholism, HIV/AIDS and drug dependency. The mortality rate among homeless people is about four times higher than the general population and a homeless person can expect to live twenty fewer years than those who have homes (Daly 1996). Being without a home or having the street as one's home is a far cry from the way the writer Witold Rybczynski (1986: 66) understands 'home' for it 'connotes a physical "place" but also has the more abstract sense of a state of "being"'.

Thus the category of homelessness may include both rough sleepers and those sleeping in shelters and similar temporary accommodations, but homes, of course, are not always havens, as those who are abused or attacked in them can testify. However, few would deny that life on the streets is tough and to survive for any length of time an individual needs to have some qualities that, apart from a physical robustness, can only be described as resilience.

Penny Woolcock's 2010 documentary *On the Streets* explores the life of London's homeless – Russian army veterans destroyed by years of war, men and women physically and sexually abused as children and as adults on the streets, people who have lost their jobs and homes, who have experienced marital or other relationship break ups, others whose stories are not told and therefore not heard but which most probably equally grim. There is a soft-spoken middle-aged man with higher degrees in mathematics; a young man who travels on trains to keep warm and dry; a young woman who, having served in the Royal Engineers, joins her 'baby uncle' to live on the pavement. He robs her.

On the Streets does not delve into the problems of those homeless people who were formerly patients in psychiatric hospitals or public health clinics or their experience of what was once absurdly referred to as 'care in the community'. Disorientation is endemic, but it would be wrong to either medicalise the issue of homelessness or assume that homelessness is a factor of personal failing or inadequacy. It is a social and economic problem that is a barometer of the level and nature of compassion, fairness and justice in a society.

Cathy Come Home, Ken Loach's seminal factually based BBC television play of 1966, was instrumental in the establishment of the homeless charity Shelter, but decades later the problem persists. Homelessness remains a troubling feature of many wealthy economies (and this is to ignore the extent and experience of homelessness in India, South America, Africa and other generally poorer places).

Homeless people are frequently abused and attacked on the street (two *Big Issue* vendors were stabbed to death in Birmingham during the writing of this chapter). They are often considered to be authors of their own problems and, in an urban culture that has been increasingly shaped by an unsympathetic neoliberalism, the sight of homeless people is frequently viewed as bad for business. Many feel that they make the place look untidy and put shoppers off the all-important business of spending money.

City centre developments and related urban regeneration projects invariably focus on the needs, culture and conditions conducive for private businesses to develop and thrive. City authorities often engage in punitive measures moving homeless people away from these increasingly commodified and often formerly public areas. Existing and newly commercialised private spaces, such as shopping malls, are tightly policed with undesirables excluded and/or chastised (Kohn 2004; Beckett and Herbert 2009). Some city politicians have spoken of the homeless as being 'the enemies within' and the need to 'cleanse' the city of this human detritus (Mitchell 1997; MacLeod 2002).

For Kohn (2004) this is a serious issue, for not only are the civil rights of homeless people being compromised by such action, but citizens generally will have less opportunity to encounter, consider and perhaps understand homeless people. This diminution and commercial sanitisation of urban inter-subjectivity breeds fear, suspicion and segregation. As Kohn (2004: 8) writes, 'without exposure to deprivation or even difference, the privileged become unable to recognise their own advantages and unlikely to question a system that produces systematic disadvantage'.

Such spaces cease to become the democratic experience of collective responsibility described by geographer Edward Soja (2010) in his work on spatial justice. The socially marginalised become spatially marginalised so that out of sight becomes out of mind, and when in sight become targets for public opprobrium, but for Stephen Robertson, group chief executive of the homeless organisation *The Big Issue* (BI), the problems are twofold: the privatisation of space, and the lack of public support and public accommodation for those who need to get off the streets:

> There are a couple of issues for me. One is the bright shiny new shopping centres, wherever they are. These are private land and in a very simplistic Big Issue world you can sell a publication unchallenged in the streets of our country without a street trader's license but not in the shopping centres.

This means that a big redevelopment of a town centre by private landowners will prevent homeless people from accessing all of those people who drive to them in their cars, park within the centre and never go out until they get back in their cars and leave. The landlords will of course be sympathetic to homelessness issues but unfortunately their tenants who have paid shed loads of money to be there really don't want homeless people upsetting their customers. In terms or urban regeneration and housing, there still remains enough housing for everyone in our country but for those people who have fallen out of the system the ways back into it are incredibly complex and some homeless people may even need to go through a programme to enable them to live indoors. In getting funding for accommodation suitable for these homeless people you are really pushing a rock up a hill.

(Robertson 2012)

Figure 8.2 Privatisation of urban space, central London
Source: John Blewitt

The Big Issue is a social enterprise. It aims to put at least some of the many marginalised, dispossessed and homeless people back on their feet. Set up in 1991 in London initially as a charity by John Bird with the assistance of Gordon and Anita Roddick of The Body Shop, it adopted and adapted the street newspaper concept first pioneered in the United States with *Street News*. Homeless people would purchase copies of the magazine from the wholesaler and then sell it on the streets to members of the public. The vendors directly benefit from the sales, generate a modest income with which they can purchase their own food and accommodation and in the process hopefully avoid being stigmatised as beggars. As Stephen Robertson believes, the BI organisation and the paper is a bridge between philanthropy and self-help. It helps develops autonomy, skill, confidence and self-respect. Vendors are in effect running micro economic enterprises but this does not prevent sellers from being verbally or physically victimised. Indeed, there is some evidence to suggest that because of their visibility BI vendors are more likely to be harassed than those homeless people who are less visible and the issues is compounded because homeless people do not always report attacks and the police do not always recognise them as victims of crime and disorder. More frequently they are perceived as being the perpetrators of it (Scurfield *et al.* 2009).

Neither does it mean that every BI vendor is able to move on and get back fully into the mainstream, return to family and community life. Both Stephen Robertson and Tessa Swithinbank (2001) in her book *Coming up from the Streets* acknowledge that selling *The Big Issue* is not a long-term or satisfactory career option, although it can, to some extent, salvage the self and help develop some personal resilience. Interestingly, in Stephen Robertson's experience the word 'resilience' is rarely if ever used by street people or BI workers and volunteers.

> Given the people we work with we are very careful to avoid professional language or language that might be associated with the homelessness sector. *Big Issue* sellers are 'vendors'. We do not call them clients although if you go to pretty much any other homeless organisation or hostel that homeless persons, you will be called a 'client'. We don't have a needs assessment. We don't talk about people as being 'needy'. We talk to people about who they are, what they want to do, in a very everyday language. We don't therefore use the word 'resilience' but in terms of getting people up and going resilience is critical. When we first encounter people they are frequently at the point of utmost crisis and they just want some money. But the proposition we offer them, when you think about it, is a face to face sales job. You buy a product and then you try and convince other people to purchase it from you so you can make a profit. That actual process is incredibly tough. Getting the public to cross that physical and psychological divide to put £2.50 in your hand is one hell of a big step for homeless people to take. The amounts of setbacks you'll experience as a vendor are immense.
>
> (Robertson 2012)

BI is also about reclaiming citizenship and the right to the city. Homelessness often comes with a personal sense of inadequacy, shame, vulnerability, loss of social worth and even ridiculousness. In his revealing personal account of being homeless and a BI seller, James Bowen, in his unexpected bestseller *A Street Cat Named Bob*, writes of being frequently be abused, ignored and reviled:

> Living on the streets of London strips away your dignity, your identity – your everything, really. Worst of all it strips away people's opinion of you. They see you are living on the streets and treat you as a non-person. They don't want anything to do with you. Soon you haven't got a friend in the world. While I was sleeping rough I managed to get a job working as a kitchen porter. But they sacked me when they found out I was homeless, even though I'd done nothing wrong at work. When you are homeless you really stand very little chance.
>
> (Bowen 2012: 33)

What helped Bowen was discovering a cat (Bob), who provided company and companionship. Bob also attracted people's attention. They asked Bowen whether they could photograph or stroke the animal. In return they would buy the *Big Issue*, perhaps revealing how animals in the city constitute part of the metropolis's living systems and an important element in the moral economy of urban social relationships. They invite others, sometimes, to return a certain humanity to disadvantaged people whose own self-esteem and with psychological resilience have been compromised. As the sociologist Thomas Scheff (1988) has shown, we often see and evaluate ourselves through the eyes of others and through a prism of social and cultural values that associates self-worth with material wellbeing.

In their study of homeless young people in New York and Toronto, Kidd and Davidson (2007) explored how homelessness leads to a painful struggle for self-definition, of self-value, of retrieving a sense of meaning and connection with others. An individual's worldview is often key to establishing a capability to survive, to cope and be resilient. Part of this may lead to a process of adaption that involves the development of a homeless self-identity, a closer affiliation with other homeless people and the culture of homelessness, and less engagement with those public or third sector services whose role has been to help. Homelessness has a seriously corrosive effect on a person's self-esteem and wellbeing which serves to re-emphasise the importance of those schemes and actions that rebuild the self and enable more or less normal human social interactions to occur, to recover their diminished rights as a citizen.

Those people who purchase the magazine tend to do so because they wish to help people help themselves. As well as wanting to do something to relieve homelessness purchasers value the idea that the magazine empowers through providing employment rather than charity although many purchasers are influenced in their decision to purchase by how needy a vendor looks (Hibbert *et al.* 2005). The magazine itself, currently selling at £2.50 and after a number of revamps, has good production values, publishes high-quality journalism and arts reviews, carries advertising, but most importantly provides a voice for the homeless who frequently contribute copy directly to it. Even though only four of the forty-eight pages of a standard issue may be allocated to the writing of homeless or ex-homeless people, BI is one of very few spaces where their voices can be heard.

Magallanes-Blanco and Pérez-Bermúdez (2009) have shown that the political empowerment of homeless people through street publications depends on them having just such a space where their voice is a presence and not an absence. When this occurs, economic developments that exclude or prevent homeless people from enjoying particular spaces or places are, at least implicitly, put under some scrutiny, and a form of communicative democracy is created (Howley 2003). In this context, the BI organisation occasionally produces films such as the twenty-minute short *The Truth About Stanley*, directed by Lucy Tcherniak. Made by the Oscar-winning Trademark film company for distribution on the internet to raise public awareness about homelessness and funding for the Big

Issue Foundation and the east London hostel Anchor House, the film features veteran African actor Oliver Litondo, who, in an interview with *The Guardian*, said he wanted people in Africa and the West to see *Stanley* because life in the developed world is not always good, or 'better'. A refugee can experience turmoil in the UK as well as in the Congo (McVeigh 2012).

For Stephen Robertson (2012), the film, available on the BI website and YouTube, is stimulating significant interest among young people about the embedded cultural prejudices against and the negative stereotyping of homeless people. 'It is part of a bigger movement which says think differently, think twice' (Robertson 2012). One aspect of this bigger movement of changing minds and perceptions is working with some financial organisations which have been willing to address homelessness and mental health issues as part of their corporate social responsibility engagement. The BI's 'Lend a Day' scheme require corporate employees to work as closely with homeless people as BI workers and volunteers do themselves. For a few hours those normally involved in selling financial products work alongside a BI vendor and attempt to sell the magazine on the street.

> They get to know their vendor and they have a very different experience on the street to what they are familiar with. It's a very vendor driven engagement activity but is very transformational. We have been working with a major high street bank in London and their sales staff has effectively been having sales training from homeless people. They think they are pretty good at selling but you stick them in a tabard and give them a big issue to sell, they learn they are not as good as they thought they were. The outputs: the vendors like it because they become the trainer for the day, they have this company with them, they're helping bankers or lawyers learn a few skills on the street which is very empowering. It has got this sort of emotional punch, a reality check for the people who engage with it, that makes them feel incredibly different. It literally transforms people in the course of six or seven hours.
>
> (Robertson 2012)

Transformative learning is invariably experiential, perspective shifting and deeply felt. It can sometimes have deep roots into a feeling, or sense of being human, and perhaps a wider cultural dignity that, as German philosopher Jürgen Habermas (2010) writes, has connotations that depend on the social recognition of a certain status (i.e. the status of democratic citizenship). With this social recognition comes self-respect, but self-respect is itself dependent on the universal nature of democratic citizenship where citizenship infers that everyone are subjects of equal actionable rights. As Mitchell writes:

> The rights of homeless people do not matter (when in competition with 'our' rights to order, comfort, places for relaxation, recreation, and unfettered shopping) simply because we work hard to convince ourselves that homeless people are not really citizens in the sense of free agents with sovereignty over

their own actions. Anti-homeless legislation helps institutionalize this conviction by assuring the homeless in public no place to be sovereign.

(Mitchell 1997: 320–1)

Interestingly, public libraries remain among of the few spaces of care open to homeless people. They are more common than day centres, are accessible to everyone, are not stigmatised places like the homeless shelter and as such they can mitigate against social marginalisation by offering opportunities for interaction with other members of the community. Although some people may argue that homeless people have no right to the library because they encroach upon the legitimate activities of other library users (Cronin 2002), many professional librarians do not seem to share this view.

Anne Hannaford, director of the first combined university–civic library in the UK, The Hive at Worcester, says that homeless people are welcome in the new £45 million multifaceted and multimedia public space so long as they, like others, do not behave in a disruptive manner. A local by-law prevents homeless people legitimately using the space to sleep but there seems to be no problem with users gently dozing off in front of a book (A. Hannaford, 2012, personal communication). To question the legitimacy of their presence is to reinforce the stigma too often conveyed through the press and broadcasting news media. The Hive building also hosts a local authority advice and guidance centre offering a great deal of important information of benefit to homeless people and as Willett and Broadley (2011) conclude, public libraries in the UK generally engage in a considerable amount of outreach work with homeless people. The library consequently is a shared civic space that cultivates a sense of belonging, a contemporary version of the commons, a living room in the city, where everyone has the right to be. In a public library a homeless person is a citizen:

> For homeless people to inhabit prime public places successfully, even when they go largely unnoticed, is to become citizens. To be denied access to such places is to be denied citizenship and to be positioned as non members of the public . . . In the library, a homeless person who engages with others, and especially with librarians, constructs a place that not only has particular meanings for space, but also for identity. Librarians who intercede on behalf of homeless people traverse spaces that the universal narrative would separate; they also transgress the identity to which authorities would have them adhere.
>
> (Hodgetts *et al.* 2008: 950–1)

As economic austerity and public expenditure cuts take hold the concept of resilience has become an increasingly common term in public policy discourse. Individuals and communities are frequently presented as authors of their own resilience and self-reliance which, of course, conveniently shifts attention away from the decline in public service delivery and the role of the state at local and national level. Individual and collective capacities for creativity and entrepreneurship are what will provide an appropriate and democratic response to social and economic crises, pecuniary hardship and loss of social entitlement. Indeed, research by the Young Foundation has shown individuals and communities can certainly be self-activating, dynamic and resilient and even without the formerly supportive and protective mechanisms of the state do not descend into despair, resignation and passivity.

But people do tire, do move on, and do sometimes lose interest and motivation. Community-based initiatives are not always autonomously driven perpetual motion machines. Strong networks and communities may provide a great deal of security and consistency but there remains a role for external and local state agencies too because many individuals may not have the necessary social capital to be part of such a collective. No individual or community is an island, and resilience is essentially derived from a whole range of social, economic and environmental relationships. For the Young Foundation (Mguni and Caistor-Arendar 2012), resilience refers to energising those dormant capacities which may bring about positive and transformative change. The Foundation has developed its own Wellbeing and Resilience Measure (WARM), whereby community resilience can be assessed and measured according to three specific but related scales:

- *Self:* the way people feel about their own lives
- *Support:* the quality of social supports and networks within the community
- *Structure and systems:* the strength of the infrastructure and environment to support people to achieve their aspirations and live a good life.

Further research by the New Economics Foundation (NEF 2012a, 2012b) shows that public expenditure cuts put immense pressure on charities and other third sector bodies and this is in turn negatively impacting on the wellbeing and resilience of deprived and disadvantaged communities. Inequalities are widening and anti-social behaviour increasing with private sector market based solutions favoured by many governments in Europe and elsewhere to poverty, inequality and homeless only exacerbating the problems.

NEF's research in Birmingham (UK) indicated that the involvement of large private sector providers often created distrust among voluntary groups and the wider community. Subcontractors, invariably small local charities, were often not paid adequately and because these companies were motivated by profit they showed little interest adding little social value to the communities they were operating within. In addition, many places are able to bring people together, where informal, creative and supportive initiatives are frequently based, are being closed down.

Given this, it is important to analyse the wider ideological discourse within which the term resilience is so liberally used. Resilience often has connotations that relate more to the imperatives of a political ideology and public relations exercise than to ecologically influenced systems theory. The resilience dynamic within academic discourse, processes of public policy formation and implementation and the actual lived experience of living and working in an unequal market society needs to be scrutinised critically, diligently and persistently.

Critique, ideology and resilience

In capitalist societies, success is measured by wealth, and wealth is understood in terms of earning power, ownership of high status consumer goods, position in the social hierarchy and the capability of exercising economic, political and symbolic power. Wealth is also about consumption and being a consumer, which is why being homeless and workless, or selling the *Big Issue* (which for many amounts to the same thing), can be so damaging. Being a consumer in a society where freedom and democracy is expressed in terms of the market means being a citizen. Wealth understood in terms of the quality of joy and pleasure experienced is seen as either part of the 'alternative' discourse on living and sustainability or a feature the elusive work-life balance mindset.

As Franco Berardi (2009) argues in his radical critique *Soul at Work*, wealth simply means having the means – money, credit, power – to consume. Wealth understood as enjoyment has decreased proportionately as wealth as economic accumulation has become dominant and this in turn fuels the need, and desire, to work to consume. For Berardi this has meant a progressive impoverishment of human social life and a re-articulation of the concept 'enterprise' away from the Renaissance humanistic meaning of transforming the world, of nature and one's relation to it, to just going into business and investing one's very self, one's imagination and feeling, in the process of production, value creation and profit. Control over the labour process is now control over the soul that which animates, gives life to, human beings. Work is globalised, fragmented spatially and temporarily and recombined in an endless network of human and material flows.

An individual's entire lived day is spent within the social factory, both consuming and producing, or both. Capital buys packets of time and neoliberalism has quite successfully sought to construct an anthropological model of *Homo economicus* where an individual's own good has become indistinguishable from economic interest. Thus, happiness is a matter of ideology for the free market works not only to democratise human needs but to maximise the general potential for these needs to be happily fulfilled through the consumption of goods, anti-depressant drugs and self-help books on stress management, leadership, personal growth and resilience:

> No desire, no vitality seems to exist anymore outside the economic enterprise, outside productive labor and business. Capital was able to renew its psychic, ideological and economic energy, specifically thanks to the absorption of creativity, desire, and individualistic, libertarian drives for self-realisation.
>
> (Berardi 2009: 96)

Freedom means deregulation of the capitalist economy, wealth creation, competition and bouncing back. Failure is not a systemic attribute, but something to bounce back from. Social norms, as articulated graphically in pop psychology, are in some ways psycho-pathological, for they 'cannot acknowledge the norm of failure without questioning its own ideological fundaments, and even its own economic efficiency' (Berardi 2009: 100). Precariousness is the true transformative element in social and economic life. Wage rates are lowered, permanent contracts an illusion, and instability and change are constants we must all learn to thrive upon. Coercion is embedded in these social relations. For Berardi:

> The real wealthy of the future will be those who will succeed in creating forms of autonomous consumption, mental models of needs reduction, habitat models for the sharing of indispensable resources. This requires the creation of dissipative wealth refrains or of frugal and ascetic wealth.
>
> (Berardi 2009: 142)

And, everything is speeding up – technology is expanding into cyberspace irrespective of the individual human brain's limited capacity. Information and communication is continually expanding too and competition and survival depends on the constant overloading of information – the signs and symbols which are the work of the symbolic analysts, the new precariat, or cognitariat, class. The information superhighway of the 1980s and 1990s has produced an information glut rather than a learning society, a fairer workplace or a greener knowledge economy.

So yoga classes may help restore a sense of personal wellbeing and build up an individual's resilience to stress at the workplace, but they won't deal with the system-wide problem (Hartfiel *et al.* 2011).

The link between redistributive social policies, democratic citizenship, meaningful work and spaces and places for discussion and learning, needs to be thoroughly rethought. There is a need for a radical transformation in the way we see and understand the world. If a number of our existing practices, conceptions and indeed ethical perceptions are failing then we clearly need to look into the future but in a way that does not tie us to the all too familiar with business as usual model.

For Simon Slater, the current economic model is clearly not working, 'but in terms of what a more sustainable economy looks like, I haven't really seen a convincing one yet' (Slater 2012). Until this future can be delineated with some degree of confidence, hope and recognition individuals, groups and organisations will continue to seek ways to deal with the symptoms of system failure rather than its cause. We need, perhaps, a new reality principle, an ethic of care and a method of understanding that does not simply soothe the iniquities of our lived experience – domination, exploitation, destruction, and homelessness.

Unfortunately, despite the evident need for systemic change, and paradigm shifts in thought and action, the campaigner George Monbiot (2001) does have a point when he remarks that proposals that require a complete transformation in the human condition is little more than a refined form of despair. However, the recognition that the world has to be in some way rebuilt and reconstituted is also a measure of the immensity and intensity of the problems we face. For

Franco Berardi (2009: 193), 'we need to rethink politics according to the metaphorical possibilities of a bioinformatics models' for networks are clearly able to direct and organise energies and information in a most functional way.

Resilience will be part of this, but resilience thinking is not necessarily an approach that automatically, logically or emotionally, suggests transformative change although change is clearly part of the discourse. We certainly know where we are but we may not necessarily be as clear as to where we want to go and how to get there. Two decades of sustainable development have been two decades of practical compromise and deep disappointment. Perhaps this is partly a result of a utopian impulse among its supporters and promoters or perhaps it is a result of the utopian impulse not being strong enough, not being fully, sufficiently, persuasively or powerfully articulated. Compromise and pragmatism allows such notions as resilient dynamism to mask business as usual.

In such a vacuum, space is filled by other things. There is no shortage of self-help books, executive coaches, business gurus, popular psychologists, politicians, community workers, conservationists talking about and preaching resilience. The term mushroomed as the global economy went into hyperdrive and then into rapid decline, as the desire and addiction to material consumption and consumerism led to a further fracturing of the global ecosystem and, particularly, as the ideology of hard work was accompanied by increases in redundancy, worklessness, poverty, ill health, risk, uncertainty and insecurity. As the power of positive thinking traded realism for delusion, the bouncing back professional optimists churned out their seven-point or ten-point plans for resilience in the face of continuing adversity.

The popular psychology and politics of Dale Carnegie's *How to Win Friends and Influence People* (Carnegie 2006), originally published in 1936, has unashamedly returned. Always look on the bright side of things. *Forbes* magazine has published its own ten ways to avoid burnout, for its mainly business readers (Lancaster 2011); the Internet site Ivestopedia has published its own 'top ten' ways for corporate financiers to avoid burnout; and there is similar guidance for church leaders and virtually every other stressed sector of society.

In fact, business gurus seem to have taken to resilience with some relish. 'Resilience is a hot topic in business these days', writes Diane Coutu (2002: 47) in an article for the *Harvard Business Review* published shortly after the 11 September 2001 terrorist attacks on the Twin Towers in New York. An important element of resilience is the ability to understand or develop meaning from what might be stressful or inexplicable. The work of the Austrian psychologist and Auschwitz survivor Viktor E. Frankl on meaning therapy and humanist therapy techniques, together with his 1959 book *Man's Search for Meaning* (Frankl 1997), has been highly influential in resilient coaching for business executives. For Coutu (2002: 55), 'resilient people and companies face reality with staunchness, make meaning of hardship instead of crying out in despair, and improvise solutions from thin air'.

Improvising solutions from thin is air is probably more difficult to do than to write. More prosaically perhaps, Clarke and Nicholson (2010) advise that resilient people rarely experience envy, and can harness the power of emotion but remain immune from its negative effects. Their research and their scientific questionnaire, administered to a number of highly resilient people top places in business, government, law, media, finance and higher education, indicated that resilience is about conveniently ignoring logical contradictions: that in thinking of others it is always important to think of yourself, to avoid making comparisons with others while acknowledging that identity and self-esteem are intimately informed by an individual's relationship with others, that having a positive mental attitude is the key to success, health and wisdom irrespective of circumstances.

Compassion is an important part of the psychological mix making up resilience, according to Clarke and Nicholson, but compassion features very little in their *Resilience: Bounce Back from Whatever Life Throws at You* for it is competition, being competitive and learning from failure that will give you the edge and enable you to compete again and this time succeed. 'Resilient people recognize that failure and disappointment are often stepping stones to success' (Clarke and Nicholson 2010: 29). Resilient people have self-esteem 'permanently on tap' and if by any chance a resilient person loses their employment, their home, their partner, their livelihood or career, they do not blame external circumstances but look deeply into the dark cloud to pull out that silver lining replete with opportunities for change, growth and advancement.

Such optimism breeds contentment, and resilient people are able to 'grow' their self-esteem like parsley in a pot. Resilient people are optimists who believe 'that things are getting better all the time' (Clarke and Nicholson 2010: 49). And so, this discourse on resilience and optimism perhaps also conveniently deflects attention away from the policy and economic system failures, the greed and hubris of business and political elites, that are responsible for both the origins and experience of the present ongoing ecological and economic crisis. By suggesting that criticism, despondency and disappointment is wrong, maybe even a psychological inadequacy or failing, it becomes easier to promote simply more of the same as remedies – more deregulation, more cuts, more exploitation, more ecological destruction, more economic growth, more resilient people, more business leaders, more discipline, and more incentives such as tax cuts for the rich and benefit cuts for the poor (Ehrenreich 2010).

Resilient people are successful, but success here is defined as success in working and living within a marketised, unsustainable, competitive, unequal, iniquitous and exploitative society. Resilient people are self-regarding people; they compete with others and themselves; they are positive and effectively selfish; self-criticism is a motivator for successful action, a competence and a 'belief that they can tackle pretty much anything life throws at them' (Clarke and Nicholson 2010: 47).

Co-operation, or rather collaboration, is also means of being successful, of winning, of realising that edge but is not a good or value in itself. For writers like Clarke and Nicholson, resilience is not about interpreting the world and certainly not changing the world, but learning how to get as much out of it as possible for you.

As such, *Resilience* (the book) and resilience (the concept) seem to be the perfect mood music to those neo-liberal ideologies and practices that have deformed and destroyed so much. It is this understanding of resilience and indeed of learning that needs to be confronted, critiqued, contested and unlearnt. Metaphors here are used carelessly in an unlabelled manner. If taken literally they are likely to preclude higher and deeper levels of learning – learning to learn, learning to critique – that enable a person to distinguish between, and communicate, different logical types in a non-falsifying manner. It is always valuable to see the joke, and to see a joke *as* a joke, a devastating experience as a devastating experience, and not necessarily a great God-given opportunity to re-enter the dragon's den. A ball bounces, a human being gets splattered. As Gregory Bateson (2000) saw it human beings use context as a guide for mode discrimination but there is another danger. What if the context itself seems to have little bearing on what could possibly be real? Competition is presented within the dominant value syntax of capitalist neo-liberalism as the key to personal and professional success, a dynamic and prosperous economy, health and vitality and to human progress itself.

Chris Johnstone is another expert in the psychology of resilience and a consultant offering a wide range of learning opportunities, training courses, advice and guidance to those who feel the need. The titles of his books clearly indicate that resilience will be found in and by the individual. *Find Your Power: A Toolkit for Resilience and Positive Change* (Johnstone 2010) presents the individual as the main focus of attention but this individual also needs to be immersed in an alternate philosophy, a world view and cultural *mentality*, that is at variance with the competitive and possessive individualism of neoliberalism. Much of Johnstone's value-based approach is drawn from Deep Ecology, and his work has been endorsed by the leading figure in the Transition movement, Rob Hopkins. In his books and succinctly in an article for *Permaculture Magazine* (Johnstone 2006) he identifies his own ten strategies to avoid burnout:

- *Value yourself as a resource*: permaculture is about conscious design to conserve and regenerate the earth's resources. If you recognise and value yourself as one such resource, you can then apply the principles of permaculture design to your life.
- *Recognise the risk*: if you're aware of the risk, you can take steps to reduce it.
- *Self-monitoring*: problems that develop slowly are often more difficult to recognise.
- *Identify hotspots*: complete the sentence 'The times I feel most under stress are when...'.
- *Commitment cropping*: like a hedge that needs to be cut back from time to time, our commitments need regular review and pruning to prevent overload.
- *Feed the soil (or the emotional bank balance)*: if you are constantly giving out your time, energy and attention, you also need to have equal measures of nourishment coming back in.

- *Companion planting:* some plants grow better with company. Relationships of mutual encouragement and support can help bring out the best in yourself and others around you.
- *Review your experience of success and failure:* failures and disappointments can be great sources of learning, but they still suck!
- *Crop rotation with fallow periods:* fallow periods allow for soil renewal. We can apply the same principle in burnout prevention – having times when we're not expecting ourselves to be productive is good for personal sustainability.
- *Grow the crops you most want to grow:* follow your enthusiasms, desires and dreams.

There are certainly lessons here for sustainability professionals who in order to make progress will constantly work with others in partnership, deal with obfuscations, the political vagaries of policy making and the ideological applications of terms such as sustainability, conservation and resilience in ways they are uncomfortable with. Director of Sustainability West Midlands, a third sector body working at both strategic and operational levels, Simon Slater (2012) has a wealth of experience in a variety of sectors:

> There is a tendency in sustainability professionals to see what they are doing as a vocation. They believe in what they are doing because they want to make a difference in the world and that sometimes tends to attract a particular type of personality and that personality can be prone to be isolated. They try to push things forwards without taking people with them and burn out. This is no different from civil rights or any other type of campaigning vocational type role. The challenge for the professional is trying to work out how many other people you can take with you to make their own change rather than seeing it as a solo effort. It's important to be challenged and inspired by other people. I need to be with others to be motivated, to get out and hear different people to be inspired but at the same time keep a reasonable attitude.
>
> (Slater 2012)

Recognition is important here too for witnessing others doing the same, or similar things, provides a sense of community, of interest and of practice, and an affirmation of status. This concern for maintaining and feeding personal resilience was something that all our interviewees acknowledged. Motivation, inspiration and recognition may be derived from all sorts of significant others. For Stephen Robertson (2012), it is about seeing and enabling the *Big Issue* vendors regain their own respect and self-esteem often emerging from the darkest of places society and the individual psyche can offer. For another interviewee, resilience was about being deluded, believing that sustainability practitioners could make a difference.

For another interviewee it was recognising that 'we are not suddenly going to be in a situation where we are in paradise and that we are engaged in activities that are in some ways about minimising rather than eliminating problems.' For another it was joining a community farm and realising that in having to get the cows back into their winter quarters you had to think about other creatures and their immediate needs rather than the cares of the world. For yet another, it was learning Spanish, or experiencing a buzz – a taste of the future and you see that another world might actually be possible, finding the whole challenge of sustainability and working with others absolutely fascinating, recognising that sustainability does not mean reinventing the wheel that there are models in the past and present that can be adapted for the future.

For many interviewees what was important was envisioning a future than is better than the present but one that is also practically possible. For all of them, resilience meant being part of something larger – a belief, a community, a movement, a hope, an intention, a will, an action, a practice. It meant being and working with others, human and non-human, connecting with self and nature. Technology works to exclude spontaneity and personal creativity. It sometimes becomes a replacement for the absence of appropriate social and political action, as the Royal Society (2009) intimated when it concluded that geo-engineering projects may be a useful complement to other mitigation and adaptation activities if they are safe and cost-effective. Nevertheless, as the Schumacher Institute argues (Harris 2012), technology has become an element of human resilience and will undoubtedly contribute to the search for sustainability solutions.

For French philosopher and theologian Jacues Ellul (1964), 'technology' should also be read as 'technique' (i.e. all those processes, methods and ways of thought that privilege rationality, efficiency, systematisation and discourse). Technique empties life of meaning, spiritual fulfilment and moral value. Technology becomes an end in itself, autonomous of human endeavour, a sublimation and retreat from self and nature. Ellul sees technology as eliminating or subordinating the natural world, preventing it from restoring itself. Technology and nature have become symbiotic even though the two worlds have little if anything in common. They both obey different laws, different imperatives and different directives. 'We are rapidly approaching the time when there will be no longer any natural environment at all. When we succeed in producing artificial *aurorae boreales*, night will disappear and perpetual day will reign over the planet', the philosopher writes (Ellul 1964: 79).

Technology may itself become an article of faith which when combined with faith in scientific ingenuity frequently works to close off debate certainly with regards the timescales of sustainable development (Hoyer and Naess 2008). Technology is not the answer by any means as many of our interviewees suggested; or if it is, then only as part of a balanced approach that also allows for spontaneity and personal creativity. Technology has to be practical and like work and consumption, meaningful and responsible, human scale.

Sustainability, resilience and the utopian method

Israeli defence and security specialist Dr Rachel Suissa has been specifically interested in the preventive connotations of the term resilience. She sees the disciplines of psychology and psychiatry as tending to explore the pathological whereas from the organisational perspective she is largely concerned with, and particularly that of the military, what is important for Suissa is what is healthy (Suissa 2012). For her, one problem with the psychological approach to resilience is that it is too reductive, emphasising emotional and related factors without taking due notice of cognitive ones. Sometimes an organisation, a society, an economic system, a military unit even, can lose its resilience because of what she terms the emergence of 'a cognitive disconnection or dissonance'. This may have nothing to do with people's emotional states. They may simply disagree with what is happening and this dissonance may be caused by a wide range of interacting factors operating with the system as a whole.

For example, a soldier is also a citizen, maybe an urbanite, certainly a human, and almost inevitably a social being. A worker will be a citizen, a lover, a home owner, an environmentalist, a business person, an environmentalist, perhaps even homeless, and so on. Resilience therefore needs to be viewed and approached holistically and when it is not or when resilience is wedded too firmly to something that is intrinsically unfair, undemocratic, exploitative, arbitrary or tyrannical, then the concept becomes basically negative.

However, echoing Thomas Homer-Dixon (2006), there is an upside to this down. This perceived 'negative resilience' may lead to a clearer understanding of what constitutes the positive. During the interview Rachel Suissa (2012) used the term 'ideal type', but equally this positive resilience could refer to a utopian future, a cleaner environment, a regenerative city, a pleasant home, decent work, self-respect and social recognition, a restored natural habitat, a rich biodiversity and so on. This is the upside of down, though it also requires an understanding of where to draw the metaphorical, and actual, line – this and no more. Even if the assessment and evaluation of risks and vulnerabilities are incomplete, knowledge uncertain and emotions frayed, there needs to be a recognition that resilience itself can only be positive if the system itself is an ethically and, in other ways, desirable one. In terms of sustainable development this will entail multidisciplinary, multi professional and participatory learning, essential democratic processes and sociocultural and biological diversity. Neither neoliberalism nor an obsession with economic growth, competition, monopoly and bouncing back will achieve this.

So, what of the future? On returning from a visit to the Soviet Union in the early 1920s, the American 'muckraking' journalist, Lincoln Steffens, famously remarked in the heat of revolutionary fervour that he had seen the brave new world. 'I have seen the future, and it works', he cried. As the history of the twentieth century so eloquently testifies, the future did not work but it is incumbent upon us today to ensure that the future actually does. There needs to be a rearticulation of the notion of wealth, work, happiness, purpose. There needs to be some more dancing in the streets whether understood literally and metaphorically, individually or collectively (Ehrenreich 2006). We must envision real utopias and create them.

The sustainability discourse has a genuine mobilising utopian potential that, as Drago Kos (2012) observes, goes beyond scenario analysis, conflict resolution and thought exercises. Utopianism is inherently practical and political. For social scientist Ruth Levitas (2010: 540), 'utopia may be understood as the expression of the desire for a better way of being or of living'. Utopian writing offers a reasonably holistic description of an alternative future, which is what drew the urbanist Lewis Mumford to the concept in his first full-length book (Mumford 1922). There is a connectedness in the best utopian writing, as William Morris demonstrated in his *News from Nowhere* (Morris [1890] 2003), where work, art, social relations, space and human happiness clearly shape each other. For Morris, utopian writing aimed to educate both hope and desire, while providing an argument for conditions that would make this new world a possibility.

Utopianism is therefore a method rather than a description of an end point, a goal. It is an imaginative reconstitution of the world, of a better society. For Levitas, this method consists of three modes:

- *archaeological* – a piecing together of a coherent political analysis and commentary on what is occurring and what their implications are, for example, of resource depletion and global warming on everyday life;
- *architectural* – a reimagining of what an alternative future might look like, of what constitutes wealth, rethinking production, work and growth, promoting equality and making sustainability central; and
- *ontological* – a reimagining of ourselves as well as our society as being other than it is. Current discussions of wellbeing and resilience are themselves ontological excursions, and the utopian method is simply another.

In this context, the work of radical thinker Roberto Unger is instructive, for Unger (2007) suggests that we do not really need to imagine ourselves as being radically different, but only slightly different, if we are to open up new possibilities. His approach is that of a 'radicalised pragmatism'. The Transition movement is full of 'ordinary people' working out an alternative future for themselves. The idea is that we can get there incrementally; we can widen those cracks within the existing system and refuse to reproduce them, refuse to live and work the way we do.

Similarly, co-operatives are now operating in many spheres, such as food production and distribution, industrial production, retail, housing, finance and energy, offering paths away from a growth-based free market model of development (Lewis and Conaty 2012). In Denmark, energy co-operatives have succeeded in rural and urban areas working with local governments and businesses in building resilience, cutting costs and cutting carbon while at the same time fashioning democratic networks.

Denmark is now perhaps the most energy-secure country in the world (Conaty 2011), and energy co-operatives are making significant impacts elsewhere. As Birmingham-based environmental activist and consultant Phil Beardmore said:

> Anything that reduces dependence on fossil fuels or relocalizes the economy is implicitly building resilience. Some of the stuff I do is about developing local supply chains. Seven or eight years ago I started to encourage social

enterprises and co-operatives in Birmingham and there was a market delivery energy efficiency programmes. I have also worked for SME [small private businesses] installers. Being resilient is about having mutually interdependent networks of people. The common-sense view of the world that it is 'dog eat dog' is based upon a metaphor which is completely false because dogs don't generally eat each other unless there are conditions of starvation. Under normal circumstances dogs are pack animals, they co-operate just like humans...People like to see that things work particularly if it is outside their everyday experience. You can never just convince people through argument. They need to see things work, like loft insulation, from people like them, people they have something in common with interns of geography, class or whatever.

(Beardmore 2012)

Locally based co-operative groups and organisations create this 'something in common' together with a sense of solidarity, possibility and value, which is why for 'the co-operative business model is unparalleled as a way of empowering people, entrepreneurs and customers, to meet a common environmental, social or economic goal and earn a good living in an ethical way' (Beardmore 2012). This utopianism, this radicalised pragmatism, creates spaces of hope. For Levitas (2007: 301–302), utopian thinking 'is the only feasible way of taking responsibility for the future of the planet'.

Figure 8.3 Occupy movement: thinking differently, Finsbury Square, London
Source: John Blewitt

Sustainable development is as much about time as it is about connectedness. It is holistic and also intergenerational. Sustainability advocates continually say we must all think of the people who will come after us. Our economic system is plundering and polluting the future, and although economically it is possible to discount the future, to render present actions harmless and virtually cost-free, nuclear waste will last for millennia, and genetic engineering parasitically and simultaneously borrows from the deep past and the deep future. But time is also money. It is traded and traversed, measured, used and organised like labour, like work. The type of future we want, and do not want, needs to be placed under severe scrutiny as we experiment with new forms of direct democracy and openly free debate, as many in the Occupy movement argued. The link between money and time, income and work, needs to be severed.

However, whatever we do, time will be of the essence. Barbara Adam writes:

> Just as the work of the majority of the world's people is air-brushed out of the globalised capitalist system of exchange, so the impact on future generations and fellow species is rendered invisible and irrelevant by the temporal strategies that form an integral part of the modern capitalist way of doing business and playing the global market. From the above we can glean that in industrial societies today the present is transcended and the future as last frontier colonised with enduring things, belief systems and institutions, with cultural and technological products, with insurance and economic practices. As such, the future is pursued, prospected, produced, polluted. It is thus traversed in the dual sense of being travelled' and negated.
>
> (Adam 2006: 125)

We are responsible for actions to and for the future. Our responsibility exceeds the lifetime of individuals because, as Adam says, we extend ourselves into the future by what we do in the present, the technologies we use and what we leave behind.

For Adam (2012), the temporal reach of our responsibilities must be consonant with the temporal reach of our actions. We have an ecological time-print as well as an ecological footprint. We need to work through the challenges and implications of these extended responsibilities and this will only occur when we have initiated the necessary paradigm shift in thought and action.

Resilience thinkers Brian Walker and David Salt (2012) would undoubtedly concur, for resilience is not only about how long a time a socio-ecological system may take to return, but whether it actually can. We are not there yet, and the concept of resilience may not get us there either. In their analysis of the new empire, Michael Hardt and Antonio Negri (2000) suggest the current world order is one where compromise and accommodation falls far short of the radical, structural and philosophic requirement to resist its cultural seductiveness.

Resistance requires an imagination and a will to be against. As the French philosopher Alain Badiou (2006: 24) writes, 'the essence of politics is not the plurality of opinions. It is the prescription of a possibility in rupture with what exists.' Following an earlier French philosopher, Henri Bergson, the moment of creativity emerges from a process of rupture, of discontinuity that can transcend the quantitative discontinuities produced by dividing the world into separate and discrete segments, disciplines and professions. These ruptures will gain strength from a re-articulation and re-apprehension of metaphor too if they are based on intuitive reflections of lived experience that imbue action with meaning and meaning with action.

For Badiou (2006), in our world, where dialogue is reduced to this plurality of opinions and where democratic individuals seem largely indifferent to injustice and vast material inequalities, only through an 'event', a radical break with the status quo, will individuals regain their subjectivity and fashion a praxis that offers a genuine alternative.

Mutual aid and co-operation will be an important element in this alternative, and examples of it are already present in our society and have been for a long time. The nineteenth-century anarchist philosopher Peter Kropotkin concluded his seminal text, *Mutual Aid: A Factor Of Evolution*, by writing:

> To attribute, therefore, the industrial progress of our century to the war of each against all which it has proclaimed, is to reason like the man who, knowing not the causes of rain, attributes it to the victim he has immolated before his clay idol. For industrial progress, as for each other conquest over nature, mutual aid and close intercourse certainly are, as they have been, much more advantageous than mutual struggle.
>
> (Kropotkin 2006: 246)

Although it is probably dangerous to look to nature for answers and attributes that make us feel good, or fuel our prejudices (Gould 1997), Kropotkin clearly recognised the supreme importance of co-operation. Metaphors, such as resilience, may be enlightening and they may be liberating, but we must beware of what we are bouncing back from, and to.

9 Destinations

Humpty Dumpty and the search for resilience

Design and technology cannot by itself create a more sustainable future. The actions and decisions of human beings will determine how unsustainable or sustainable, resilient or vulnerable, ecologically intelligent or stupid we will be. The systems thinker and environmental scientist Hartmut Bossel (1998, 2000) clearly recognises this, seeing human individuals themselves as self-organising systems. It is obvious to all but economists, he believes, that the model of the rational economic decision making individual is wrong. For Bossel, this model does not enable sustainable development, for only a systems model that incorporates normative concepts, social knowledge of the world, possibly can.

All things change – societies, environments, knowledge, technologies, values and aspirations and a sustainable society must allow change and adaptation to occur. The actual results of this process including the decisions people make, the interactions between the various co-evolving social and ecological systems, are difficult to predict with certainty. However, sustainable development can only occur within strict boundaries and constraints – physical, ecological, temporal, cultural, psychological, political and social. The 'basic orientators' of human beings are derived from their fundamental (self-organising) system interests. These include survival, viability, and success in their environment whatever, or wherever, that may be.

For Bossel, this environment is comprised of six fundamental properties:

- normal environmental states – such as legal, political and social arrangements;
- resource scarcity – consumer goods, energy, food, shelter ,and so on;
- variety – cultural, social, ethnical and other diversities;
- variability – the fluctuations may occasionally take the environment away from its normal state;
- change – such as the introduction of new technologies, economic cycles and aging; and
- other actors – including non-human others, the interests of neighbours and corporations.

Bossel further builds on this process of identifying orientators, indicators and needs to produce a model that can show how system needs are being met (or not being met) and consequently how healthy or resilient the system is or may become.

Resilience is increasingly coming into its own as a concept that suggests solutions, practical actions, new dispositions, states of mind and perhaps even states of being. In the first chapter we asked whether resilience is a process and what can be learnt about the concept from studying systems, communities and individuals that have been referred to as resilient or in some ways lacking resilience. We have seen that resilience is an important element of the public policy discourse around sustainability, sustainable development, risk and vulnerability. We have noted that at times resilience is used in a dual and sometimes confusing way referring simultaneously as both an outcome and a variable. It clearly has a popular meaning, which is inevitably envisaged as the ability to 'bounce back', conjuring up rather unfortunate images of rubber balls. People may be resilient, but they are not rubber balls. You can use metaphors and analogies that obstruct and obfuscate as well as enlighten and resilience is a term that seems increasingly adaptable, flexible and politically versatile.

Certainly, as Morgan Williams, Molly Scott Cato and a number of our other interviewees reminded us, resilience from an ecological systems perspective has a fairly well defined meaning but there have been many attempts to broaden this systems approach, and with it the concept of resilience, to other spheres. The ultimate aim here is being to realise a holistic embrace of social, psychological, environmental, scientific and other systems creating single worldview – the systems worldview. This has not always been successful for there are always points of detail or elements of interpretation that simply do not fit or derail a systems approach from being politically radical. In the social sciences systems approaches have frequently been tied to functionalism.

Thus systems theory, and with it resilience, has become part of an endeavour to produce a grand narrative of sustainable development which quite possibly could go the way of most other grand narratives that have illuminated human history. This leads to the question of whether the concept of sustainable development is itself sustainable or resilient. It certainly has had its fair share of criticism, reworking, reinterpretations and has shown itself to be adaptable. Perhaps too adaptable; perhaps too flexible. Sustainable development and sustainability are terms that are used in virtually every discursive context you can imagine and many of these have little common sense or meaning beyond lasting a long time. It has frequently been noted that there are many adjectival educations or adjectival businesses or adjectival persons. There is now another – resilient education, resilient business, resilient individual.

However, something undesirable may be sustainable and, by extension, resilient, and this resilience or sustainability will not necessarily relate to living or working within ecological limits or, in other ways, relate to being 'a good thing'. In other words, it seems that there is a certain Humpty Dumpty quality to the concepts 'sustainable development' and 'resilience'. As Lewis Carroll wrote in another context:

'When I use a word,' Humpty Dumpty said, in rather a scornful tone, 'it means just what I choose it to mean – neither more nor less.'

'The question is,' said Alice, 'whether you can make words mean so many different things.'

(Carroll 1872)

A violent dictatorship or an abusive relationship or an exploitative economic system may be resilient, and even sustainable, but it is not necessarily a good thing. To say nothing lasts forever is no comfort for those presently suffering in them. So, apart from the metaphorical application resilience may otherwise have in particular contexts, it must also reference what is essentially right and good, meaning that its ethical and moral dimension is something that must always be to the fore in any discussion of resilience – its use, application or meaning. The same must go for sustainable development and sustainability too, for it is the ethical imperative that moves sustainable development, conservation and resilience beyond the pale of business as usual, coping with, bouncing back and other convenient short hands turns of phrase. They must point to something else, something better, something utopian – a good place, a work in progress, a sustainable future.

Thus a resilient green economy has to be something other than a simple tweaking of current failed neoliberal policies and perspectives, or a conservation practice that sacrifices the greater good for pragmatic goals that may ultimately serve to maintain the vested interests of powerful economic and political groups while the Red List of endangered species gets bigger and bigger and the price of horn ripped from rhinos and elephants exceeds that of gold. A resilient person certainly needs to be able to cope with the slings and arrows of austerity's misfortune and she may even benefit from thinking with concepts and images rooted in permaculture and the transition movement. Resilience in learning may even benefit from its framing as a doughnut. The latter, though, given its association with unhealthy eating and obesity, is perhaps a rather unfortunate association, albeit in other ways a readily comprehensible one.

For some sociologists and philosophers the natural world may be an ideological construct but many sustainability practitioners look to the natural world for inspiring models and metaphors; and, learning for sustainability and for resilience also makes strong allusions to an ecological model of human behaviour which at times even includes grappling with the uncomfortable realities of politics and power. Given all this, it does seem that with climate change, population growth, unsustainable economic development, the stubborn survival (resilience?) of poverty, hardship and exploitation, human civilisation is in need of securing a means to ensure its own sustainability and resilience. We have lost a great deal of the resilience that comes from action, activity, technology, and ambition that may be termed human scale. We have perhaps lost touch with each other with ourselves and clearly with non-human others, the natural world. If we lack resilience, if human civilisation is in danger, then it is because of what we as a species have done in the past and are continuing to do in the present and almost certainly will continue to do in the future.

But to say the fault, or the problem, lies with humanity is both too obvious and too easy. The origins of the present crisis are not really a crisis of a species, or of humanity as a cultural entity, although of course it is definitely a crisis for the planet's many other species. It is, though, a crisis and a product of the way certain political and economic systems have developed, of how benefits have been produced and inequitably shared, of how competition has overshadowed co-operation, of how class and gender inequality and exploitation has not only been tolerated but actually supported, nurtured and reinforced over the decades if not centuries.

However, as Steven Pinker (2012) has shown, human society may actually be less violent than it once was and even the big corporate funders of climate change denial and skepticism now don the cloak of corporate responsibility. The idea of progress is not dead yet. There may indeed be twenty-first century enlightenment. From some perspectives things are looking better. The language and metaphors of sustainability practitioners, models derived from an under-standing of nature, are being applied in many spheres and forums where they previously were not; but there is still a need to be critical and look beyond appearance, beyond the face value of political rhetoric, corporate public relations and educational strategies and mission statements (Blewitt 2013). Pragmatism and compromise may simply not be enough – a first step maybe but one that leads to a journey of a few rather than a thousand miles. We need to know where we need to go. Constant adaptation may not be the same as being a bouncing ball or being mindful of initiating actions or processes that culminate in paradigmatic and so genuinely transformative change.

Having said that, the work of Roel Van Raij, Peter Head, Paul Clarke, Rob Hopkins, Herbert Girardet and many others demonstrates that there are clear examples of change and adaptation; and, indeed revolutionary proposals, para-digm shifting, transformative action and radical thinking. We have gone beyond sustainability and resilience towards regeneration and renewal. We've discussed conservation measures, local food movements, eco-city developments, big issues, co-operative work, sustainable education practice, and perspectives of economic and business transformation. There are still a great many reasons why we all need to be concerned about the continuing destruction of natural habitats and species lost.

We seem to be very good at counting the numbers of threatened species, analysing the problems of unsustainability and suggesting possible solutions. Clearly, there are some very innovative and courageous conservation activities taking place engaging a far wider range of stakeholders than occurred only a few years ago. There are new business models being developed and new media tech-nologies are being to play an important part in making new things happen. Graham Wallington's WildLife TV is just one example.

We have also shown examples, or offered interpretations, of actions and achievements that need to be further developed, scaled up, sharpened, or perhaps even abandoned. We have tried to be reflective and reflexive. We have also tried to show, although often by implication or inference, that positive change does happen and that faith in the human capacity, and capability, for pro-sustainable change is very real although often subject to challenge, manipulation and doubt. This is not to say that those who seem to exhibit faith are religious zealots in green clothing. Scratch the surface and the pessimist of the intellect often seems to trump the optimist of the will or the beholder of a very insecure faith. Education, business, governments, community, society, people, can change, and are changing. There are new global frameworks for sustainability in all these fields being developed. They simply need to be applied critically, rigorously and courageously.

We can live in harmony with the planet's natural ecological systems. and we may even be able to see and treat them as not just another service that can carry a dollar sign. Technology may be able to fix the future or we might all have to go back to the land assuming there is enough of it to go round. Who knows? There are clearly doubts surrounding both of these presumptions. So, our search for resilience in sustainable development leads us to a number of destinations. One of which is, perhaps, that although our knowledge and understanding of risks and vulnerabilities, resilience and sustainable development, are undoubtedly incomplete, a strong possibility emerges that even if it was not, even if knowledge was somehow magically complete and understanding total, it would still not be enough. The deadweight of past generations, of routines and established habits of mind, weigh heavily upon us. Systems will and do change and human actions will, and do change them.

But do we really want to change? Are we able to? Can that ethic of care sustainability educators and practitioners speak and write of be nurtured to the extent necessary to initiate the necessary changes? We do have a responsibility for and to the future, but it is not totally clear whether our future has already been used up; or whether the title of Franny Armstrong's 2009 documentary, *The Age of Stupid*, is actually the most appropriate epithet for our times or not.

Our search for resilience in sustainable development tells us that we are by no means stupid or ignorant but that something is nonetheless missing. Pessimism of the intellect; optimism of the will. The talk of the need for resilience does not necessarily strike us as being an indicator of optimism or faith in the effectiveness of current sustainability practices. Where resilience is needed is in our determination to make the changes that are necessary for a more sustainable world to take shape, and to remember that, as Nietzsche put it, faith does not want to know what is actually true.

Notes

1 Introduction

1   See Ethical Performance website at www.ethicalperformance.com. Ethical Performance hosts over 200 CSR and sustainability reports, mostly from multinational corporations.
2   Daniella Tilbury was a formal delegate at the Rio+20 Summit. These are her observations of the process and outcomes of this international gathering.

3 Shifting tactics?

1   Dr Morgan Williams convincingly argued that 'The ecological sustainability of many whole ecosystems, and the species they support, face a dire future. So by definition the act of conservation is failing and this fact is challenging the future of the conservation movement itself'.
2   The largest US-based conservation organisation.
3   De Zoysa (2012) believes that, traditionally, local people did not destroy their own land and environment. The development quest in the West delinked people from their environment and the modern conservation discourse is an effort to reconstruct relationships. The Western imperialism of the South (through colonisation to postcolonial exploitation and open market tactics) has delinked many communities in the south from their natural environment – hence the Western construct of conservation is being similarly applied in a universal way across the world.
4   In Chapter 4 readers can connect with 'WildEarth TV', which is creating a model of ecotourism that is designed to directly benefit local communities.
5   Such as the WWF MEdPO 'Across the Waters Programme' or the WWF/Adena Spain 'Local Action Groups initiative.
6   Daniella Tilbury was an official delegate of Rio+20 and observed the gap between the positions taken at the negotiating table and the examples of good practices showcased through various official side-events. She noted that there were new frames and discourses but not always new approaches or ways of working.
7   WWF was involved in setting up the Assisi meeting in 1986.

4 Contesting market logics

1   James Robertson (1998) has argued this case for decades too.

7 Education and conservation

1   The WWF document does not identify these specific studies. Australian studies, however, have come to similar conclusions (see Tilbury *et al.* 2005; Skamp *et al.* 2007).
2   There were exceptions. Ann explained that WWF UK had followed a different pathway from the late 1980s exploring different pedagogies and seeking systems change. It embraced education for sustainability in the early 1990s with the establishment of the WWF South Bank ESD postgraduate course. Also, Sweden and Colombia were also moving away from traditional conservation approaches, adopting community-based approaches towards the end of the 1980s.
3   Daniella Tilbury had an opportunity to review this programme and see first-hand the changes that had resulted during the programme offering, but more recently as part of a Rio+20 visit.
4   These included socially critical thinking, systemic thinking, values clarification, participation in decision-making and futures thinking, which have since been associated with sound and effective educational practices for sustainability (UNESCO 2005; Tilbury 2011).
5   Framed around the work of John Huckle's (1993) education for sustainability approach, underpinned by critical reflective thinking and participatory methodologies which challenge the traditional role of the educator as the source of knowledge.
6   Daniella Tilbury evaluated Phase 1 of this programme (1997–1999) and involved in framing and continuing development of the programme until 2005.
7   Although resilience did not figure as a term. This work recognised the importance of creating opportunities for personal and critical reflection as well as the building social engagement strategies – concepts implicit within the resilience literature today.
8   This links with the views that visioning and utopian thinking must underpin resilience (see Chapter 8) but contradicts Zolli's (2012) interpretation of resilience, which, he argues, needs to be pragmatic and focused on problem-solving and risk reduction.
9   Risk and climate change were key words often associated with resilience in the documentation circulated at Rio+20, as represented in Figure 1.3.
10   Commentators such as Gonzalo Guadiano (2012) would argue that environmental education has always intended to have that critical edge, but as an evaluator, Daniella Tilbury observed that few initiatives developed under this label practice the socially-critical approach.
11   Showcased in the WWF China and Brazil exemplary programmes.

References

Books

Alvares, C. and Faruqi, S. (eds) (2012) *Decolonising the University: The Emerging Quest for Non-Eurocentric Paradigms*. Pulau Pinang: Penerbit Universiti Sains Malaysia.

Aronowitz, S. and DiFazio, W. (2010) *The Jobless Future*. Minneapolis, MN: University of Minnesota Press.

Badiou, A. (2006) *Metapolitics*. Jason Barker (trans.). London: Verso.

Baeumler, A., Ijjasz-Vasquez, E. and Mehndiratta, S. (eds) (2012) *Sustainable Low-Carbon City Development in China*. Washington, DC: World Bank.

Barry, J. and Quilley, S. (2009) The Transition to Sustainability: Transition Towns and Sustainable Communities. In Leonard, L. and Barry, J. (eds), *The Transition to Sustainable Living and Practice: Advances in Ecopolitics, Vol 4*. Bingley: Emerald Group Publishing Ltd.

Barry, J. (2012) *The Politics of Actually Existing Unsustainability: Human Flourishing in a Climate-Changed, Carbon Constrained World*. Oxford: Oxford University Press.

Bateson, G. (2000) *Steps to and Ecology of Mind*. Chicago, IL: Chicago University Press.

Beatley, T. (2004) *Native to Nowhere: Sustaining Home and Community in the Global Age*. Washington, DC: Island Press.

Beatley, T. (2009) *Green Urbanism Down Under*. Washington, DC: Island Press.

Beck, U. (1992) *Risk Society: Towards a New Modernity*. London: Sage.

Beckett, K. and Herbert, S. (2009) *Banished: The New Social Control in Urban America*. New York: Oxford University Press.

Beecher, J., Scott Cato, M. and Weir, N. (2012) The Resilience of Co-operative Food Networks: A Case Study from Stroud, England. In MacDonald, D. and MacKnight, E. (eds), *The Co-operative Model in Practice: International Perspectives*. Aberdeen, University of Aberdeen/CETS.

Berardi, F. (2009) *The Soul at Work: From Alienation to Autonomy*. Los Angeles, CA: Semiotext(e).

Blewitt, J. (2013) EfS: contesting the market model of higher education. In Sterling, S., Maxey, L. and Luna, H. (eds), *The Sustainable University: Progress and Prospects*. London: Routledge.

Blewitt, J. (forthcoming 2014) Digital Media and the Right to the City. In Atkinson, H. and Wade, R. (eds), *The Challenge of Sustainability: Linking Politics, Education and Learning*. Bristol: Policy Press.

Blythman, J. (2004) *Shopped: The Shocking Power of British Supermarkets*. London: Fourth Estate.

Boone, G.C. and Modarres, A. (2006) *City and Environment*. Philadelphia, PA: Temple University Press.

Borrini-Feyerabend, G. (ed.) (1997) Beyond Fences: Seeking Social Sustainability in *Conservation, Vol. 1*. Gland: IUCN.

Bossel, H. (1998) *Earth at a Crossroads: Paths to a Sustainable Future*. Cambridge: Cambridge University Press.

Bowen, J. (2012) *A Street Cat Named Bob*. London: Hodder & Stoughton.

Brown J.H, D'Emidio-Caston, M. and Bernard, B. (2000) *Resilience Education*, Thousand Oaks, CA: Corwin Press/Sage Publications.

Brugmann J. (2009) *Welcome to the Urban Revolution: How Cities are Changing the World*. New York: Bloomsbury Press.

Campbell, A., Kapos, V., Scharlemann, J.P.W., Bubb, P., Chenery, A., Coad, L., Dickson, B., Doswald, N., Khan, M.S.I., Kershaw, F. and Rashid, M. (2009) *Review of the Literature on the Links between Biodiversity and Climate Change: Impacts, Adaptation and Mitigation*. Technical Series no. 42. Montreal: Secretariat of the Convention on Biological Diversity.

Carnegie, D. (2006) *How to Win Friends and Influence People*. London: Vermillion.

Carroll, L. (1871) *Through the Looking-Glass, and What Alice Found There*. London: Macmillan.

Chase-Dunn, C. and Hall, T.D. (1997) *Rise and Demise: Comparing World-Systems*. Boulder, CO: Westview Press.

Clarke, J. and Nicholson, J. (2010) *Resilience: Bounce Back from Whatever Life Throws at You*. Richmond: Crimson Publishing. Available at www.cbd.int/sp/targets (accessed 22 December 2012).

Cleaver, H. (2000) *Reading Capital Politically*. Leeds: AK Press.

Conaty, P. (2011) *A Co-operative Green Economy: New Solutions for Energy and Sustainable Social Justice*. Manchester: Co-operatives UK, available at www.uk.coop/sites/default/files/docs/greeneconomy_v1_0_0.pdf.

Costanza, R., Graumlich, L. and Steffen, W. (eds) (2007) *Sustainability or Collapse? An Integrated History and Future of People on Earth*. Cambridge, MA: MIT Press.

Crompton, T. (2010) *Common Cause: The Case for Working with our Cultural Values*. Godalming: WWF.

Crouch, C. (2011) *The Strange Non Death of NeoLiberalism*, London: Polity Press.

Crouch, D. and Ward, C. (1997) *The Allotment: Its Landscape and Culture*. Nottingham: Five Leaves Publications.

Daly, G. (1996) *Homeless*. London: Routledge.

Darnton, A. and Kirk, M. (2011) *Finding Frames: New Ways to Engage the UK Public in Global Poverty*. London: Bond.

Despommier, D. (2011) *The Vertical Farm: Feeding the World in the 21st Century*. New York: Picador.

Diamond, J. (2005) *Collapse: How Societies Choose to Fail or Survive*. London: Penguin Books.

Dowie, M. (2009) *Conservation Refugees: The Hundred-Year Conflict between Global Conservation and Native Peoples*. Cambridge, MA: MIT Press.

Dudley, M. (ed.) (2013) *Public Libraries and Resilient Cities*. Chicago, IL: American Library Association.

Ehrenreich, B. (2006) *Dancing in the Streets: A History of Collective Joy*. New York: Metropolitan Books.

Ehrenreich, B. (2010) *Bright-sided: How the Relentless Promotion of Positive Thinking Has Undermined America*. New York: Picador.

Ellul, J. (1964) *The Technological Society*. New York: Vintage.

Evans, S. and Boyte, H.C. (1986) *Free Spaces: The Sources of Democratic Change in America*. New York: Harper & Row.

Food and Agricultural Organization of the United Nations (2011) *State of the World's Forests 2011*. Rome: Food and Agricultural Organization of the United Nations.

Folke, C. et al. (2002) *Resilience and Sustainable Development: Building Adaptive Capacity in a World of Transformations*. Stockholm: Ministry of the Environment.

Forsyth, T. (2005) Critical Realism and Political Ecology. In Lopez, J. (ed.), *After Postmodernism: An Introduction to Critical Realism*. London: Continuum, pp. 146–52.

Foster, J.B., Clark, B. and York, R. (2010) *The Ecological Rift: Capitalism's War on the Earth*. New York: Monthly Review Press.

Frankl, V.E. (1997) *Man's Search for Meaning*. New York: Simon & Schuster.

Gardner, K. and Lewis, D. (1996) *Anthropology, Development and the Post-Modern Challenge*. London: Pluto Press

Girardet, H. (1996) *The Gaia Atlas of Cities: New Directions for Sustainable Urban Living*. London: Gaia Books.

Girardet, H. (2004) *Creating a Sustainable Adelaide*. Adelaide: Department of the Premier and Cabinet.

Girardet, H. (2010) *Regenerative Cities*. Hamburg: World Future Council.

Girardet, H. and Mendonca, M. (2009) *A Renewable World: Energy, Ecology, Equity*. Totnes: Green Books.

Gleick, J. (1988) *Chaos*. London: Sphere.

Global University Network for Innovation (2011) *Higher Education in the World 4: Higher Education's Commitment to Sustainability: From Understanding to Action*. Basingstoke: Palgrave Macmillan.

Goffman, E. (1968) *Asylums*. Harmondsworth: Penguin Books.

Gorgolewski, M., Komisar, J. and Nasr, J. (2011) *Carrot City: Creating Places for Urban Agriculture*. New York: Monacelli Press.

Gorz, A. (1999) *Reclaiming Work: Beyond the Wage Based Society*. Cambridge: Polity Press.

Gunderson, L.H. and Holling, C.S. (eds) (2002) *Panarchy: Understanding Transformations in Human and Natural Systems*. Washington, DC: Island Press.

Hardt, M. and Negri, A. (2000) *Empire*. Cambridge, MA: Harvard University Press.

Harvey, D. (1996) *Justice, Nature and the Geography of Difference*. Oxford: Blackwell.

Harvey, D. (2000) *Spaces of Hope*. Edinburgh: Edinburgh University Press.

Harvey, D. (2011) *The Enigma of Capitalism and the Crises of Capitalism*, London: Profile Books.

Heinberg, R. (2011) *The End of Growth: Adapting to Our New Economic Reality*. West Hoathly: Clairview Books.

Heynen, N., McCarthy, J., Prudham, S. and Robbins, P. (eds) (2007) *Neoliberal Environments: False Promises and Unnatural Consequences*. London: Routledge.

Hirsch, F. (1977) *Social Limits to Growth*. London: Routledge & Kegan Paul.

Holling, C.S., Schindler, D.W., Walker, B.H. and Roughgarden, J. (1995) Biodiversity in the Functioning of Ecosystems: An Ecological Primer and Synthesis. In Perrings, C., Maler, K.-G., Folke, C., Holling, C.S. and Jansson, B.O. (eds), *Biodiversity Loss: Ecological and Economic Issues*. Cambridge: Cambridge University Press, pp. 44–83.

Homer-Dixon, T. (2006) *The Upside of Down: Catastrophe, Creativity and the Renewal of Civilisation*. London: Souvenir Press.

Honore, C. (2004) *In Praise of Slow*. London: Orion.

Hopkins, R. (2008) *The Transition Handbook: From Oil Dependency to Local Resilience.* Totnes: Green Books. Free version available at www.transitie.be/userfiles//transition-handbook(1).pdf (accessed 28 August 2012).

Hopkins, R. (2011) *The Transition Companion: Making Your Community More Resilient in Uncertain Times.* Totnes: Transition Books.

Hutchins, G. (2012) *The Nature of Business: Redesigning for Resilience.* Totnes: Green Books.

Johnstone, C. (2010) *Find Your Power: A Toolkit for Resilience and Positive Change.* East Meon: Permanent Publications.

Joss, S., Tomozeiu, D. and Cowley, R. (2011) *Eco-cities: A Global Survey 2011.* London: University of Westminster.

Keen, M., Brown, V.A. and Dyball, R. (2005) Social Learning: A New Approach to Environmental Management. In Dyball, R. and Keen, M. (eds), *Social Learning in Environmental Management: Towards a Sustainable Future.* London: Earthscan.

Kohn, M. (2003) *Radical Space: Building the House of the People.* Ithaca, NY: Cornell University Press.

Kohn, M. (2004) *Brave New Neighbourhoods: The Privatization of Public Space.* London: Routledge.

Kropotkin, P. (2006) *Mutual Aid: A Factor of Evolution.* New York: Dover Books.

Lakoff, G. (2004) *Don't Think of an Elephant: Know Your Values and Frame the Debate.* White River Junction, VT: Chelsea Green.

Lakoff, G. (2008) *The Political Mind.* New York: Viking Books.

Lakoff, G. and Johnson, M. (1999) *Philosophy in the Flesh: The Embodied Mind and its Challenge to Western Thought.* New York: Basic Books.

Lapham, L. (1998) *The Agony of Mammon: The Imperial Global Economy Explains Itself to the Membership in Davos, Switzerland.* London: Verso.

Lawrence, F. (2004) *Not On the Label: What Really Goes into the Food on Your Plate.* London: Penguin.

Lazzarato, M. (1996) Immaterial Labour. In Hardt, M. and Virno, P. (eds), *Radical Thought in Italy: A Potential Politics.* Minneapolis, MN: University of Minnesota Press.

Mattern, S. (2007) *The New Downtown Library: Designing with Communities.* Minneapolis, MN: University of Minnesota Press.

Maxwell, R. and Miller, T. (2012) *Greening the Media.* Oxford: Oxford University Press.

McAnany, P.A. and Yoffee, N. (eds) (2009) *Questioning Collapse: Human Resilience, Ecological Vulnerability, and the Aftermath of Empire.* Cambridge: Cambridge University Press.

Meadows, D.H. (2009) *Thinking in Systems: A Primer.* London: Earthscan.

Meadows, D.H., Meadows, D.L., Randers, J. and Behrens III, W.W. (1972) *The Limits to Growth.* New York: Signet.

Millennium Ecosystem Assessment (2005) *Ecosystems and Human Wellbeing: Policy Responses, vol. 3.* Washington, DC: Island Press.

Mitchell, W.J. and Townsend, A.M. (2005) Cyborg Agonistes: Disaster and Reconstruction in the Digital Electronic Era. In Vale, L.J. and Campanella, T.J. (eds), *The Resilient City: How Modern Cities Recover from Disaster.* Oxford: Oxford University Press.

Moffat, S., Suzuki, H. and Iizuka, R. (2012) *Eco2 Cities Guide: Ecological Cities and Economic Cities.* Washington, DC: World Bank.

Monaghan, P. (2012) *How Local Resilience Creates Sustainable Societies: Hard to Make, Hard to Break.* London: Earthscan.

Morris, W. ([1885] 1962) Useful Work versus Useless Toil. In Briggs, A. (ed.), *William Morris: Selected Writing and Designs*. Harmondsworth: Penguin Books.

Morris, W. ([1890] 2003) *News from Nowhere*. Oxford: Oxford University Press.

Mumford, L. (1922) *The Story of Utopias*. New York: Boni & Liveright.

Mumford, L. (1934) *Technics and Civilization*. New York: Harcourt Brace.

Mumford, L. (1938) *The Culture of Cities*. New York: Harcourt Brace.

Mumford, L. (1961) *The City in History*. Harmondsworth: Penguin.

Negri, A. (1989) *The Politics of Subversion: A Manifesto for the Twenty-first Century*. James Newell (trans.). Cambridge: Polity Press.

Newman, P. and Jennings, I. (2008) *Cities as Sustainable Ecosystems*. Washington, DC: Island Press.

Norman, D. (2008) Foreword. In Crompton, T., *Weathercocks and Signposts: The Environment Movement at a Crossroads* London: WWF UK.

Ostrom, E. (1990) *Governing the Commons: The Evolution of Institutions for Collective Action*. Cambridge: Cambridge University Press.

Pearce, D., Markandya, A. and Barbier, E. (1989) *Blueprint for a Green Economy*. London: Earthscan.

Pelling, M. (2011) *Adaptation to Climate Change*. London: Routledge.

Perez, A.A., Fernandez, B.H. and Gatti, R.C. (2010) *Building Resilience to Climate Change: Ecosystem-Based Adaptation and Lessons from the Field*. Gland: IUCN.

Pinker, S. (2012) *The Better Angels of Our Nature: A History of Violence and Humanity*. London: Penguin.

Procee, P. and Brecht, H. (2012) Adapting to Climate Risks: Building Resilient Cities in China. In Baeumler, A., Ijjasz-Vasquez, E. and Mehndiratta, S. (eds), *Sustainable Low-Carbon City Development in China*. Washington, DC: World Bank.

Register, R. (2006) *Ecocities: Rebuilding Cities in Balance with Nature*. Gabriola Island: New Society Publishers.

Rifkin, J. (2000) *The End of Work*. London: Penguin Books.

Roberts, P. (2005) *The End of Oil: The Decline of the Petroleum Economy and the Rise of a New Energy Order*. London: Bloomsbury Publishing.

Robertson, J. (1998) *Transforming Economic Life: A Millennial Challenge*. Schumacher Briefing 1. Totnes: Green Books.

Rose, C. (2011) *What Makes People Tick: The Three Hidden Worlds of Settlers, Prospectors and Pioneers*. Leicester: Matador.

Roseland, M. (1997) *Eco-City Dimensions: Healthy Communities, Healthy Planet*. Gabriola Island: New Society Publishers.

Rybczynski, W. (1986) *Home: The Short History of an Idea*. New York: Viking.

Schlosser, E. (2002) *Fast Food Nation: What The All-American Meal is Doing to the World*. London: Penguin.

Schumacher, E.F. (1974) *Small is Beautiful*. London: Abacus.

Schumacher, E.F. (1980) *Good Work*. London: Sphere.

Scott, G., Tilbury, D., Sharp, L. and Deane, E. (2012) *Turnaround Leadership for Sustainability in Higher Education*. Sydney: Office of Learning and Teaching.

Scott Cato, M. (2012) *The Bioregional Economy*. London: Earthscan.

Smith, J., with Akpadio, S., Bushnaq, H., Campbell, A., Hassan, L. and Pal, S. (2008) *Valuable Lives: Capabilities and Resilience Amongst Single Homeless People*. London: Crisis.

Soja, E.W. (2010) *Seeking Spatial Justice*. Minneapolis, MN: University of Minnesota Press.

Standing, G. (2009) *Work After Globalization: Building Occupational Citizenship*. Cheltenham: Edward Elgar.

Standing, G. (2011) *The Precariat: The New Dangerous Class*. London: Bloomsbury Acacemic.

Steel, C. (2009) *Hungry City: How Food Shapes Our Lives*. London: Vintage.

Sterling, S. (2001) *Sustainable Education: Revisioning Learning and Change*. Totnes: Green Books.

Sterling, S. *et al.* (eds) (2013) *The Sustainable University: Process and Prospects*. Abingdon: Routledge.

Stern, N. (2007) *The Stern Review: The Economics of Climate Change*. Cambridge: Cambridge University Press.

Suzuki, H., Dastur, A., Moffatt, S., Nanae, Y. and Hinako, M. (2010) *Eco2 Cities: Ecological Cities as Economic Cities*. Washington, DC: World Bank, available at www.worldbank.org/eco2

Swithinbank, T. (2001) *Coming Up from the Streets: The Story of The Big Issue*. London: Earthscan.

Thayer, R.L. (2003) *LifePlace: Bioregional Thought and Practice*. Berkeley, CA: University of California Press.

Thomashow, M. (2002) *Ecological Identity: Becoming a Reflective Environmentalist*. Cambridge, MA: MIT Press.

Tilbury, D. (1999a) WWF-China PO – The Environmental Education Initiative for China. In Fien, J. (ed.), *Education and Conservation: An Evaluation of the Contributions of Educational Programmes to Conservation within the WWF Network*. Gland: WWF, pp. 32–6.

Tilbury, D. (1999b) WWF-Brazil Change the World Raimundo! Programme. In Fien, J. (ed.), *Education and Conservation: An Evaluation of the Contributions of Educational Programmes to Conservation within the WWF Network*. Gland: WWF, pp. 48–53.

Tilbury, D. (1999c) WWF South Africa – The School Water Action Project. In Fien, J. (ed.), *Education and Conservation: An Evaluation of the Contributions of Educational Programmes to Conservation within the WWF Network*. Gland: WWF, pp. 59–70.

Tilbury, D. (2011a) Higher Education for Sustainability: A Global Overview of Commitment and Progress. In GUNI (ed.), *Higher Education's Commitment to Sustainability: from Understanding to Action*. Higher Education in the World 4. Barcelona: GUNI, pp. 18–28.

Tilbury, D. (2011b) *Education for Sustainable Development: An Expert Review of Processes and Learning*. Paris: UNESCO.

Tilbury, D. (2013) Another World is Desirable: A global rebooting of higher education for sustainable development. In Sterling, S. *et al.* (eds), *The Sustainable University: Process And Prospects*. Abingdon: Routledge.

Tilbury, D. and Wortman, D. (2004) *Engaging People in Sustainability*. Gland: IUCN. Available at www.iucn.org/dbtw-wpd/edocs/2004-055.pdf (accessed 1 May 2005).

UNESCO (2005) *Education for Sustainability: From Rio to Johannesburg – Lessons Learnt from a Decade of Commitment*. Paris: UNESCO.

Unger, R.M. (2007) *Self Awakened: Pragmatism Unbound*. Harvard, MA: Harvard University Press.

Upton, S. and Ibrahim, M. (2012) *Resilience in Practice*. Rugby: Practical Action.

Vale, L.J. and Campanella, T.J. (eds) (2005) *The Resilient City: How Modern Cities Recover from Disaster*. Oxford: Oxford University Press.

Van Matre, S. (1978) *Sunship Earth*. Martinsville, IN: American Camping Association.

Van Matre, S. (1988) *Earth Keepers.*Warrenville, IL: The Institute for Earth Education.

Walker, B. and Salt, D. (2006) *Resilience Thinking: Sustaining Ecosystems and People in a Changing World.* Washington, DC: Island Press.

Walker, B. and Salt, D. (2012) *Resilience Practice: Building Capacity to Absorb Disturbance and Maintain Function.* Gabriola Island: Island Press.

Wallerstein, I. M. (1974) *The Modern World-System, vol. 1. Capitalist Agriculture and the Origins of the European World-Economy in the Sixteenth Century.* Cambridge: Cambridge University Press.

Wals, A.E.J., van der Hoeven, N. and Blanken, H. (2009) *The Acoustics of Social Learning: Designing Learning Processes that Contribute to a More Sustainable World.* Wageningen: Wageningen Academic Publishers.

Weeks, K. (2005) The Refusal of Work as Demand and Perspective. In Murphy, T.S. and Mustapha, A.-K. (eds), *The Philosophy of Antonio Negri: Resistance in Practice.* London: Pluto Press.

Wilkinson, R. and Pickett, K. (2010) *The Spirit Level: Why Equality is Better for Everyone.* London: Penguin.

Worldwatch Institute (2012a) *The State of the World 2012: Moving Toward Sustainable Prosperity.* Washington, DC: Worldwatch Institute.

Worldwatch Institute (2012b) *Vital Signs 2012: The Trends That are Shaping our Future.* Washington, DC: Worldwatch Institute.

Zolli, A. and Healy, A.M. (2012) *Resilience: Why Things Bounce Back.* New York: Free Press.

Journals

Adam, B. (2006) Time. *Theory, Culture and Society,* 23 (2–3): 119–38.

Ahmed, A. and Stein. J.A.(2004) Science, Technology and Sustainable Development: A World Review. *World Review of Science, Technology and Sustainable Development,* 1: 5–24.

Altieri, M.A., Companioni, N., Cañizares, K., Murphy, C. Rosset, P., Bourque, M. and Nicholls, C.I. (1999) The Greening of the 'Barrios': Urban Agriculture for Food Security in Cuba. *Agriculture and Human Values,* 16: 131–40.

Amin, A. (2005) Local Community on Trial. *Economy and Society,* 34 (4): 612–33.

Anon (2008) Health Consequences of Cuba's Special Period. *Canadian Medical Association Journal,* 179 (3), available at www.ncbi.nlm.nih.gov/pmc/articles/PMC2474886.

Audebrand, L.K. (2010) Sustainability in Strategic Management Education: The Quest for New Root Metaphors. *Academy of Management Learning and Education,* 9 (3): 413–28.

Banerjee, S.B. (2008) Corporate Social Responsibility: The Good, the Bad and the Ugly. *Critical Sociology,* 34 (1): 51–79.

Barr, S., Gilg, A. and Shaw, G. (2011) Citizens, Consumers and Sustainability: (Re)Framing Environmental Practice in an Age of Climate Change. *Global Environmental Change,* 21 (4): 1224–33.

Bengtsson, J., Angelstam, P., Elmqvist, T., Emanuelsson, U., Folke, C., Ihse, M., Moberg, F. and Nyström, M. (2003) Reserves, Resilience and Dynamic Landscapes. *Ambio,* 32 (6): 389–96.

Berkes, F. and Turner, N.J. (2006) Knowledge, Learning and the Evolution of Conservation Practice for Social-Ecological System Resilience. *Human Ecology,* 34 (4): 479–94.

Blewitt, J. (2011) Critical Practice and Public the Pedagogy of Environmental and Conservation Media. *Environmental Education Research*, 17 (6): 719–34.

Blewitt, J. (2012) The Future of the Public Library: Reimagining the Moral Economy of the 'People's University'. *Power and Education*, 4 (1): 107–17.

Blewitt, J. and Gambles, B. (2010) The Library of Birmingham Project: Lifelong Learning for the Digital Age. *Journal of Adult Continuing Education*, 16 (2): 52–66.

Bossel, H. (2000) Policy Assessment and Simulation of Actor Orientation for Sustainable Development. *Ecological Economics*, 34: 37–355.

Brand, F.S. and Jax, K. (2007) Focusing the Meaning(s) of Resilience: Resilience as a Descriptive Concept and a Boundary Object. *Ecology and Society*, 12 (1): 23, available at www.ecologyandsociety.org/vol12/iss1/art23

Brown, J.H. (2001) Systemic Reform Concerning Resilience in Education. *Tech Trends*, 45 (4): 47–54.

Butchart, S.H.M. *et al.* (2010) Global Biodiversity: Indicators of Recent Declines. *Science*, 328 (5982): 1164–8.

Campanella, T.J. (2006) Urban Resilience and the Recovery of New Orleans. *Journal of the American Planning Association*, 72 (2): 141–6.

Cao, S., Chen, L., Shankman, D., Wang, C., Wang, X. and Zhang, H. (2011) Excessive Reliance on Afforestation in China's Arid and Semi-arid Regions: Lessons in Ecological Restoration. *Earth-Science Reviews*, 104 (4): 240–5.

Castree, N. (2003) Commodifying What Nature? *Progress in Human Geography*, 27 (3): 273–97.

Clarke, S. (2005) Future Technologies, Dystopic Futures and the Precautionary Principle. *Ethics and Information Technology*, 7: 121–6.

Cole, R.J. (2012): Transitioning from Green to Regenerative Design. *Building Research and Information*, 40 (1): 39–53.

Cook-Greuter, S.R. (2000) Mature Ego Development: A Gateway to Ego Transcendence? *Journal of Adult Development*, 7: 227–40.

Costanza, R. *et al.* (1997) The Value of the World's Ecosystem Services and Natural Capital. *Nature*, 387: 253–60.

Coutu, D.L. (2002) How Resilience Works. *Harvard Business Review*, May, pp. 46–55.

Cronin, B. (2002) What a Library is Not. *Library Journal*, 127 (19): 46.

Crouch, D. and Parker, G. (2003) 'Digging-Up' Utopia? Space, Practice and Land Use Heritage. *Geoforum*, 34: 395–408.

Dixon, J., Omwega, A.M., Friel, S., Burns, C., Donati, K. and Carlisle, R. (2007) The Health Equity Dimensions of Urban Food Systems. *Journal of Urban Health: Bulletin of the New York Academy of Medicine*, 84 (1): 118–29.

Duffy, R., and L. Moore (2010) Neoliberalizing Nature? Elephants as Imperfect Commodities. *Antipode*, 42 (3): 742–66.

Du Plessis, C. (2012) Towards a Regenerative Paradigm for the Built Environment. *Building Research and Information*, 40 (1): 7–22.

Evans, J.P. (2011) Resilience, Ecology and Adaptation in the Experimental City. *Transactions of the Institute of British Geographers*, 36: 223–37.

Fadeeva, Z. and Mochizuki, Y. (2010). Higher Education for Today and Tomorrow: University Appraisal for Diversity, Innovation and Change towards Sustainable Development. *Sustainability Science*, 5 (2): 249–56.

Fan, P. and Qi, J. (2010) Assessing the Sustainability of Major Cities in China. *Sustainability Science*, 5: 51–68.

Fazey, I. (2010) Resilience and Higher Order Thinking. *Ecology and Society*, 15 (3): 9, available at www.ecologyandsociety.org/vol15/iss3/art9

Fazey, I., Gamarra, J.G.P., Fischer, J., Reed, M.S., Stringer, L.C. and Christie, M. (2010) Adaptation Strategies for Reducing Vulnerability to Future Environmental Change. *Frontiers in Ecology and the Environment*, 8 (8): 414–22.

Fien, J., Scott, W., and Tilbury, D. (2001) Education and Conservation: Lessons from an Evaluation. *Environmental Education Research*, 7 (4): 379–95.

Flecha, R. and Santa Cruz, I. (2011) Cooperation for Economic Success: The Mondragon Case. *Analyse and Kritik*, 33: 157–70.

Fischer, J., Peterson, G. D., Gardner, T. A., Gordon, L. J., Fazey, I., Elmqvist, T., Felton, A., Folke, C. and Dovers, S. (2009) Integrating Resilience Thinking and Optimisation for Conservation. *Trends in Ecology and Evolution*, 24 (10): 549–54.

Folke, C. (2006) Resilience: The Emergence of a Perspective for Social-Ecological Systems Analyses. *Global Environmental Change*, 16: 253–67.

Folke, C., Holling, C.S. and Perrings, C. (1996) Biological Diversity, Ecosystems and the Human Scale. *Ecological Applications*, 6: 1018–24.

Folke, C., Carpenter, S., Elmqvist, T., Gunderson, L., Holling, C.S. and Walker, B. (2002) Resilience and Sustainable Development: Building Adaptive Capacity in a World of Transformations. *Ambio*, 31 (5): 437–40.

Galaz, V. *et al.* (2012) 'Planetary boundaries' – Exploring the Challenges for Global Environmental Governance. *Current Opinion in Environmental Sustainability*, 4: 80–7.

Gill, R. and Pratt, A. (2008) In the Social Factory? Immaterial Labour, Precariousness and Cultural Work. *Theory, Culture and Society*, 25 (7–8): 1–30.

Girardet, H. (2012) Regenerative Adelaide. *Solutions*, 5 (3): 46–54.

Gotts, N.M. (2007) Resilience, Panarchy, and World-Systems Analysis. *Ecology and Society*, 12 (1): 24–38.

Gould, S.J. (1997) Kropotkin was No Crackpot. *Natural History*, 106 (June): 12–21.

Gunnestad, A. (2006) Resilience in Cross Cultural Perspective: How Resilience is Generated in Different Cultures. *Journal of Intercultural Communication*, (11), available at www.immi.se/jicc/index.php/jicc/article/view/99/68 (accessed 27 Match 2013).

Habermas, J. (2010) The Concept of Human Dignity and the Realistic Utopia of Human Rights. *Metaphilosophy*, 41 (4): 464–80.

Hartfiel, N., Havenhand, J. Khalsa, S.B., Clarke, G. and Kraya, A. (2011) The Effectiveness of Yoga for the Improvement of Well-being and Resilience to Stress in the Workplace. *Scandinavian Journal of Work and Environmental Health*, 37 (1): 70–6.

Harvey, D. (1998) Marxism, Metaphors and Ecological Politics. *Monthly Review*, 49: 17–31.

Hibbert, S., Hogg, G., and Quinn, T. (2005) Social Entrepreneurship: Understanding Consumer Motives for Buying The Big Issue. *Journal of Consumer Behaviour*, 4 (3): 159–72.

Hodgetts, D., Stolte, O., Chamberlain, K., Radley, A., Nikora, L., Nabalarua, E. and Groot, S. (2008) A Trip to the Library: Homelessness and Social Inclusion. *Social and Cultural Geography*, 9 (8): 933–53.

Hollands, R.G. (2008) Will the Real Smart City Please Stand Up? *City*, 12 (3): 303–20.

Holling, C.S. (1973) Resilience and Stability of Ecological Systems. *Annual Review of Ecology and Systematics*, 4: 1–23.

Holling, C.S. (2001) Understanding the Complexity of Economic, Ecological, and Social Systems. *Ecosystems*, 4: 390–405.

Holling, C.S. (2004) From Complex Regions to Complex Worlds. *Ecology and Society*, 9 (1): 11–21.

Hopkins C. (2012) Reflections on 20+ Years of ESD. *Journal of Education for Sustainable Development*, 6 (1): 21–36.

Howley, K. (2003) A Poverty of Voices: Street Papers as Communicative Democracy. *Journalism*, 4 (3): 273–92.

Hoyer, K.G. and Naess, P. (2008) Interdisciplinarity, Ecology and Scientific Theory: The Case of Sustainable Urban Development. *Journal of Critical Realism*, 7 (2): 179–207.

Igoe, J., Neves, K. and Brockington, D. (2010) A Spectacular Eco-tour around the Historic Bloc: Theorising the Convergence of Biodiversity Conservation and Capitalist Expansion. *Antipode*, 42 (3): 486–512.

International Institute for Educational Planning (2009) Rebuilding Resilience: The Education Challenge. *IIEP Newsletter*, 27 (1): 1–2.

Jackson, R.B. and Salzman, J. (2010) Pursuing Geoengineering for Atmospheric Restoration. *Issues in Science and Technology*, summer, pp. 67–76.

Janssen, M.A., Schoon, M.L., Ke, W. and Borner, K. (2006) Scholarly Networks on Resilience, Vulnerability and Adaptation within the Human Dimensions of Global Environmental Change. *Global Environmental Change*, 16 (3): 240–52.

Johnstone, C. (2006) Ten Strategies for Avoiding Burnout. *Permaculture Magazine* (50): 21–2.

Joss, S. (2010) Eco-cities a Global Survey 2009. *WIT Transactions on Ecology and the Environment*, 129: 239–50.

Joss, S. (2011) Ecocities. *MODUS*, June, pp. 32–35.

Kenworthy, J.R. (2006) The Eco-city: Ten Key Transport and Planning Dimensions for Sustainable City Development. *Environment and Urbanization*, 18 (1): 67–85.

Khono, M., Masuyama, Y. Kato, N. and Tobe, A. (2011) Hitachi's Smart City Solutions for New Era of Urban Development. *Hitachi Review*, 60 (2): 79–88.

Kidd, S.A. and Davidson, L. (2007) 'You Have to Adapt Because You Have No Other Choice': The Stories of Strength and Resilience of 208 Homeless Youth in New York City and Toronto. *Journal of Community Psychology*, 35 (2): 219–38.

Kirmayer, L. J., Sehdev, M., Whitley, R., Dandeneau, S.F. and Isaac, C. (2009) Community Resilience: Models, Metaphors and Measures. *Journal de la santé autochtone*, Novermber, pp. 62–117.

Koller, S.H. (2011) Resilience: Definitions, Measurements, and Conclusions. *International Society for the Study of Behavioural Development Bulletin*, 1 (59): 15–19.

Kos, D. (2012) Sustainable Development: Implementing Utopia? *Sociologija*, 54 (1): 7–20.

Krasny, M.E., Lundholm, C. and Plummer, R. (2010): Resilience in Social–Ecological Systems: The Roles of Learning and Education. *Environmental Education Research*, 16 (5–6): 463–74.

Lakoff, G. (2010) Why it Matters How We Frame the Environment. *Environmental Communication: A Journal of Nature and Culture*, 4 (1): 70–81.

Langley, P. and Mellor, M. (2002) 'Economy', Sustainability and Sites of Transformative Space. *New Political Economy*, 7 (1): 49–65.

Levitas, R. (2007) Looking for the Blue: The Necessity of Utopia. *Journal of Political Ideologies*, 12 (3): 289–306.

Levitas, R. (2010) Back to the Future: Wells, Sociology, Utopia and Method. *The Sociological Review*, 58 (4): 530–47.

Levkoe, C.Z. (2006) Learning Democracy through Food Justice Movements. *Agriculture and Human Values*, 23: 89–98.

Lewis, M. and Conaty, P. (2012) *The Resilience Imperative: Co-operative Transitions to a Steady-State Economy*. Gabriola Island: New Society Publishers.

Macedo, J. (2004) City Profile: Curitiba. *Cities*, 21 (6): 537–49.

MacLeod, G. (2002) From Urban Entrepreneurialism to a 'Revanchist City'? On the Spatial Injustices of Glasgow's Renaissance. *Antipode*, 34 (3): 602–4.

Magallanes-Blanco, C. and Pérez-Bermúdez, J.A. (2009) Citizens' Publications that Empower: Social Change for the Homeless. *Development in Practice*, 19 (4–5): 654–64.

Mang, P. and Reed, B. (2012) Designing from Place: A Regenerative Framework and Methodology. *Building Research and Information*, 40 (1): 23–38.

Marvier, M., Kareiva, P. and Lalasz, R. (2012) Conservation in the Anthropocene: Beyond Solitude and Fragility. *The Breakthrough Journal* Winter, available at www.thebreakthrough.org/index.php/journal/past-issues/issue-2/conservation-in-the-anthropocene/ (accessed 21 December 2012).

Masten, A. (2001) Ordinary Magic: Resilience Processes in Development. *American Psychologist*, 56 (3): 227–38.

Masten, A.S. and Obradovic, J. (2007) Disaster Preparation and Recovery: Lessons from Research on Resilience in Human Development. *Ecology and Society*, 13 (1): 9, available at www.ecologyandsociety.org/vol13/iss1/art9

Masten, A., Best, K.M. and Garmezy, N. (1990) Resilience and Development: Contributions from the Study of Children who Overcome Adversity. *Development and Psychpathology*, 2: 425–44.

Mezher, T., Fath, H., Abbas, Z. and Khaled, A. (2011) Techno-economic Assessment and Environmental Impacts of Desalination Technologies. *Desalinisation*, 266 (1–3): 263–73.

Mitchell, D. (1997) The Annihilation of Space by Law: The Roots and Implications of Antihomeless Laws in the United States. *Antipode*, 29: 303–35.

Nader, S. (2009) Paths to a Low-Carbon Economy: The Masdar Example. *Energy Procedia*, 1: 3951–8.

Nelson, D.R., Adger, W.M. and Brown, K. (2007) Adaptation to Environmental Change: Contributions of a Resilience Framework. *Annual Review of Environment and Resources*, 32: 395–419.

Nevárez, J. (1999) The Urban Challenge of Socially and Environmentally sound Community Research in 'Tropical Suburbia.' *Global Development Studies*, 1 (3–4): 262–72.

Newman, P. (2006) The Environmental Impact of Cities. *Environment and Urbanization*, 18: 275–95.

Norris, F.H., Stevens, S.P., Pfefferbaum, B., Wyche, K.F. and Pfefferbaum, R.L. (2008) Community Resilience as a Metaphor, Theory, Set of Capacities, and Strategy for Disaster Readiness. *American Journal of Community Psychology*, 41: 127–50.

Orr, D. (1999) Rethinking Education. *The Ecologist*, 29 (3): 232–4.

Peterson, G.D., Cumming, G.S. and Carpenter, S.R. (2003) Scenario Planning: a Tool for Conservation in an Uncertain World. *Conservation Biology*, 17 (2): 358–66.

Polletta, F. (1999) 'Free Spaces' in Collective Action. *Theory and Society*, 28 (1): 1–38.

Prudham, S. (2009) Pimping Climate Change: Richard Branson, Global Warming, and the Performance of Green Capitalism. *Environment and Planning A*, 41: 1594–613.

Rees, W. and Wackernagel, M. (1996) Urban Ecological Footprints: Why Cities Cannot Be Sustainable and Why They Are a Key to Sustainability. *Environmental Impact Assessment Review*, 16: 223–48.

Rockström, J. *et al.* (2009) A Safe Operating Space for Humanity. *Nature*, 461 (24 September): 472–5.

Rose, J. (2009) Sandstorms Shrink UAE's Solar Power Generation. *TOBOC*, 8 October, available at www.toboc.com/tradenews/Sandstorms-Shrink-Uae'S-Solar-Power-Generation/1347.aspx (accessed 1 October 2012).

Safian, R. (2012) The Secrets of Generation Flux. *Fast Company*, 15 October, available at www.fastcompany.com/3001734/secrets-generation-flux

Sassen, S. (2010) A Savage Sorting of Winners and Losers: Contemporary Versions of Primitive Accumulation. *Globalizations*, 7 (1): 20–53.

Satterthwaite, D. (1997) Sustainable Cities or Cities that Contribute to Sustainable Development? *Urban Studies*, 34 (10): 1667–91.

Scheff, T. J. (1988) Shame and Conformity: The Deference-Emotion System. *American Sociological Review*, 53 (3): 395–406.

Schwartz, A. (1982) Meaningful Work. *Ethics*, 92 (4): 634–46.

Scott Cato, M. and Hillier, J. (2010) How Could we Study Climate-Related Social Innovation? Applying Deleuzean Philosophy to Transition Towns. *Environmental Politics*, 19 (6): 869–87.

Scurfield, J., Rees, P. and Norman, P. (2009) Criminal Victimisation of the Homeless: An Investigation of Big Issue Vendors in Leeds. *Radical Statistics*, 99: 3–11.

Smith, B. (2011) Resilient Communities, Resilient Environments. *IUCN CEC Newsletter*, 14 April, available at www.iucn.org/what/tpas/climate/resources/news/?7255/Resilient-Communities-Resilient-Environments (accessed 28 August 2012).

Standing, G. (2008) Economic Insecurity and Global Casualisation: Threat or Promise? *Social Indicators Research*, 88 (1): 15–30.

Stanton, C. (2010) Masdar City Searches for Clean Water. *The National*, 3 April, available at www.thenational.ae/news/uae-news/technology/masdar-city-searches-for-cleaner-water# (accessed 1 October 2012)

Sterling, S (2011) Transformative Learning in Sustainability: Sketching the Conceptual Ground. *Learning and Teaching in Higher Education*, 5: 17–33.

Surjan, A.K. and Shaw, R. (2008) 'Eco-city' to 'Disaster-Resilient Eco-community': A Concerted Approach in the Coastal City of Puri, India. *Sustainability Science*, 3: 249–65.

Tàbara, J.D. and Pahl-Wostl, C. (2007) Sustainability Learning in Natural Resource Use and Management. *Ecology and Society*, 12 (2), available at www.ecologyandsociety.org/vol12/iss2/art3

Tilbury, D. (1995) Environmental Education for Sustainability; Defining the New Focus of Environmental Education. *Environmental Education Research*, 1 (2): 195–212.

Tilbury, D. (2011c) Are We Learning to Change? Mapping Global Progress in Education for Sustainable Development in the Lead Up to 'Rio Plus 20.' *Global Environmental Research*, 14 (2): 101–7.

Turnbull, S. (1997) Stakeholder Cooperation. *Journal of Co-operative Studies*, 29 (3): 18–52.

Unger, M. (2011) The Social Ecology of Resilience: Addressing Contextual and Cultural Ambiguity of a Nascent Construct. *American Journal of Orthopsychiatry*, 81 (1): 1–17.

Urry, J. (2005) The Complexities of the Global. *Theory Culture Society*, 22 (5): 235–54.

Verma, S., Sta Maria, M. and Morojele, N. (2011) A Cross-Cultural View to the Study of Resilience among Street Children. *International Society for the Study of Behavioural Development Bulletin*, 1 (59): 11–14.

Walker, B., Gunderson, L., Kinzig, A., Folke, C. Carpenter, S. and Schultz, L. (2006) A Handful of Heuristics and Some Propositions for Understanding Resilience in Social-Ecological Systems. *Ecology and Society*, 11 (1), available at www.ecologyandsociety.org/vol11/iss1/art13.

Whitmarsh, L. and O'Neill, S. (2010) Green Identity, Green Living? The Role of Pro-environmental Self-identity in Determining Consistency Across Diverse Pro-environmental Behaviours. *Journal of Environmental Psychology*, 30 (3): 305–14.

Willett, P. and Broadley, R. (2011) Effective Public Library Outreach to Homeless People. *Library Review*, 60 (8): 658–70.

Zhang, X, Shen, G.Q.P., Feng, J. and Wu, Y. (2013) Delivering a Low-Carbon Community in China: Technology vs. Strategy? *Habitat International*, 37: 130–7.

Thesis

Podger, D. (2009) Contribution of a Faith Organisation to Education for Sustainability: Infusing Spirituality into Learning for Sustainability. PhD Study undertaken at Macquarie University, Sydney, Australia.

Newspaper articles

Bunting, M. (2009) Beyond Westminster's Bankrupted Practices, a New Idealism is Emerging. *The Guardian*, 31 May, available at www.guardian.co.uk/commentisfree/2009/may/31/reform-transition-a-new-politics (accessed 24 October 2012).

Chakrabortty, A. (2013) An Action-Packed Thriller is about to Unfold in Davos, Switzerland. *The Guardian*, 21 January, available at http://m.guardian.co.uk/commentisfree/2013/jan/21/davos-switzerland-rich-plotting-richer.

Chasek, P. (2012) Beyond Rio+20: What It Means for Global Higher Education. *The Chronicle of Higher Education*, July 2, available at http://chronicle.com/blogs/worldwise/beyond-rio20-what-it-means-for-global-higher-education/299755 (accessed 1 February 2013).

Marsh, J. (2011) Why Education is Not an Education Panacea. *Chronicle of Higher Education*, 28 August, available at http://chronicle.com/article/Why-Education-Is-Not-an/128790 (accessed 24 January 2013).

McVeigh, T. (2012) 21st-Century Cathy Come Home: Will Highlight the Rise of UK Homelessness. *The Guardian*, 1 April, available at www.guardian.co.uk/society/2012/apr/01/truth-about-stanley-film-homelessness.

Monbiot, George (2001) Turn the Screw. *The Guardian*, 24 April, available at www.guardian.co.uk/world/2001/apr/24/mayday.business.

Platt, E. (2011) Edible Hackney. *The Guardian*, 1 September, available at www.guardian.co.uk/lifeandstyle/2011/sep/01/edible-hackney (accessed 20 October 2012).

Zolli, A. (2012) Learning to Bounce Back. *The New York Times*, Opinion Column, 2 November, available at www.nytimes.com/2012/11/03/opinion/forget-sustainability-its-about-resilience.html?pagewanted=all&_r=1&(accessed 15 February 2013).

Conference papers and proceedings

Boon, J.K.T. (2012) WWF-Malaysia's Proposed Environmental Education Model with Curriculum as its Central Focus. Conference presentation at International Greening Education Event, Karlsruhe, Germany, available at www.etechgermany.com/en/IGEE2012/resources/Day_2/Johleen_Koh/WWF-Malaysia%E2%80%99s%20Proposed_Environment_Education_Model.pdf

Convention on Biological Diversity (2012) Cities and Biodiversity Outlook. CBD, Montreal, available at www.cbd.int/en/subnational/partners-and-initiatives/cbo

Knowles, J. (2012) Sustainable Development: The Indicators Paper. Rio+20 side event, North South Forum, 20 June.

Kumetat, D. (2009) Climate Change in the Persian Gulf -Regional Security, Sustainability Strategies and Research Needs. Paper presented at Climate Change, Social Stress and Violent Conflict, Hamburg, 19–20 November.

Trieb, F. (2007) Concentrating Solar Power for Seawater Desalination. *Proceedings of MENAREC 4*, Damascus, Syria, 20–24 June.

Wals, A.E.J. (2010) Message in a Bottle. Inaugural lecture upon taking up the posts of Professor of Social Learning and Sustainable Development, and UNESCO Chair at Wageningen University, 27 May.

Corporate publications

Adam, B. (2012) *Responsibility to Future Generations*. Schumacher Institute Challenge Paper. Available at www.schumacherinstitute.org.uk/sites/schumacherinstitute.org.uk/files/downloadable/Challenge%20Papers/BAdam%20Challenge%20-%20Responsibility%20to%20Future.pdf.

Australian Government (2011) Insuring the Future: The Impacts of Climate Change on the Insurance Industry in Australia. Unpublished report. Canberra: Australian Government.

BioRegional (2009) *BedZed: Seven Years On*. London: BioRegional.

BioRegional/WWF (2005) *London 2012: Candidate City – Towards a One Planet Olympics*. London: BioRegional/WWF.

Co-operative Bank (2011) *Annual Ethical Consumerism Report 2011*. Available at www.co-operative.coop/PageFiles/416561607/Ethical-Consumerism-Report-2011.pdf (accessed 7 November 2012).

Defra (2008) *A Framework for Pro-environmental Behaviours*. London: Defra.

Department of Energy and Climate Change (2012) *Energy Consumption in the United Kingdom*. Available at www.decc.gov.uk/en/content/cms/statistics/publications/ecuk/ecuk.aspx# (accessed 2 November 2012).

Dobbs, R., Oppenheim, J. Thompson, F., Brinkman, M. and Zornes, M. (2011) *Resource Revolution: Meeting the World's Energy, Materials, Food and Water Needs*. Available at www.mckinsey.com/Insights/MGI/Research/Natural_Resources/Resource_revolution

European Commission DG INFSO (2008) *Final Report: Impacts of ICT on Energy Efficiency*. Brussels: European Union.

Fien, J., Scott, W. and Tilbury, D. (1999) *Education and Conservation: An Evaluation of the Contributions of Educational Programmes to Conservation within the WWF Network*. Gland: WWF.

González-Gaudiano, E. (2012) *The Latin American Perspective on the Debate on Education for Sustainable Development*. Available at www.anea.org.mx/docs/Gonzalez-EnvironmentalCommunicator.pdf (accessed 11 November 2012).

Green New Deal Group (2008) *A Green New Deal*. London: New Economics Foundation, available at www.neweconomics.org/sites/neweconomics.org/files/A_Green_New_Deal_1.pdf.

Hargreaves, T. (2010) *Putting Foucault to Work on the Environment: Exploring Pro-environmental Behaviour Change as a Form of Discipline*. CSERGE Working Paper EDM 10–11, available at www.cserge.ac.uk/sites/default/files/edm_2010_11.pdf.

Hibbard, K.A., Costanza, R., Crumley, C., van der Leeuw, S., Aulenbach, S., Dearing, J., Morais, J., Stelen, W. and Yasuda, Y. (2010) *Developing an Integrated History and Future of People on Earth (IHOPE): Research Plan*. IGBP Report no. 59. Stockholm: IGBP Secretariat.

International Labour Office (2010) *The Global Wage Report 2010–2011: Wage Policies in Times of Crisis*. Geneva: International Labour Office.

International Labour Office (2012) *Global Employment Trends 2012: Preventing a Deeper Jobs Crisis*. Geneva: International Labour Office.

International Union for the Conservation of Nature (2011) *Transitioning to a Green Economy: Building on Nature – IUCN's Position on Green Economy for the Rio 2012 Conference*. Position paper on Green Economy. Gland: IUCN, available at http://cmsdata.iucn.org/downloads/position_paper_on_green_economy_22march2012 .pdf (accessed 28 August 2012).

International Union for the Conservation of Nature (2012) *IUCN Knowledge Products*. Gland: IUCN.

Lancaster, A. (2011) 10 Ways to Avoid Burnout as an Entrepreneur. *Forbes*, 16 October 2011, available at www.forbes.com/sites/thebigenoughcompany/2011/10/16/10-ways-to-avoid-burnout-as-an-entrepreneur

Mguni, N. and Caistor-Arendar, L. (2012) *Rowing Against the Tide: Making the Case for Community Resilience*. London: Young Foundation, available at http://youngfoundation.org/publications/rowing-against-the-tide-making-the-case-for-community-resilience

National Audit Office (2011) *The Financial Stability Interventions*. London: HM Treasury.

NEF (2012a) *The New Austerity and the Big Society*. London: New Economics Foundation, available at www.neweconomics.org/publications/the-new-austerity-and-the-big-society

NEF (2012b) *Cutting it in Birmingham: Why the Grassroots Aren't Growing Anymore*. London: New Economics Foundation, available at www.neweconomics.org/ publications/cutting-in-in-birmingham

Parry M., Arnell, N., Berry P., Dodman D.,Fankhauser, S. Hope, C. Kovats, S., Nicholls, R., Satterthwaite, D., Tiffin, R. and Wheeler T. (2009) *Annual Cost of Climate Assessing the Costs of Adaptation to Climate Change: A Review of the UNFCCC and Other Recent Estimates*. London: International Institute of Sustainable Development, available at www.astrid-online.it/clima—ene/documenti/archivio-22/Assessing_the_ costs_of_adapatation_to_cliamate_change_agosto2009.pdf (accessed 2 November 2012)

Rose, C., Dade, P. and Kerr, J. (2007) *Research Into Motivating Prospectors, Settlers and Pioneers To Change Behaviours That Affect Climate Emissions*. Paper, available at www.campaignstrategy.org/articles/behaviourchange_climate.pdf

Royal Society (2009) *Geoengineering the Climate: Science, Governance and Uncertainty*. London: Royal Society.

Skamp, K., Bergmann, I., Taplin, R. and Cooke, K. (2007) *A Review of Air Quality Education: Australian Research Institute in Education for Sustainability*. Canberra: Australian Government Department of the Environment and Water Resources.

Tilbury, D., Coleman, V., Jones, A. and MacMaster, K. (2005) *A National Review of Environmental Education and its Contribution to Sustainability in Australia: Community Education*. Canberra: Australian Government Department for the Environment and Heritage and Australian Research Institute in Education for Sustainability (ARIES), available at www.aries.mq.edu.au/projects/national_review/files/volume3

WBCSD (2010) *Vision 2050: The New Agenda for Business*. Geneva: WBCSD, available at www.wbcsd.org/pages/edocument/edocumentdetails.aspx?id=219&nosearchcontext key=true

World Bank (2009) *Africa: Making Development Climate Resilient: A World Bank Strategy for Sub-saharan Africa*. Washington, DC: World Bank.

World Economic Forum (2013) *Resilient Dynamism – Executive Summary*. Davos: WEF, available at www3.weforum.org/docs/AM13/WEF_AM13_ExecutiveSummary.pdf

WWF (2012) *Living Planet Report 2012 – Special Edition – On the Road to Rio+20*. Gland: WWF International.

Electronic or audiovisual

Adams, A. M. (2012) *The Education Link: Why Learning is Central to the Post-2015 Global Development Agenda*. Working Paper 8. Centre for Universal Education at the Brookings Institution, available at www.brookings.edu/research/papers/2012/12/education-post-2015-adams (accessed 20 March 2013).

American Association for the Advancement of Science (AAAS) *Is the Future of Conservation at a Crossroads?* AAAS 2013 Annual Meeting, available at www.aaas.confex.com/aaas/2013/webprogram/Session5931.html (accessed 12 January 2013).

ARC (2012) What is ARC? Available at www.arcworld.org (accessed 19 December 2012).

ARC (2013) About ARC. Available at www.arcworld.org/about.asp?pageID=2 (accessed 21 Feb 2013).

BioRegional (n.d.) What is One Planet Living? Available at www.bioregional.com/oneplanetliving/what-is-one-planet-living (accessed 19 March 2013).

Chapple, K. (2008) *Defining our Green Economy: A Premier on Green Economic Development*. Berkeley, CA: Centre for Community Innovation, University of Berkeley, available at www.communityinnovation.berkeley.edu/reports/Chapple%20-%20Defining%20the%20Green%20Economy.pdf (accessed 22 December 2012).

Copernicus Alliance and Treaty Circle (2012) *The People's Sustainability Treaty on Higher Education*, available at http://sustainabledevelopment.un.org/index.php?page=view&type=1006&menu=1348&nr=135 (accessed 18 March 2013).

Elmqvist, T. (2012) Cities and Biodiversity Outlook: Unprecedented Opportunities Lie Ahead in Greening Urban Expansion. *The Nature of Cities*, blogpost, 3 October. Available at www.thenatureofcities.com/2012/10/03/cities-and-biodiversity-outlook-unprecedented-opportunities-lie-ahead-of-us-in-greening-urban-expansion (accessed 27 March 2013).

Global Forest Coalition (2012) IUCN Officially Blocks Participation by Jeju Villagers who Opposed Naval Base Construction Near Convention. Article posted 5 September, available at www.peopleforestsrights.wordpress.com/2012/09/05/iucn-officially-blocks-participation-by-jeju-villagers-who-oppose-naval-base-construction-near-convention (accessed 10 January 2013).

Green Economy Group (2012) *The Green Economy*, available at www greeneconomy-group.com/company/green-economy-definition/?doing_wp_cron=1357603482.402713 0603790283203125 (accessed 10 December 2012).

Head, P. (2008) Entering the Ecological Age. Available at www.arup.com/Publications/Entering_the_Ecological_Age.aspx (accessed 19 March 2013).

Hainmueller J., Hiscox, M. J. and Sequiera, S. (2011) *Consumer Demand for the Fair Trade Label: Evidence from a Field Experiment*. Cambridge, MA/London: Massachusetts

Institute of Technology and London School of Economics, available at www.mit.edu/~jhainm/Paper/hhs.pdf (accessed 2 November 2012).

Harris, S.R. (2012) Nuclear Energy: one strand of hope for environmental and social justice on a crowded planet? Schumacher Institute Challenge Paper. Available at: www.schumacherinstitute.org.uk/sites/schumacherinstitute.org.uk/files/downloadable/Challenge%20Papers/SRH%20Challenge%20-%20Nuclear%20 %26%20SD.pdf

International Union for Conservation of Nature (2011) *IUCN Red List of Threatened Species.* Version 2011.2, available at www.iucnredlist.org

International Union for the Conservation of Nature (2012) News. Available at www.iucn.org/news_homepage/events/iucn_rio_20 (accessed 30 October 2012).

Kareiva P., Lalaz, R. and Marvier, M. (2012) Conservation in the Anthropocene: Beyond Solitude and Fragility. Available at www.thebreakthrough.org/index.php/journal/past-issues/issue-2/conservation-in-the-anthropocene (accessed 1 November 2012).

Letman, J. (2012) Jeju Island Base Divides Korean, International Green Groups. 20 August 2012, available at www.ipsnews.net/2012/08/jeju-island-base-divides-korean-international-green-groups (accessed 13 January 2013).

Mott MacDonald (n.d.) About Mott MacDonald. Available at www.mottmac.com/aboutmottmac (accessed 19 March 2013).

Nature Conservancy (2012) *What will Rio+20 Mean?* Available at www.blog.nature.org/2012/06/what-will-rio20-mean (accessed 12 December 2012).

Newport, D. (2013) Has 'Sustainability' Run its Course? Is it Time for the Next Big Thing? *The Dept of Change*, 3 January, available at http://davenewportblog.blogspot.co.uk/2013/01/2013-resilience-vs-campus-sustainability.html.

NICE (2009) Green Digital Charter. Available at www.greendigitalcharter.eu/greendigitalcharter (accessed 20 March 2013).

Park, S. (2012) JEJU-Island Navy-Base Controversy Divides IUCN. 14 September, available at www.biodiversitymedia.ning.com/profiles/blogs/jeju-island-navy-base-controversy-divides-iucn (accessed 11 January 2013).

Person, D. (2011) Conservation at a Crossroads. *The Bozeman Daily Chronicle*, 27 March, available at www.bozemandailychronicle.com/news/article_0244bfd2-5734-11e0-8c33-001cc4c002e0.html (accessed 9 January 2013).

Philosophical Primate (2011) Education IS a Panacea. Sort of. Available at http://thephilosophicalprimate.wordpress.com/2011/08/ (accessed 4 February 2013).

Pressenza International Press Agency (2012) Worlds Largest Environmental Organisation in Ethical Quandary. 14 September, available at www.pressenza.com/2012/09/south-korea-worlds-largest-environmental-organization-in-ethical-quandary (accessed 13 January 2013).

Red Cross (2012) *Do You Want to Know What Resilience Is?* Available at www.ifrcmedia.org/blog/do-you-want-to-discover-what-resilience-is (accessed 15 November 2012).

Resilience Doughnut (n.d.) What is the Resilience Doughnut, and How Does it Build Resilience? Available at www.theresiliencedoughnut.com.au/details.php?p_id=25 (accessed 19 March 2013).

Rio Tinto (2012) *Business Resilience and Recovery*. Available at www.riotinto.com/ourapproach/17216_business_resilience_recovery.asp (accessed 8 November 2012).

SGS (2012) *Care Share Appraisal: Final Report*. Report for the NSW Government of Australia, available at www.cityofsydney.nsw.gov.au/aboutsydney/parkingandtransport/documents/CarShareEconomicAppraisalFINALREPORT.pdf (accessed 2 November 2012).

Steiner, A. (2012) Remarks of the UNEP Executive Director at the opening session of the High Level Segment of the 11th Conference of the Parties to the Convention on Biological Diversity, available at www.unep.org/newscentre/Default.aspx?DocumentID=2696&ArticleID=9304&l=en (accessed 16 October 2012).

Stockholm Resilience Centre (2012) *What is Resilience?* Available at www.stockholmresilience.org/21/research/what-is-resilience.html (accessed 2 November 2012).

Tollefson, J. and Gilbert, N. (2012) *Earth Summit: Rio Report Card: The World has Failed to Deliver on Many of the Promises it Made 20 years Ago at the Earth Summit in Brazil.* Available at www.nature.com/news/earth-summit-rio-report-card-1.10764 (accessed 22 December 2012).

Totnes EDAP (n.d.) Lighting. Available at http://totnesedap.org.uk/book/part2/stories/lighting (accessed 20 March 2013).

Toulmin, C. (2012) *IUCN World Conservation Congress Begins.* 6 September, available at www.iied.org/iucn-world-conservation-congress-begins (accessed 12 January 2013).

Toulmin, C. (2013) *Five Moments from 2012 that Could Spell Change for the Planet 7 January 2013.* Available at www.iied.org/five-moments-2012-could-spell-change-for-planet (accessed 13 January 2013).

Transition Network (n.d.) Why do Transition? Available at www.transitionnetwork.org/why-do-transition#economic-crisis (accessed 30 December 2012).

UNECE (2011) *Learning for the Future: Competences in Education for Sustainable Development.* ECE/CEP/AC.13/2011/6, available at www.unece.org/fileadmin/DAM/env/esd/6thMeetSC/Learning%20for%20the%20Future_%20Competences%20for%20Educators%20in%20ESD/ECE_CEP_AC13_2011_6%20COMPETENCES%20EN.pdf (accessed 13 January 2013).

UNEP/IETC (2002) *Melbourne Principles for Sustainable Cities: Integrative Management.* Series no. 1. Osaka: UNEP. Available at www.unep.or.jp/ietc/focus/melbourneprinciples/english.pdf.

United Nations (2012) *The Future We Want: Rio+20 Outcomes Document.* Available at www.uncsd2012.org/content/documents/727The%20Future%20We%20Want%2019%20June%201230pm.pdf (accessed 2 November 2012).

United Nations Commission on Sustainable Development (2012) *Issues Brief 6 – SDGs and Indicators.* Available at www.docs.google.com/gview?url=www.uncsd2012.org/rio20//content/documents/218Issues+Brief+6++SDGs+and+Indicators_Final+Final+clean.pdf&chrome=true (accessed 26 December 2012).

United Nations Development Programme (2012) *Fast Facts: Millennium Development Goals.* Available at www.undp.org/content/undp/en/homelibrarypage/results/fast_facts/millennium-development-goals (accessed 2 November 2012).

United Nations Environment Programme (2007) *Emerging Issues for Biodiversity Conservation.* Technical Series 29. Paris: Secretariat of the Convention of Biological Diversity, United Nations Environment Programme. Available at www.cbd.int/doc/publications/cbd-ts-29.pdf (accessed 2 November 2012).

United Nations Environment Programme (n.d.) *The Green Economy.* Available at www.unep.org/greeneconomy/AboutGEI/FrequentlyAskedQuestions/tabid/29786/Default.aspx (accessed 12 December 2012).

United Nations Environment Programme (2011) Global Universities Partnership on Environment and Sustainability (GUPES). Available at www.unep.org/training/programmes/gupes.asp (accessed 19 March 2013).

United Nations Environment Programme World Conservation Monitoring Centre

(2012) *World Database on Protected Areas*. Available at www.unep-wcmc.org/world-database-on-protected-areas_164.html

United Nations Global Pulse (2012) Overview. Available at www.unglobalpulse.org/about-new (accessed 22 December 2012).

United Nations Secretary-General's High-level Panel on Global Sustainability (2012) *Resilient People, Resilient Planet: A Future Worth Choosing*. New York: United Nations, available at www.un.org/gsp/sites/default/files/attachments/GSP_Report_web_final.pdf (accessed 29 August 2012).

Vallila Library (n.d.) Green Library. Available at www.helmet.fi/en-US/Libraries_and_services/Vallila_Library/Whats_going_on/Vallila_Library__Green_Library(1983) (accessed 27 March 2013).

Wohlsen, M. (2012) It's the End of the World, and I Feel Fine: 10 Questions with Andrew Zolli. Available at www.wired.com/business/2012/07/its-the-end-of-the-world-and-i-feel-fine-10-questions-with-andrew-zolli (accessed 7 December 2012).

WWF (2013) Brief History of WWF. Available at www.wwf.org.uk/what_we_do?about_us/history (accessed 15 January 2013).

Film

The Age of Stupid (2009) Directed by Franny Armstrong, GB.

Cathy Come Home (1966) Directed by Ken Loach, GB.

Food (2009) Directed by Robert Kenner, USA.

McLibel (2005) Directed by Franny Armstrong and Ken Loach, UK.

On the Streets (2010) Directed by Penny Woolcock, GB.

The Power of Community: how Cuba survived peak oil (2006) Directed by Faith Morgan, USA.

Supersize Me (2004) Directed by Morgan Spurlock, USA.

The Truth About Stanley (2012) Directed by Lucy Tcherniak, GB. Available at http://thetruthaboutstanley.com.

Interviews

Beardmore, P. (2012) Interviewed 6 February 2012.

Bourne, G. (2012) Interviewed 3 December 2012.

Budden, K. (2012) Interviewed 21 February 2012.

Clarke, P. (2012) Interviewed 26 March 2012.

De Zoysa, U. (2012) Interviewed 12 November 2012.

Finlayson, A. (2013) Interviewed 1 February 2013.

Girardet, H. (2012) Interviewed 22 February 2012.

Head, P. (2012) Interviewed 26 April 2012.

Hopkins, R. (2012) Interviewed 27 April 2012.

Houben, F. (2012) Interviewed 1 May 2012.

Kerr, A. (2012) Interviewed 2 March 2012.

McKenna, S. (2012) Interviewed 15 March 2012.

Monaghan, P. (2012) Interviewed 13 July 2012.

Porritt, J. (2012) Interviewed 9 August 2012.

Pradhan, M. (2013) Interviewed 22 February 2013.

Puntenney, P. (2013) Interviewed 1 February 2013.

Riddlestone, S. (2012) Interviewed 17 May 2012.
Robertson, S. (2012) Interviewed 17 April 2012.
Sarabhai, K. (2013) Interviewed 18 February 2013.
Scott Cato, M. (2012) Interviewed 16 February 2012.
Slater, S. (2012) Interviewed 25 April 2012.
Suissa, R. (2012) Interviewed 13 September 2012.
Thomashow, M. (2012) Interviewed 4 October 2012.
Ullah, F. (2013) Interviewed 10 January 2013.
Van Raaij, R. (2012) Interviewed 18 December 2012.
Wallington, G. (2010) Interviewed 14 October 2010.
Wheeler, K.A. (2012) Interviewed 20 November 2012.
Williams, M.J. (2012) Interviewed 27 November 2012.
Zeidler, J. (2012) Interviewed 29 November 2012.

Index